Rich Dad's
ADVISORS ™

My poor dad often said, "What you know is important." My rich dad said, "If you want to be rich, *who* you know is more important than *what* you know." Rich dad explained further, saying, "Business and investing is a team sport. The average investor or small-business person loses financially because they do not have a team. Instead of a team, they act as individuals who are trampled by very smart teams." That is why the Rich Dad's Advisors book series was born. Rich Dad's Advisors will guide you to help you know who to look for and what questions to ask so you can go out and gather your own great team of advisors.

Robert T. Kiyosaki

Author of the *New York Times* Bestsellers
Rich Dad Poor Dad™
Rich Dad's CASHFLOW Quadrant™
Rich Dad's Guide to Investing™
and *Rich Dad's Rich Kid Smart Kid*™

Rich Dad's™ Classics

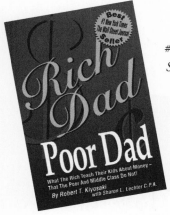

#1 *New York Times,* #1 *Wall Street Journal,*
#1 *Business Week,* #1 *Publishers Weekly,* as well as a
San Francisco Chronicle and *USA Today* bestseller.
Also featured on the bestseller lists of
Amazon.com, Amazon.com UK and Germany,
E-trade.com, *Sydney Morning Herald* (Australia),
Sun Herald (Australia), *Business Review Weekly*
(Australia), Borders Books and Music (U.S. and
Singapore), and Barnes & Noble.com.

Wall Street Journal, New York Times
business and *Business Week* bestseller.
Also featured on the bestseller lists of the
Sydney Morning Herald (Australia), *Sun
Herald* (Australia), *Business Review Weekly*
(Australia), and Amazon.com, Barnes &
Noble.com, Borders Books and Music
(U.S. and Singapore).

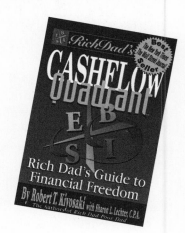

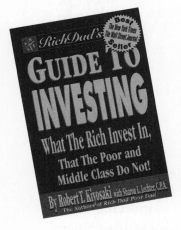

*USA Today, Wall Street Journal, New York
Times* business, *Business Week,* and
Publishers Weekly bestseller.

Wall Street Journal, New York Times,
and *USA Today* bestseller.

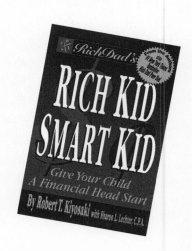

Rich Dad's Advisors™ Series

Rich Dad said,
"Business and Investing is a team sport."

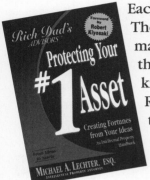

Each of us has a million-dollar idea in our head. The first step in turning your idea into millions, maybe even billions of dollars, is to protect that idea. Michael Lechter is an internationally known intellectual property attorney who is Robert Kiyosaki's legal advisor on all his intellectual property matters. His book is simply written and is an important addition to any businessperson's library.

Loopholes of the Rich is for the aspiring as well as the advanced business owner who is looking for better and smarter ways to legally pay less tax and protect his or her assets. It gives real solutions that will be easy to apply to your unique situation. Diane Kennedy offers over twenty years of experience in research, application, and creation of innovative tax solutions and is Robert Kiyosaki's personal and corporate tax strategist.

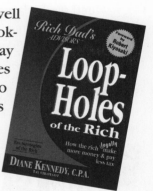

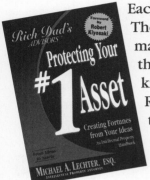

Your most important skill in business is your ability to communicate and sell! SalesDogs® is a highly educational, inspirational, and somewhat "irreverent" look at the world of sales, communications, and the different characters that occupy that world. All of us sell in one way or another. It is important for you to find your own unique style. Blair Singer is respected internationally as an extraordinary trainer, speaker, and consultant in the fields of sales, communication, and management.

Rich Dad's Advisors™ *Series*

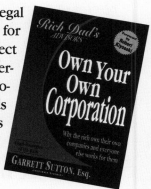

Dolf de Roos is a real estate investor who bought his first property as an undergraduate student. After completing eight years of university education and earning a Ph.D. in electrical engineering, he was offered a job at $32,000 per year. The week before, he had completed a real estate deal worth $35,000. Consequently, he didn't accept the job, and to this day, has never had one. Dolf willingly shares his enthusiasm for real estate, and has rattled cages in audiences in over sixteen countries. He passionately believes that the Deal of the Decade comes along about once a week.

Own Your Own Corporation reveals the legal secrets and strategies that the rich have used for generations to run their businesses and protect their assets. Written in a clear and easily understandable style, *Own Your Own Corporation* provides the necessary knowledge to save thousands of dollars in taxes and protect your family assets from the attacks of creditors.

Rich Dad's ADVISORS™

Own Your Own Corporation

Why the rich own their own companies
and everyone else works for them

GARRETT SUTTON, Esq.

WARNER
BUSINESS
BOOKS™

Published by Warner Books

An AOL Time Warner Company

Published by Warner Books in association with CASHFLOW Technologies, Inc., and BI Capital, Inc.

CASHFLOW, Rich Dad, and Rich Dad's Advisors are trademarks of CASHFLOW Technologies, Inc.

 is a trademark of
CASHFLOW Technologies, Inc.

 Warner Business Books are published by Warner Books, Inc.,
1271 Avenue of the Americas, New York, NY 10020

Visit our Web site at www.twbookmark.com.

 An AOL Time Warner Company

The Warner Business Book logo is a trademark of Warner Books, Inc.

Printed in the United States of America

First Printing: October 2001
10 9 8 7 6 5

Library of Congress Cataloging-in-Publication Data

Sutton, Garrett.
    Own your own corporation : why the rich own their own companies and everyone else works for them / Garrett Sutton.
        p. cm.
    ISBN 0-446-67861-9
    1. Small business—Management.   2. Home-based businesses—Management.
3. Self-employed.   I. Title.

HD62.7 .S977   2001
658'.041—dc21   2001026877

Designed by imagesupport.com, LLC.
Book design by Stanley S. Drate / Folio Graphics Co. Inc.

Acknowledgments

This book is dedicated to my wonderful wife, Jenny, and our terrific kids, Teddy, Emily, and Sarah. Thank you for your understanding as this book was being written.

I would like to thank Robert Paul Turner, Megan Hughes, Andrew Smetana, and Cammie Warburton for their invaluable assistance in the creation of this book.

Special thanks are also extended to Robert Kiyosaki, Sharon Lechter, and Diane Kennedy for allowing me the opportunity to participate as a Rich Dad's Advisor.

And thanks to all my clients. Assisting you to reach your business, financial, and personal goals is a very satisfying activity.

Contents

Foreword by Robert Kiyosaki

When I was ten years old and in the fifth grade, I began to read about the great explorers, such as Columbus, Magellan, Cortez, DaGama, Cook. I dreamed of someday traveling the world in a wooden ship, in search of treasures in unexplored lands. I read every book I could about their lives and adventures. In the fifth grade, I often had the highest scores on the tests and quizzes about the great explorers.

"You read about the explorers who were successful," said rich dad. "What about the explorers who failed?" Rich dad was helping me prepare for my final exam in the fifth grade.

"The ones who failed?" I asked.

"Yes, the ones who failed," said rich dad. "In school they teach you about the successful explorers or the famous explorers. There were many more explorers who were not successful and not famous whom we have never heard about, nor will we ever hear about them."

"Why is studying about the explorers who failed so important?" I asked.

"Because you need to know how the owners and the investors in those failed voyages protected themselves against the repercussions from such failures," said rich dad.

"Repercussions?" I asked. "What kind of repercussions?"

"Such things as the loss of life," said rich dad. "The owners and investors wanted to protect themselves and their fortunes from the families of the explorer and his crew in the event there was a loss of life on the voyage."

"You mean the men on the ship risked and sometimes lost their lives, and all the owners and investors on land wanted to do was protect themselves from losing money? That's one of the repercussions you're talking about?"

Rich dad nodded his head. He then began to tell me about the Dutch East India Company and the British East India Company, two of the more powerful and famous corporations behind some of those explorers. Some of these corporations even had their own navy and army to control access to their nation's overseas wealth. He told me how these corporations in many ways took over whole countries, such as New Zealand, Hawaii, Australia, Malaysia, Indonesia, South Africa, and other parts of the world. One of those countries was one day to become the United States of America. Rich dad pointed out to me that the flag of the United States was originally the flag of the British East Company, reportedly modified by Betsy Ross. While England may have lost control over its colonies, the British East India Company simply changed its name—a simple d.b.a.—and kept on trading.

The more rich dad told me about the corporations behind these great explorers and how they shaped world history, the more interested I became in global business and doing business through a corporation. When I was sixteen, I began applying for a congressional appointment to the U.S. Merchant Marine Academy, the federal military school that trains young men to sail ships of the merchant marine. Kings Point, which the school is also known as, continues to train young people to replace the great seafaring explorers. Only two students from Hawaii are admitted to this little known federal academy each year, so I felt fortunate to be accepted after passing rigorous exams and interviews. At age eighteen, I began sailing as a student onboard ships carrying cargo along the same trade routes established by Ferdinand Magellan and Captain James Cook. I quickly realized that although the early explorers are gone, some of those corporations rich dad talked about still exist today, and the U.S. government funds the education of these corporations' leaders. I began to understand why rich dad told me years ago, "Don't just study the explorer and his ships, study the power of the corporations behind the explorer and his ships."

747 Replaces Cargo Ships

Today I travel by 747 rather than by cargo ship. Although my mode of transportation has changed, I have heeded rich dad's advice and learned my lessons well. Today I travel as a representative of several corporations—the difference is that I own those corporations rather than simply work for them.

As I stated in *Rich Dad Poor Dad,* my poor dad thought it was a good idea to be a good employee and climb the corporate ladder, while my rich dad said, "Don't climb the corporate ladder, why not own the corporate ladder?" Rich dad also said, "The problem with climbing the corporate ladder is that when you look up, you see somebody's big fat butt above you." On a more serious note, he said, "The two main reasons you need to own your own corporation are for protection against law suits and against excessive taxes, yet there are many other reasons and other strategies. The point is, if you are serious about being rich and keeping your wealth, understanding corporations and other legal structures is an important part of your ongoing financial education."

Introducing Garrett Sutton

I am pleased to introduce Garrett Sutton to you. Often in my classes, students ask me questions about corporations and legal structures. My standard reply is, "I did not go to law school and I am not an attorney, so I do not give advice on that subject. I suggest you do as I do: Find a good attorney and use him or her as your advisor on this very important subject." I am pleased to introduce to you my advisor in these matters, Garrett Sutton. He is a pleasure to work with, and he is more than a great advisor, he is a great teacher. As rich dad said to me years ago, "If you are serious about being rich and keeping your wealth, understanding corporations and other legal structures is an important part of your ongoing financial education."

AUDIO DOWNLOAD

In each of our books we like to provide an audio inter-view as a bonus with additional insights. As a thank-you to you for reading this book, you may go to the Web site www.richdad.com/advisors.

Thank you for your interest in your financial educa-tion.

Introduction

Congratulations. You are about to undertake a powerful and enlightening journey. By reading this book you will learn quickly and easily the legal secrets and strategies that the rich have used to run their businesses and protect their assets. In short order you will clearly understand exactly how certain entities—corporations, limited liability companies, and limited partnerships—can not only save you thousands and thousands of dollars in taxes but can also save your house and savings and family assets from the attacks of creditors.

These are the same lessons that Robert Kiyosaki's rich dad taught him. Own nothing and control everything. Use the techniques of the rich to improve your financial standing and protect your family. And above all, work smarter instead of harder.

By the time you finish this book you will have the legal savvy of an experienced entrepreneur and the knowledge necessary to immediately implement your own custom legal strategy.

Let's begin . . .

OWN YOUR
OWN CORPORATION

Chapter 1

Your Entity Menu

- C corporation
- S corporation
- Limited Liability Company (LLC)
- Limited Partnership (LP)
- General Partnership
- Sole Proprietorship

As legal business systems and traditions have developed over the last five hundred years, several structures for running a business have evolved. Each structure (or entity) has its own advantages and drawbacks, which we will explore.

As a frame of reference for making your selection, it is important for you to clarify your strategy in this planning. The purpose of this chapter is for you to clearly understand and choose the best entity for your unique and specific purpose. To that end, the following checklist should be considered:

1. Protection of family assets and investments
2. Management control
3. Avoiding family disputes
4. Flexibility of decision making
5. Succession of children and other family members to management
6. The nature of the business to be operated

7. The nature of the asset to be held
8. The number of owners involved
9. Estate planning and gifting of assets
10. Who may legally obligate the business
11. Effect upon an owner's death or departure
12. The need for start-up funding
13. Taxation
14. Privacy of ownership
15. Consolidation of assets and investments

These and other issues will become apparent as we review your choices. And please note, your decision does not have to be made alone. It is recommended that these issues be discussed with your attorney, accountant, or other professional advisor. An individual well versed in these areas will provide excellent insight into which entity is right for you.

It is important to know that in entity selection one size *does not* fit all. If your attorney or accountant suggests only one entity, a general partnership for example, for each and every business venture you have him or her review, you will want to question why they believe one entity fits all situations. Or you may want to seek out a new professional advisor.

We will discuss which entities work well in various business and asset-holding scenarios. But before doing so, we must point out which entities do not work well in any situation. For as important as knowing which entity to use for running your business, protecting your assets, and limiting your liability is knowing which entity NOT to use.

Bad Entities

- Sole proprietorships
- General partnerships

In my legal practice I represent various businesses, from small and basic to large and complicated. I enjoy helping entrepreneurs and business owners make money, provide for their families and employees, and secure a stable future.

I cannot do my job if a client insists on using a bad entity. Sole proprietorships and general partnerships provide no asset protection. One lawsuit against your business, and your house, savings, and personal assets can all be lost. Our first case is illustrative.

Case No. 1—Johnny

Johnny was a plumber. He had been at it for five years and was starting to succeed. His customers were satisfied with his work and the word of mouth for Johnny's Ace Plumbing was good.

While Johnny was a good plumber, he felt intimidated by legal matters. Lawyers and accountants were supposed to be smart, so the work they did must be difficult. When Johnny was a young boy his father had been unfairly treated by a lawyer. He remembered it to this day, and wanted nothing to do with them.

So instead of consulting with a professional on how best to conduct his business, Johnny let his part-time bookkeeper select an entity off the menu. The results were disastrous.

Johnny's part-time bookkeeper knew only that forming a corporation required filing special documents with the state but did not know how to file them. He knew that a corporation needed to file a separate tax return but was not sure of the ins and outs of preparing one. As so he suggested Johnny use a sole proprietorship because he knew how to handle one and always suggested one for his clients. One size fits all.

The problem was that a sole proprietorship provides absolutely no asset protection. By operating as a sole proprietorship Johnny has unlimited liability for the debts, claims, and obligations of the business. This unlimited liability meant that his house and savings and personal assets were exposed to the claims of others.

Of course, as in all horror stories, a demon entered Johnny's business. He had hired Damien as an employee to assist with his growing workload. Damien seemed like a decent guy and appeared to know the plumbing business. Johnny did not bother to do a background check on Damien. Johnny was new to the business world and not aware of the need to do so.

After one week on the job, Damien assaulted one of Johnny's customers while they were alone in her house. Without going into the sordid details, this woman was so severely traumatized by what Damien did to her in her own home that she and her family had to move away.

Within three weeks of the incident Johnny's business was sued. Because Johnny was a sole proprietor, this meant that *he*, and not the business itself, as with a corporation, was sued and had to defend himself.

The lawyers suing for the woman did the background check of Damien that Johnny did not do. Damien was a recently released ex-convict with a history of sexual assaults. Johnny did not have the insurance to cover such a claim. The case went forward. The lawyers argued to a jury that Johnny's business was irresponsible for failing to check up on Damien and was responsible for the consequences. They presented to the jury what was true—a business is vicariously liable, or responsible, for the acts of its employees. The jury was horrified by the whole case and awarded damages of $10 million.

Johnny was wiped out. As a sole proprietor he was completely and personally responsible for every claim the business incurred. And he had attorneys with a one-third contingent interest in the collection of $10 million after him.

Johnny lost his house, his savings, and his family. The stress of it all resulted in his wife divorcing him, obtaining custody of the children, and moving away. Johnny declared bankruptcy. He ended up a broken man despising lawyers and our legal system all the more.

The irony, of course, is that by consulting with a lawyer and using the legal system to *his* advantage, Johnny could have prevented the disastrous consequences that resulted from relying on a part-time bookkeeper with a one-size-fits-all mentality for entity selection.

A competent lawyer would have told Johnny that there were risks—known and unknown—in running any business. To protect yourself from such risks you need to limit your liability by establishing a corporation or other good entity.

A good entity is one that shields and protects your personal assets from business risk. A bad entity is one that provides you no protection whatsoever. By using a good entity Johnny could have used the legal system—which has evolved to encourage business activity and limit the liability of risk takers—to his advantage.

Other Sole Proprietorship Disadvantages

As if personal liability was not bad enough, there are two other disadvantages to using a sole proprietorship:

- *Sale.* It is hard to sell a sole proprietorship, since its value is based on the owner and not the business.
- *Death.* When a sole proprietor dies, the sole proprietorship terminates. The sole proprietor's successors can only sell assets, not the business as a going concern.

A general partnership is also a bad entity. In fact it is twice as bad as a sole proprietorship because you have twice the personal exposure: personal liability for your acts and your partners' acts. This will be illustrated in Case No. 2 ahead.

Whenever two or more persons agree to share profits and losses a partnership has been formed. Even if you never sign a partnership agreement, state law provides that under such circumstances you have formed a general partnership.

A written partnership agreement is not required by law. A handshake is acceptable for formation. In the event you do not sign a formal document, you will be subject to your state's applicable partnership law. This may not be to your advantage, since such general rules rarely satisfy specific situations. As an example, most states provide that profits and losses are to be divided equally among the partners. If your oral understanding is that you are to receive 75 percent of the profits, state law and your handshake will not help you. You are better advised to prepare a written agreement addressing your rights and rewards.

Unlike a sole proprietorship, in which only one individual may participate, by definition, a general partnership must consist of two or more people. You cannot have a one-person partnership. On the other hand, you may have as many partners as you want in a general partnership. This may sound like a blessing but it is actually a curse.

The greatest drawback of a general partnership is that each partner is liable for the debts and obligations incurred by all the other general partners. While you may trust the one general partner you have not to improperly obligate the partnership, the more general partners you bring aboard the greater risk you run that someone will create serious problems.

And remember, just as with a sole proprietorship, your personal assets are at risk in a general partnership. Your house and your life savings can be lost through the actions of your partner. While you may have had nothing to do with the decision that was made and you may have been five thousand miles away when it was made and you may have voiced your opposition to it when you found out it was made, you are still personally responsible for it as a general partner.

As such, a general partnership is much riskier than a sole proprietorship. In a sole proprietorship, only the proprietor can bind the business. In a general partnership, any general partner—no matter how wise or, unfortunately, how ignorant—may obligate the business. By contrast, limited liability companies, limited partnerships, and corporations offer much greater protection. All of them offer owners limited personal liability for business debts and the acts of others.

It should be noted that because of these unlimited risks the last thing you want to do is become a general partner of an enterprise in which you do not have day-to-day management control. If you do not thoroughly know what is going on in the company you should not put your future on the line as a general partner.

Case No. 2—Louise

Louise had worked for someone else all her life. For the last ten years she had worked in the gift section of a large department store. She did not like the floor manager insisting she do things a certain way when she knew her way would generate more sales for the company. It was all petty politics. She looked forward to the day when she could open her own business and make her own decisions.

Then one day, Maxine came to work at the department store. The two of them hit it off immediately. Maxine had a certain style and attitude that appealed to Louise. They had similar interests, the same feel for what the customers wanted, and the same desire to escape working for a faceless corporation filled with narrow-minded managers who stifled their every idea for improvement. Soon they were talking about opening their own gift boutique.

Louise had managed to save $10,000 to pursue her dream. Maxine did not have any money to contribute, but convinced Louise that she would contribute her first $5,000 in profits back into the business.

Louise was not aware that by agreeing to form a partnership with Maxine without getting a written agreement as to distributions meant that they were automatically 50-50 partners. While Louise put up all the money and Maxine orally agreed to put her profits back later, the law treated them as each owning 50 percent of their new business, L & M Gifts.

In nine businesses out of ten there are problems when only one partner puts up all the money. L & M Gifts was no exception.

Maxine wanted the store to have the right atmosphere. She decided on leasing a storefront in a nice area and obligated the partnership to a three-year lease at an above-market rate. She decided on stylish tenant improvements to achieve the right look for her dream store. She then obligated the partnership to buy a large quantity of gifts in order to stock the store.

Before L & M Gifts opened its doors the partnership had obligated itself to spend $12,000 on improvements. They were also obligated to pay $1,500 per month in rent for the next three years. Louise was not aware of these transactions. However, as general partner, Maxine could obligate the partnership without informing or getting the approval of her other partner.

Louise wanted to announce their grand opening by placing an ad in the newspaper. Because they were a new business, the paper wanted a check up front. When Louise went to write a check it hit her. They were out of money. Maxine had spent Louise's entire $10,000, and then some, to open the store.

When Louise confronted Maxine with this Maxine was unconcerned. She asked Louise if she could put up any more cash. But Louise did not have any more money. Her life savings, her dream of her own business and control of her future, was the $10,000 that Maxine had already spent.

Maxine said she did not have a credit card but asked if Louise had or could get a credit card to help them get over this hump. Maxine said that if they could just get the doors open together they would be rolling in profits. It was with this comment that Louise realized that she was putting up all the money and taking all the risk so that Maxine could share in all the profits.

Louise was shaken by this realization but remained composed. She said she did not have a credit card nor did she have good enough credit to get one.

At this, Maxine flew off the handle. She said that she had invested all her ideas of style and atmosphere into the business. All Louise had to do was put up the money. She was furious that her creative vision for L & M Gifts was to be dimmed by Louise's refusal to put in more money.

Louise was stunned by her partner's reaction. She had put her life savings into the business. Maxine, without telling her, had squandered it. And now Maxine was angry that she could not put in more.

As one would expect, things soured very quickly between the two. As soon as Maxine learned that no more money was forthcoming, she reignited a relationship with an old boyfriend who lived two thousand miles away. She picked up and left town within forty-eight hours. No one heard from her again.

Louise was left with all the bills. Because Maxine had obligated the partnership, even though Louise had no knowledge of such obligations, Louise as the remaining general partner was personally responsible.

The landlord, the contractor who did the tenant improvements, and the suppliers of the inventory all sued Louise. While Maxine was equally responsible (if not more so) for these debts, the creditors did not even bother to pursue her. She had no money and she was on the other side of the country. Why would someone spend the time and money to chase her? The sole burden of the partnership's debts fell upon Louise.

With her life savings gone and her vision of her own business dashed, Louise unhappily went back to work at the department store.

As Case No. 2 illustrates, with a general partnership you have double the exposure of a sole proprietorship. Not only you—but your partner—can put your personal assets at risk. All of the risk and double (or triple or more depending on the number of general partners you have) the exposure is not a good way to do business.

As our first two cases point out, it is important to select the correct entity at the start. (And, please note, not all of our stories will be so dire. It is just that right now we are dealing with bad entities.)

> ## *Other General Partnership Disadvantages*
>
> As if all of the risk and double the exposure were not bad enough, there are other disadvantages to operating as a general partnership:
>
> - *Termination.* A partnership terminates when one partner dies, leaves, or goes bankrupt. You may be surprised by some unexpected event.
> - *Sale.* Most sophisticated buyers do not want the risk of being in a general partnership. This will hinder the ability to sell your interest in a general partnership.

Rich Dad Tip

- The longer you operate as a sole proprietorship or general partnership the longer you are going to be personally responsible for every bad thing that can happen in your business.
- If you are currently operating as a sole proprietorship or general partnership, see a professional immediately about switching to a good entity.
- If you are considering getting into a business, do not start out on the wrong foot by using a bad entity.

Good Entities

- C corporations
- S corporations
- Limited liability companies (LLCs)
- Limited partnerships (LPs)

To succeed in business, to protect your assets, and to limit your liability, you will want to select from one of the good entities listed above. Each one has its own advantages and specific uses. Each one is utilized by the rich and the knowledgeable in their business and personal financial affairs. And, depending on your state's fees, each one can be formed for $900 or less so that you can achieve the same benefits and protections that sophisticated businesspeople have enjoyed for centuries.

Before we discuss the relative strengths of corporations, LLCs, and LPs, it is important to know the language of each. While their basic structure is similar, the terms for each structural facet are different. Here then is the language for the good entities.

The Language of Corporations, Limited Liability Companies, and Limited Partnerships

Term	Corporation	Limited Liability Company	Limited Partnership
Owner	Shareholder	Member	General and limited partner
Senior management	Chairman of the board; chief executive officer (CEO); president	Manager(s)	General partner(s)
Organizational document filed with state	Articles of incorporation	Articles of organization	Certificate of limited partnership
Operational road map	Bylaws	Operating agreement	Limited partnership agreement

Corporations

The best place to start the discussion of good entities is with corporations. They have evolved over the last five hundred years to become the most commonly used entity for conducting business.

As Robert Kiyosaki learned during his study of admiralty law, corporations came into common usage in the 1500s to protect investors in maritime ventures. Prior to the popular use of corporations, investors would come together as a partnership, outfit a ship, and send it out for trading purposes. If the ship was lost at sea, the investors could not only lose everything but also be personally sued by various creditors. Of course, this exposure deterred people from risk taking and discouraged economic activity. Seeing this, the English Crown and courts allowed for the charter of corporations whereby risks and liabilities could be limited to the corporation itself.

The shareholders, the investors in the corporation, were liable only to the extent of their contribution to the business. This was a significant development in world economic history.

Case No. 3—The *English Rose*/Sir Richard Starkey

In the late 1500s maritime activity was increasing. The New World beckoned with the promise of riches and opportunity. The then small segment of Europeans with money were investing in sailing ships to pursue trading opportunities. If your ship could make it across the Atlantic with supplies, sell them or trade them for commodities, and return with a valuable cargo, you could make a fortune. This scenario was the origin of the phrase: "When my ship comes in."

During this time, two groups of London promoters were soliciting investors to outfit a ship and send it to the Caribbean in search of trading opportunities. A ship known as the *Royale Returne* had just recently arrived at the London docks and its investors had reaped profits of 1,000 percent. Investors were excited by these opportunities. The first group was outfitting a ship known as the *English Flyer.* The promoters brought investors in as general partners, offering 10 percent of the profits in exchange for £250. In Elizabethan England, as today, there was no special requirement to get permission to operate as a general partnership.

Two British gentlemen, Sir Richard Starkey and Master John Fowles, were potential investors. Master John Fowles was astounded by the profits the *Royale Returne* had generated for its investors. He wanted to invest in the very next ship set to sail. It didn't matter that the *English Flyer* was a partnership. The personal liability of a general partnership did not trouble him—not when huge profits were in sight. Master John Fowles invested £250 in the *English Flyer* as soon as he could.

The second group of promoters was outfitting the *English Rose.* They wanted the limited liability of a new entity called a corporation. The problem was that, like today, it cost extra money to form and you had to wait for the Crown to give you a charter. But the second group of promoters was more careful than the first. They did not want to put themselves or their investors at risk in case the ship never returned. Sir Richard Starkey, being prudent and cautious, chose to invest in the *English Rose.* He knew there was risk in venturing across the Atlantic. He wanted to limit his exposure to just £250.

As it turned out, the *English Rose* and the *English Flyer* left London for the Caribbean at about the same time. As they set sail the risks to the investors in each enterprise were as follows:

	The English Flyer	*The* English Rose
Business entity	General partnership	Corporation
Investment	£250 for 10% of general partnership interests	£250 for 10% of corporation's shares
Liability	Unlimited joint and several	Limited to £250
If ship does not return	Each investor personally liable for all debts and obligations	Each investor's liability limited only to the £250 put into corporation

As luck would have it, the *English Flyer* was lost near the Bermuda Triangle. The promoters had leased the boat, provided their own captain, and were now responsible to the owners for its loss. The promoters and 90 percent of the general partners did not have as much money as Master John Fowles did. As we learned in Louise's case, and as has been the case for centuries, creditors will go after the easiest target with the deepest pockets. As so Master John Fowles, only a 10 percent general partner, was sued and held responsible for the entire loss of the *English Flyer.* He learned the hard way what happens when your ship does not come in, and you are responsible for it.

As Sir Richard Starkey's luck would have it, the *English Rose* did well on each side of the Atlantic and provided a huge return to its investors. Unlike Master John Fowles, Sir Richard Starkey was willing to lose £250 and no more. By using a corporation instead of a partnership he was able to establish his downside risk, while allowing for his upside advantage to be unlimited.

Sir Richard Starkey and other knowledgeable and sophisticated investors have used corporations, and other good entities, to limit their liability for centuries.

Forming a corporation is simple. Essentially, you file a document that creates an independent legal entity with a life of its own. It has its own name, business purpose, and tax identity with the IRS. As such, it—the corporation—is responsible for the activities of the business. In this way, the owners, or shareholders, are protected. The owners' liability is limited to the monies they used to start the corporation, not all of their other personal assets. If an entity is to be sued it is the corporation, not the individuals behind this legal entity.

A corporation is organized by one or more shareholders. Depending upon each state's law, it may allow one person to serve as all officers and directors. In certain states, to protect the owners' privacy, nominee officers and directors may be utilized. A corporation's first filing, the articles of incorporation, is signed by the incorporator. The incorporator may be any individual involved in the company, including, frequently, the company's attorney.

The articles of incorporation set out the company's name, the initial board of directors, the authorized number of shares, and other major items. Because it is a matter of public record, specific, detailed, or confidential information about the corporation should not be included in the articles of incorporation. The corporation is governed by rules found in its bylaws. Its decisions are recorded in meeting minutes, which are kept in the corporate minute book.

When the corporation is formed, the shareholders take over the company from the incorporator. The shareholders elect the directors to oversee the company. The directors in turn appoint the officers to carry out day-to-day management.

The shareholders, directors, and officers of the company must remember to follow corporate formalities. They must treat the corporation as a separate and independent legal entity, which includes holding regularly scheduled meetings, conducting banking through a separate corporate bank account, filing a separate corporate tax return, and filing corporate papers with the state on a timely basis.

Failure to follow such formalities may allow a creditor to disregard the corporate veil and seek personal liability against the corporate officers, directors, and shareholders. This is known as "piercing the corporate veil"—a legal maneuver in which the creditor tries to establish that the corporation failed to operate as a separate and distinct entity; if this is the case, then the veil of corporate protection is pierced and the individuals involved are held personally liable. Adhering to corporate formalities is not at all difficult or particularly time-consuming. In fact, if you have your attorney handle the corporate filings and preparation of annual minutes and direct your accountant to prepare the corporate tax return, you should spend no extra time at it with only a very slight increase in cost. The point is that if you spend the extra money to form a corporation in order to gain limited liability it makes sense to spend the extra, and minimal, time and money to ensure that protection is achieved.

One disadvantage of utilizing a regular, (or C) corporation to do business is that its earnings may be taxed twice. This generally happens at the end of the corporation's fiscal year. If the corporation earns a profit it pays a tax on the gain. If it then decides to pay a dividend to its shareholders, the shareholders are taxed once again. To avoid the double tax of a C corporation, most C corporation owners make sure there are no profits at the end of the year. Instead, they use all the write-offs allowed to reduce their net income.

The potential for double taxation does not occur with the other good entities, a limited liability company or a limited partnership. In those entities profits and losses flow through the entity directly to the owner. Thus, there is no entity tax but instead there is a tax obligation on your individual return. Depending on your situation, an LLC or LP with flow-through taxation may be to your advantage or disadvantage. Again, one size does not fit all.

It should be noted here that a corporation with flow-through taxation features does exist. The Subchapter S corporation (S corporation), named after the IRS code section allowing it, is a flow-through corporate entity. By filing Form 2553, "Election by a Small Business Corporation," the corporation is not treated as a distinct entity for tax purposes. As a result, profits and losses flow through to the shareholders as in a partnership.

While a Subchapter S corporation is the entity of choice for certain small businesses, it does have some limits. It can only have seventy-five or fewer shareholders. All shareholders must be American citizens. Corporations, limited partnerships, limited liability companies, and other entities, including certain trusts, may not be shareholders. A Subchapter S corporation may have only one class of stock.

In fact, it was the above-named limitations that led to the creation of the limited liability company. Because many shareholders wanted the protection of a corporation with flow-through taxation but could not live within the shareholder limitations of a Subchapter S corporation, the limited liability company was born.

The Subchapter S corporation requires the filing of Form 2553 by the 15th day or the third month of its tax year for the flow-through tax election to become effective. A limited liability company or limited partnership receives this treatment without the necessity of such a filing.

Another issue with the Subchapter S corporation is that flow-through taxation can be lost when one shareholder sells his stock to a nonpermitted owner, such as a foreign individual or trust. By so terminating the Subchapter S election, the business is then taxed as a C corporation and the company cannot reelect S status for a period of five years. The potential for this problem is eliminated by using a limited liability company.

Both C and S corporations require that stock be issued to their shareholders. While limited liability companies may issue membership interests and limited partnerships may issue partnership interests, they do not feature the same ease of transferability and liquidity (or salability) of corporate shares. Neither limited liability companies nor limited partnerships have the ability to offer an ownership incentive akin to stock options. Neither entity should be considered a viable candidate for a public offering. If stock incentives and public tradeability of shares are your objective, you must eventually become a C corporation.

Rich Dad Tips

- If you think you may want to go public at some point in the future but want initial losses to flow through, consider starting with an S corporation or a limited liability company.
- You can always convert to a C corporation at a later date, after you have taken advantage of flowing through losses.

Limited Liability Companies

The limited liability company is a good entity to use in certain situations. Because it provides the limited liability protection of a corporation and the flow-through taxation of a partnership, some have referred to the LLC as an incorporated partnership.

There are two more features that make the LLC unique:

- Flexible management structure
- Flexible allocation of profit and loss

These features will be illustrated in our next case.

Case No. 4—Thelma/Millennium Salsa

Thelma was looking to start a salsa business with two partners, Pepe and Hans. They had taken the beneficial step of preparing a business plan. They analyzed the market and their competition. They calculated their expenses, projected conservative revenues, and figured that Millennium Salsa could break even in two years.

The problem was that each partner had his or her own agenda that was difficult to reconcile. They had agreed that for their efforts each was to receive a one-third interest in Millennium Salsa. But beyond that it was looking doubtful that they could structure the business in such a way that it would work. Pepe was putting in $200,000 of start-up money to get the business going. He wanted no part of managing the business but wanted, first, to use any losses to offset other business/personal income; and, second, that all of the first profits be paid directly to him until he was paid back $300,000, or one and one half times what he had invested. Hans, on the other hand, was putting his salsa recipe into the company. It was a well-known and world-famous recipe renowned for its freshness and long shelf life, but beyond that Hans's contribution to the company would be limited. He had offered to work for the company, but for Thelma and Pepe, who both knew of Hans's odd work habits and culinary eccentricities, that was more of a threat than a promise.

Thelma was going to work in the business. Her contribution was to spend the next two years—or however long it took—working for a very low wage to make a go of it. She had learned from her cousin Louise that a general partnership was a bad entity to use. The last thing Thelma wanted was for Hans to be out obligating their business to another bizarre food project like the banana-shaped onion fiasco.

The management of the business, and keeping Hans out of it, was one issue. But an even bigger issue was how to satisfy Pepe's demands for all the losses to flow through to him and the first $300,000 in profits to go to him.

Thelma knew that in a Subchapter S corporation when profits and losses flowed through the entity, they flowed rigidly according to the shareholder's ownership percentage. If you owned 50 percent, then 50 percent flowed through to you. In the case of Millennium Salsa, each person would have a one-third interest in whatever entity was to be used. But they needed to initially distribute more than one third to Pepe.

How could they satisfy Pepe's demands? Thelma knew she had to figure out some way to get it done or Pepe would not agree to the project.

Thelma went to her part-time bookkeeper, who told her she had to use an S corporation. Thelma was told that Pepe's demands could not be met and that the only way to handle the corporate structure was to allocate profits and losses on a one-third basis to each Millennium Salsa shareholder. The bookkeeper said she used an S corporation for every such situation and that most of her clients were satisfied.

Thelma then sought the advice of a local attorney who specialized in business formation and structure. It was during her initial consultation that Thelma learned of the limited liability company for the first time. She learned that special allocations according to partnership formulas could be made to accommodate Pepe's conditions. She learned that a flexible LLC management structure could be implemented so that neither Pepe nor Hans would be involved as decision makers.

The attorney charted for her the difference between the rigidity of an S corporation and the flexibility of an LLC when it came to distributions.

Millennium Salsa, Inc., an S Corporation

Owner and Interest	Year One $60,000 Loss	Year Two $30,000 Loss	Year Three $300,000 Gain	Year Four $600,000 Gain
Pepe—33⅓%	<$20,000>	<$10,000>	$100,000	$200,000
Hans—33⅓%	<$20,000>	<$10,000>	$100,000	$200,000
Thelma—33⅓%	<$20,000>	<$10,000>	$100,000	$200,000

In Millennium Salsa, Inc. the flow-through distributions have to be made according to each shareholder's percentage ownership. Because Pepe owns one third there is no way to allocate him 100 percent of either profits or losses. He is stuck with what flows through to him strictly according to his ownership interest. However, Thelma liked what could be accomplished with an LLC:

Millennium Salsa, Limited Liability Company

Owner and Interest	Year One $60,000 Loss	Year Two $30,000 Loss	Year Three $300,000 Gain	Year Four $600,000 Gain
Pepe—33⅓%	<$60,000>	<$30,000>	$300,000	$200,000
Hans—33⅓%	0	0	0	$200,000
Thelma—33⅓%	0	0	0	$200,000

In the LLC scenario, Pepe's goals are achieved. He is able to take the first losses and receive the first $300,000 in profits. It should be noted that special allocations such as this must be based on legitimate economic circumstances as opposed to simply shifting tax obligations from one taxpayer to another. For an excellent discussion on these rules see Chapters 11–15 of Diane Kennedy's *Loopholes of the Rich*. The attorney informed Thelma she needed to work with a tax professional so that Millennium Salsa's objectives were properly documented and carried out.

The attorney also noted that money flowing through the LLC to Thelma, as an employee, was subject to self-employment taxes of 15.3 percent to the statutory maximum of $80,400 for 2001 and 2.9 percent over that for the Medicare portion. Because Pepe and Hans were not employees but rather investors, their flow through of monies was not subject to self-employment tax. It was noted that an S corporation, where self-employment taxes were only paid on monies deemed to be salaries and profits above that were not taxed as self-employment income, may be an option for Thelma's distributions. But again, the attorney noted the flexible distributions Pepe wanted could not be achieved in an S corporation. One entity did *not* fit all situations.

Thelma also learned that the management structure was different, and much more flexible, than that of a corporation. A corporation had directors elected by shareholders, officers elected by directors, and employees hired by officers. By contrast, an LLC could be managed by all its members, which are akin to shareholders in a corporation, or be managed by just some of its members or by a nonmember. The first was called a member-managed LLC, the second a manager-managed LLC. Because Pepe wanted no management responsibility and neither Thelma nor Pepe wanted Hans anywhere near management authority, it was decided that Thelma would be the sole manager of a manager-managed LLC. As manager she had complete authority for the company's affairs. In corporate terms, she was the board of directors, the president, secretary, treasurer, and all vice presidents of Millennium Salsa. And all her business card had to say was "Manager, Millennium Salsa, LLC."

Pepe liked the plan that Thelma brought back from the attorney's office. He funded the project and they were in business.

The LLC was designed to overcome the problems corporations faced in attempting to avoid double taxation. In the process, as we have seen, some unique and useful features were created as additional benefits to the entity. The main features are as follows:

LIMITED LIABILITY PROTECTION

In an LLC, like a corporation, the owners do not face personal liability for business debts or for legal claims made against the company. In this day and age when litigation can unexpectedly wipe out a lifetime of savings, limited liability protection is of paramount importance.

It is important to note that in an LLC, as with a corporation, you may become personally liable for certain debts of the company if you sign a personal guarantee. As an example, most landlords will require the owners or officers of a new business to personally guarantee that the lease payments will be made. If the business goes under, the landlord has the right to seek monthly payments against the individual guarantors until the premises are leased to a new tenant. Likewise, loans backed by the Small Business Administration will require a personal guarantee. The SBA's representative will state that they will only loan to those persons committed enough to put their own assets at risk. In truth, as with any bank, they want as much security as they can get. Such personal guarantees are standard business requirements that will not change.

The important point to remember is that you are not going to sign a personal guarantee for each and every vendor agreement and customer transaction you enter. And in these matters, you will be protected through the proper use of an LLC. To obtain such protection it is important to sign any agreement as an officer of the LLC. By signing an agreement "Joe Doe" without adding "Manager, XYZ, LLC" you can become personally liable. The world must be put on notice that you are operating as an independent entity. To that end, it is important to include LLC—or Inc. if you use a corporation, or LP for a limited partnership—on all your stationery, checks, invoices, promotional literature, and especially written agreements.

UNLIMITED OWNERSHIP

One of the reasons people have a problem utilizing the S corporation is the limits on owners. An S corporation can only have seventy-five or fewer shareholders. As well, some foreign citizens and certain entities are prohibited from becoming shareholders of an S corporation.

The LLC offers the flexibility of allowing for one member to an unlimited number of members, each of whom may be a foreign citizen, spendthrift trust, or corporate entity. And unlike an S corporation, you won't have to worry about losing your flow-through taxation in the event one shareholder sells their shares to a prohibited shareholder.

FLEXIBLE MANAGEMENT

LLCs offer two very flexible and workable means of management. First, they can be managed by all of their members, which is known as member-managed. Or they can be managed by just one or some of their members or by an outside nonmember, which is called manager-managed.

It is very easy to designate whether the LLC is to be member- or manager-managed. In some states, the articles of organization filed with the state must set out how the LLC is to be managed. In other jurisdictions, management is detailed in the operating agreement. If the members of an LLC want to change from manager-managed to member-managed, or vice versa, it can be accomplished by a vote of the members.

In most cases, the LLC will be managed by the members. In a small, growing company, each owner will want to have an active say in how the business is operated. Member management is a direct and simple way to accomplish this.

It should be noted that in a corporation there are several layers of management supervision. The officers—president, secretary, treasurer, and vice presidents—handle the day-to-day affairs. They are appointed by the board of directors, which oversees the larger, strategic issues of the corporation. The directors are elected by the shareholders. By contrast, in a member-managed LLC, the members are the shareholders, directors, and officers all at once.

In some cases, manager management is appropriate for conducting the business of the LLC. The following situations may call for manager management:

1. One or several LLC members are only interested in investing in the business and want no part of management decision making.

2. A family member has gifted membership interests to his children but does not want them or consider them ready to take part in management decisions.

3. A nonmember has lent money to the LLC and wants a say in how the funds are spent. The solution is to adopt manager management and make him a manager.

4. A group of members come together and invest in a business. They feel it is prudent to hire a professional outside manager to run the business and give him management authority.

As with a corporation, it is advisable to keep minutes of the meetings held by those making management decisions. While some states do not require annual or other meetings of an LLC, the better practice is to document such meetings on a consistent basis in order to avoid miscommunication, claims of mismanagement, or attempts to assert personal liability.

DISTRIBUTION OF LLC PROFITS AND LOSSES/SPECIAL ALLOCATIONS

One of the remarkable features of an LLC is that partnership rules provide that members may divide the profits and losses in a flexible manner. This is a significant departure from the corporate regime whereby dividends are allocated according to percentage ownership.

For example, an LLC can provide 40 percent of the profits to a member who only contributed 20 percent of the initial capital. This is achieved by making what is called a special allocation.

To be accepted by the IRS, special allocations must have a "substantial economic effect." In IRS lingo this means that the allocation must be based upon legitimate economic circumstances. An allocation cannot be used to simply reduce one owner's tax obligations.

By including special language in your LLC's operating agreement you may be able to create a safe harbor to insure that future special allocations will have a substantial economic effect. (As with ships at sea, a safe harbor for IRS purposes is a place of comfort and certainty.) The required language deals with the following:

1. Capital accounts, which represent the investment of the owner plus accumulated undistributed earnings, less accumulated losses less any distribution of capital back to the owners. Each member's capital account must be carried on the books under special rules set forth in the IRS regulations. Consult with your tax advisor on these rules. They are not unusual or out of the ordinary.

2. Liquidation based upon capital accounts. Upon dissolution of the LLC, distributions are to be made according to positive capital account balances.

3. Negative capital account paybacks. Any members with a negative capital account balance must return their account to a zero balance upon the sale or liquidation of the LLC, or when the owner sells his interest.

It should be noted that complying with the special allocation rules and qualifying under the safe harbor provisions is a complicated area of the law. Be sure to consult with an advisor who is qualified to assist you in this arena.

FLOW-THROUGH TAXATION

As has been mentioned throughout, one of the most significant benefits of the LLC, and a key reason for its existence, is the fact that the IRS recognizes it as a pass-through tax entity. All of the profits and losses of the business flow through the LLC without tax. They flow through to the business owner's tax return and are dealt with at the individual level.

Again, a C corporation does not offer such a feature. In a C corporation, the profits are taxed at the corporate level and then taxed again when a dividend is paid to the shareholder. Thus, the issue of double taxation. Still, with proper planning, the specter of C corporation double taxation can be minimized.

In an S corporation, profits and losses flow through the corporation, thereby avoiding double taxation, but may only be allocated to the shareholders according to their percentage ownership interest. As described above, LLC profits and losses flow through the entity and may be freely allocated without regard to ownership percentages. As such, the LLC offers the combination of two significant financial benefits that other entities do not.

LACK OF PRECEDENT

One of the drawbacks to the LLC is the fact that it is a new entity. As such, there are not many court decisions defining the various aspects of its use. With corporations and partnerships, on the other hand, you have several hundred years of court cases creating a precedent for their operation.

Most legal commentators anticipate that the courts will look to corporate law to define the limited liability and corporate features of the LLC and to partnership law to define the partnership aspects of the entity. In time, a cohesive body of LLC law will emerge.

Until that day arrives, owners of an LLC must be cognizant that the courts may interpret a feature, a benefit, or even a wrinkle of LLC law in a way that does not suit them. If you are on the fence between selecting a limited partnership, a corporation, or an LLC and do not like the uncertainty associated with a lack of legal precedent, you may want to consider utilizing an entity other than an LLC.

───────────────── **Rich Dad Tips** ─────────────────

- California residents must be cautious when considering the use of an LLC. The fees are onerous.
- In addition to the annual LLC tax of $800 the state of California hits LLCs with a fee based on their gross income. This fee has nothing to do with whether your company is profitable or not. It is only based on revenue generated, so you can lose money and still owe the fee.
- On gross income of $250,000 to $499,999 the fee is $1,042. The fee gradually rises to $9,377 on gross income of over $5 million. Be sure to consider this fee when analyzing which entity to use in California.

Limited Partnership

A limited partnership is similar to a general partnership with the exception that it has two types of partners. The first type is a general partner who is responsible for managing the partnership. As with a general partnership, the general partner of a limited partnership has broad powers to obligate the partnership and is also personally liable for the business's debts and claims. If there is more than one general partner involved they are all jointly and severally liable, meaning that a creditor can go after just one partner for the entire debt. However, a corporation or an LLC can be formed to serve as a general partner of a limited partnership, thus isolating unlimited liability in a good entity.

The second type of limited partnership partner is a limited partner. By definition, a limited partner is "limited" to his contribution of capital to the partnership and may not become actively involved in the business of the partnership. A limited partner may then be owner but have absolutely no say in how the entity operates. This was exactly what Jim wanted.

Case No. 5—Jim

Jim was the proud father of three boys in high school. Aaron, Bob, and Chris were coming of age. They were active, athletic, and creative boys almost ready to embark upon their own careers. The problem was that they were sometimes too active, too athletic, and too creative.

Aaron was seventeen years old and every one of the seemingly unlimited hormones he had was shouting for attention. He loved the girls, the girls loved him, and his social life was frenetic and chaotic. Jim knew his son was smart but worried whether he would ever settle down enough to complete one homework assignment, much less go to college.

Bob was sixteen years old and sports was all that mattered. He played sports, watched sports, and lived and breathed sports. Bob was hoping to get a college scholarship to play football and/or baseball. But Jim worried that if a scholarship wasn't offered whether Bob would ever get into or be interested in going to college.

Chris was fifteen years old and the lead guitarist in a heavy metal band known as Shrike. When Shrike practiced in Jim's garage the neighbors did not confuse them with the Beatles. The members of Shrike had pierced appendages, graphic tattoos, and girlfriends who looked like wild animals. Jim worried about the company that Chris kept. When you could hear the lyrics, Shrike's songs made frequent reference to school as a brainwashing tool of the elite. And while Jim may have also believed that to be true when he was fifteen, he worried that Chris would still embrace the idea at age twenty-one.

Compounding Jim's concerns was that he had five valuable real estate holdings that he wanted to go to the boys. His wife had passed on several years before and he needed to make some estate planning decisions. But given the boys' energy level and lack of direction he did not want them controlling or managing the real estate.

Jim knew that if he left the assets in his own name, when he died the IRS would take 55 percent of his estate, which was valued at over $2 million. And while estate taxes were to be gradually eliminated, Jim knew that Congress could always reinstate them. Jim had worked too hard, and had paid income taxes once already before buying the properties, to let the IRS's estate taxes take away half his assets. But again, he could not let his boys have any sort of control over the assets. While the government could squander 55 percent of his assets, he knew that his boys could easily top that with a 100 percent effort.

Jim asked his friends to refer him to a good attorney who could put together a plan to assist him. The attorney he met with suggested that Jim place the five real estate holdings into five separate limited partnerships.

It was explained to Jim that the beauty of a limited partnership was that all management control was in the hands of the general partner. The limiteds were not allowed to get involved in the business. Their activity was "limited" to being passive owners.

It was explained that the general partner can own as little as 1 percent of the limited partnership, with the limited partners owning the other 99 percent of it, and yet the general partner can have 100 percent control in how the entity was managed. The limited partners, even though they own 99 percent, cannot be involved. This was a major and unique difference between the limited partnership and the limited liability company or a corporation. If the boys owned 99 percent of an LLC or a corporation they could vote out their dad, sell the assets, and have a party for the ages. Not so with a limited partnership.

The limited partnership was perfect for Jim. He could not imagine his boys performing any sort of responsible management. At least not now. And at the same time he wanted to get the assets out of his name so he would not pay a huge estate tax. The limited partnership was the best entity for this. The IRS allowed discounts when you used a limited partnership for gifting. So instead of gifting $10,000 tax free to each boy he could gift $12,500 or more to each boy. Over a period of years, his limited partnership interest in each of the limited partnerships would be reduced and the boys' interest would be increased. When Jim passed on, his estate tax would be based only on the amount of interest he had left in each limited partnership. If he lived long enough he could gift away his entire interest in all five limited partnerships.

Except for his general partnership interest. By retaining his 1 percent general partnership interest, Jim could control the entities until the day he died. While he was hopeful his boys would straighten out, the limited partnership format allowed him total control in the event that did not happen.

Jim also liked the attorney's advice that each of the five properties be put into five separate limited partnerships. It was explained to him that the strategy today is to segregate assets. If someone gets injured at one property and sues, it is better to only have one property exposed. If all five properties were in the same limited partnership, the person suing could go after all five properties to satisfy his claim. By segregating assets into separate entities the person suing can only go after the one property where they were injured.

An added benefit to segregating assets in Jim's case was the boys were interested in different activities. One of the properties housed a batting cage business and another a laundromat. He could see Bob being interested in the batting cage business and Aaron meeting girls while owning the laundromat. (Jim owned nothing that would currently appeal to Chris.) As the boys got older he could gift more of one limited partnership to one boy and more of another to another.

Jim liked the control and protections afforded by the limited partnership entity and proceeded to immediately form five of them.

To organize a limited partnership you must file a certificate of limited partnership, otherwise known as an LP-1, with your state secretary of state's office. This document contains certain information about the general partner and, depending on the state, limited partners and is akin to the filing of articles of incorporation for a corporation or articles of organization for a LLC.

As with the LLC, the LP offers certain unique advantages not found in other entities. These features include:

LIMITED LIABILITY

Limited partners are not responsible for the partnership's debts beyond the amount of their capital contribution or contribution obligation. So, as discussed, unless they become actively involved, the limited partners are protected.

As a general rule, general partners are personally liable for all partnership debts. But as was mentioned above, there is a way to protect the general partner of a limited partnership. To reduce liability exposure, corporations or LLCs are formed to serve as general partners of the limited partnership. In this way, the liability of the general partner is encapsulated in a limited liability entity. Assume a creditor sues a limited partnership over a business debt and seeks to hold the general partner liable. If the general partner is a corporation or LLC, that is where the liability ends. No one's personal assets are at risk.

As such, many, if not most, limited partnerships are organized using corporations or LLCs as general partners. In this way, both the limited and general partners achieve limited liability protection.

RETAINED MANAGEMENT

Because by definition limited partners may not participate in management, the general partner maintains complete control. In many cases, the general partner will hold only 1 percent or 2 percent of the partnership interest but will be able to assert 100 percent control over the partnership. This feature is valuable in estate planning situations where a parent is gifting or has gifted limited partnership interests to his children. Until such family members are old enough or trusted enough to act responsibly, the senior family members may continue to manage the LP even though only a very small general partnership interest is retained.

RESTRICTIONS ON TRANSFER

The ability to restrict the transfer of limited or general partnership interests to outside persons is a valuable feature of the limited partnership. Through a written limited partnership agreement, rights of first refusal, prohibited transfers, and conditions to permitted transfers are instituted to restrict the free transferability of partnership interests. It should be noted that LLCs can also afford beneficial restrictions on transfer. These restrictions are crucial for achieving the creditor protection and estate and gift tax advantages afforded by limited partnerships.

PROTECTION FROM CREDITORS

Creditors of a partnership can only reach the partnership assets and the assets of the general partner, which is limited by using a corporate general partner. Thus if, for example, you and your family owned three separate apartment buildings, it may be prudent to compartmentalize these assets into three separate limited partnerships, using three separate corporate gen-

eral partners. If a litigious tenant sued over conditions at one of the properties, the other two buildings would not be exposed to satisfy any claims.

Creditors of the individual partners can only reach that person's partnership interest and not the partnership assets themselves. Assume you've
gifted a 25 percent limited partnership interest in one of the apartment
building partnerships to your son. He is young and forgets to obtain automobile insurance. Of course, in this example, he gets in a car accident and
has a judgment creditor looking for assets. This creditor cannot reach the
apartment building asset itself because it is in the limited partnership. He
can only reach the limited partnership interest, and then only through a
charging order procedure; a charging order allows the creditor of a judgment debtor who is in a partnership with others to reach the debtor's partnership interest without dissolving the partnership. Charging orders, which
can result in phantom income to the creditor, are not favored by creditors.
This is because phantom income is the allocation of a tax obligation to the
creditor without the receipt of money to pay the taxes on such income. Not
many creditors enjoy paying taxes on an uncollectable debt.

FAMILY WEALTH TRANSFERS

With proper planning, transfers of family assets from one generation to the
next can occur at discounted rates. As a general rule, the IRS allows one individual to give another individual a gift of $10,000 per year. Any gifts valued
at over $10,000 are subject to a gift tax starting at 18 percent. In the estate
planning arena, senior family members may be advised to give assets away
during their lifetimes so that estate taxes of up to 55 percent are minimized.

By using a family limited partnership, a limited partnership used for the
management, and gifting of family assets, gifting can be accelerated with an
IRS-approved discount. As discussed, because limited partnership interests
do not entitle the holder to take part in management affairs and are frequently restricted as to their transferability, discounts on their value are permissible. In other words, even if the book value of 10 percent of a certain
limited partnership is $12,500, a normal investor wouldn't pay that much for
it because, as a limited partner, they would have no say in the partnership's
management and would be restricted in their ability to transfer their interest
at a later date. So, instead of valuing that limited partnership interest at
$12,500, the IRS recognizes that it may be worth more like $10,000.

The advantage of this recognition comes into play when parents are ready to gift to their children. Assume a husband and wife have four children. Each spouse can gift $10,000 per year to each child without paying a gift tax. As such, a total of $80,000 can be gifted each year (two parents times four children times $10,000). With the valuation discount reflecting that the $12,500 interest is really only worth $10,000 to a normal investor, each parent gifts a 10 percent limited partnership interest to each child. Their combined gifts total an $80,000 valuation, thus incurring no gift tax. However, of the partnership valued at $125,000 they have gifted away 80 percent of the limited partnership with a book value of $100,000. Had they not used a limited partnership they would have had to pay a gift tax on the $20,000 difference between the $80,000 discounted gifted value and the $100,000 undiscounted value of eight $12,500 10 percent partnership interests that were gifted.

As the example illustrates, transfers of family wealth can be accelerated through the use of limited partnership discounts. Once this technique is appreciated, the question always becomes: How much of a discount will the IRS allow? Is it 25 percent, 35 percent, or can you go as high as 65 percent? While there is no brightline test or number, the simple answer is found in this maxim: Pigs get fat, hogs get slaughtered. If you get greedy with your discounting, the IRS will call into question all of your planning. In my practice, I do not advise my clients to go over a 30 percent discount. That may be conservative. I have dealt with some professionals who with certainty assert higher discounts are easily justified. Again, there is no correct answer. You and your advisor should establish your own comfort level.

FLEXIBILITY
The limited partnership provides a great deal of flexibility. A written partnership agreement can be drafted to tailor the business and family planning requirements of any situation. And there are very few statutory requirements that cannot be changed or eliminated through a well-drafted partnership agreement.

TAXATION
Limited partnerships, like general partnerships, are flow-through tax entities. The limited partnership files an informational partnership tax return

(IRS Form 1065, "U.S. Partnership Return of Income," the same as a general partnership), and each partner receives an IRS Schedule K-1 (1065), "Partner's Share of Income, Credits and Deductions," from the partnership. Each partner then files the K-1 with their individual IRS 1040 tax return.

Following is a table comparing the good and bad entities we have discussed. From there we will further explore the advantages of C and S corporations.

Entity Comparison

	C Corporation	S Corporation	Limited Liability Company	Limited Partnership	General Partnership	Sole Proprietorship
Personal liability for business debts	No personal liability of shareholders	No personal liability of shareholders	No personal liability of members	General partner(s) personally liable; limited partners not personally liable	General partners personally liable	Sole proprietor personally liable
Who can legally obligate the business?	Officers and directors	Officers and directors	In member-managed, any member; in manager-managed, any manager	Any general partner, not limited partners	Any general partner	Sole proprietor
Responsibility for management decisions	Board of directors, officers	Board of directors, officers	Same as above	Same as above	General partners	Sole proprietor
Ownership restrictions	Most states allow one-shareholder corporations; some require at least two	No more than 75 shareholders allowed; no foreign entities or individuals or domestic entities allowed	Most all states allow one-member LLCs	At least one general partner and at least one limited partner required	At least two general partners	Only one sole proprietor and no more
Start-up and ongoing formalities	Articles filed with state; bylaws and annual meetings required	Articles filed with state; form 2553 filed with IRS; bylaws and annual meetings required	Articles filed with state; operating agreement and annual meetings not required, but strongly recommended	LP-1 filed with state, partnership agreement and annual meeting not required but recommended	No state filing; partnership agreement recommended, no meetings required	No state filing, no meetings required

	C Corporation	S Corporation	Limited Liability Company	Limited Partnership	General Partnership	Sole Proprietorship
Limits on transferability of interests	Transfers may be limited by agreement or by securities laws	Transfers may be limited by agreement or by securities laws; transfers to nonqualified persons may cause loss of S corporation status	Unanimous or super-majority consent may be required by nontransferring members	Consent of all partners may be required	Consent of all partners may be required	Can sell business to another
Business effect on death or departure of owner	Corporation continues	Corporation continues	In some states, dissolution unless members vote to continue	Automatic dissolution unless provided for in partnership agreement	Automatic dissolution unless provided for in partnership agreement	Automatic dissolution
Taxation of business profits	Corporate profits taxed at corporate rates; dividends taxed at individual rates of shareholders	Individual tax rates of shareholders	Individual tax rates of members unless LLC elects corporate taxation (Californians beware of additional state fees)	Individual tax rates of general and limited partners	Individual tax rates of general partners	Individual tax rate of sole proprietor

Chapter 2

How to Take Maximum Advantage of a C Corporation

As we have learned, one entity size does not fit all business scenarios. There are situations when an LLC is called for and times when an LP is the best vehicle.

But in terms of maximizing deductions and taking advantage of the tax laws for fringe and other benefits, nothing beats a C corporation.

Consider this chart on the availability of tax deductible fringe benefits.

Entity Comparison—Fringe Benefits

Sole Proprietorship	General and Limited Partnerships	Limited Liability Company	S Corporation	C Corporation
IRA or Keogh retirement plans permitted; may deduct a portion of medical insurance premiums	For general partners and employees, IRA or Keogh retirement plans permitted; may deduct a portion of medical insurance premiums	Depending on tax treatment can get benefits associated with corporation, partnership, or sole proprietorship	Employee shareholders owning 2 percent or more of corporate stock have fringe benefits treated as income; otherwise same as general partnership	Full fringe benefits package tax deductible to corporation and not treated as income to shareholder

The full fringe benefits package that C corporations may offer includes:

- Medical insurance premiums
- Group life and disability insurance
- Reimbursement of employees' medical expenses

Also, unlike other entities, a C corporation may make contributions to plans even though doing so creates a net operating loss for the business. If the full panoply of deductions and their continued availability is important to you, a C corporation should be your entity of choice.

Case No. 6—Tony and Theresa

Tony and Theresa were happily married with two young children, a dog, and a monthly mortgage. Tony worked as a lab technician at a local hospital. Theresa took care of the children and did part-time floral arranging for a local florist while they were in school. While Tony made a decent salary they never seemed to have enough money at the end of the month. They had not started to save for their children's college tuition, nor had they really started to save for their own retirement.

Tony and Theresa knew a number of other couples who faced the same situation. In many cases both spouses were working at full-time jobs and still not getting ahead. Many were resigned to the hope that somehow things would work out. Their children would get college scholarships and student loans. Social Security would provide comfort in retirement.

But Theresa could not rely on such fuzzy hopes. She did not want her children starting out with huge student loans to pay back. And she certainly did not believe that Social Security would be there for her. Not with millions upon millions of baby boomers set to retire.

So Tony and Theresa talked about how they could improve their financial situation. They reviewed their current situation and needs. Tony was a full-time employee at the hospital. He received medical insurance but had to pay for the rest of the family's coverage with after-tax dollars. He also received a small retirement benefit. The two of them liked to travel and tried to take one or two decent trips per year. In terms of cars, Tony had a newer Ford Taurus that served them well. But Theresa had a beat-up Dodge Shadow that she did not like taking the children around in. They also noted that the children were getting older and needed to start using a computer at home in order to keep up in school. The family did not own a computer.

Tony and Theresa listed these and many other factors on a piece of paper. Upon review, it seemed that Tony was in a good position to provide for the family. What was needed was a way for Theresa to be able to work and provide some benefits for the family.

Theresa had learned that a friend of hers recently went into a network marketing business. In network marketing, one can benefit from the sale of a product that is personally distributed, as well as from sales of a product sold by persons he or she has brought into the program. In some cases these outside salespeople can be quite lucrative for the person at the top of the network. While she knew network marketing was not for everyone, her friend said she had formed a C corporation so that she could take pretax deductions for expenses that benefited the family.

Theresa was personable and confident and felt she could do well in network marketing. And she liked the idea of using the corporate tax laws to benefit her family.

With the help of a professional Theresa formed T & T, Inc. to pursue her network marketing business. She investigated a number of network businesses very carefully and found a good opportunity for growth and income. Soon she was bringing money into the corporation. And, as importantly, she was benefiting her family as follows:

Office Rent Expense

Theresa set up a spare bedroom in her house as her office. She learned that to rent 140 square feet (the size of the bedroom) in her town would cost $1.75 per square foot, or $245.00 per month. T & T, Inc. then paid this amount to her and Tony for the use of the office. This payment to them was rental income against which they wrote off a pro rata portion of the property taxes, mortgage interest, insurance, and utilities.

Start-up Expenses

The cost of printing up business cards, incorporating, joining the network marketing program, and the like were all expenses that T & T, Inc. could and did deduct.

Meals

Theresa, along with Tony and their children, could have meals at T & T, Inc.'s expense as long as they were furnished on the premises of the business. That was easy: On occasion they went into the spare bedroom for a tax-free business meal.

It should be noted that caution is required in this realm. Remember, pigs get fat and hogs get slaughtered. You are not going to eat every possible meal in the spare bedroom and hope to get a year's deduction on meals. Be prudent. Also note that only 50 percent of your meal costs can be deducted while traveling.

Computer Expense

Theresa needed a computer for her business. She learned that she could deduct $24,000 a year (the law at this edition) for the purchase of equipment and business assets. Amounts over $24,000 in purchases needed to be depreciated (written off) over a five-year period. So Theresa spent $1,500 on a new computer and printer and wrote the whole amount off against income. If she had purchased the computer outside the business she would have had to use after-tax dollars, monies already reduced by Tony and Theresa's 28 percent tax bracket. In essence the computer equipment would have cost her another $420.

The family had needed a computer. While its actual main use was for T & T, Inc.'s business, the fact that the children used it now and then to explore the Internet and play computer games was de minimis, meaning not enough for T & T, Inc. to charge Theresa for its personal use. And now there was a way for Theresa to keep upgrading her computer with pretax dollars.

Telephone Expense

The IRS does not allow a family's main telephone line to be a business deduction. That was okay with Theresa. The company needed its own line listed in its own name anyway. And the second line was useful when people were on the Internet or the fax machine was being used. The business line was a fully deductible expense.

Employee Expense

As Theresa began to succeed in her network marketing business and money flowed into T & T, Inc., it came time for her to draw an employee paycheck.

This means calculating payroll taxes and making mandatory tax deposits with the IRS.

It is not that hard to do. On salary up to $72,600 (as of this edition), the employee and the corporation split the 15.3 percent tax that goes for Social Security and Medicare. On salary above $72,600 (again, as of this writing) the Medicare tax of 2.9 percent is split between employee and employer (T & T, Inc.). Your accountant can easily calculate these numbers for you. It is important to note that if Theresa did not use a corporation but rather was self-employed, she would have to pay the 15.3 percent herself, without half of it being a deduction to the corporation.

Now that she was an employee, Theresa had even more benefits available to her.

Auto Allowance
The Dodge Shadow was on its final lap. It was time to get another car. Theresa had the choice of buying or leasing a car herself and charging T & T, Inc. for its use, or having T & T, Inc. buy or lease the car itself. For Theresa the deciding factors were that she could use the Shadow personally as a trade-in and that T &T, Inc. was a new corporation and not likely to get financing.

Theresa traded in the Dodge Shadow for a three-year-old Ford Windstar minivan coming off a lease. It was a good vehicle for transporting her network marketing products. And it was safe and roomy for the children. She and Tony worked out the deal and arranged to purchase it over a five-year period. She estimated her miles at 1,000 per month and had T & T, Inc. pay her an auto allowance of $345 per month (1,000 miles × 34.5¢ per mile IRS car allowance). It was her responsibility to pay for the gas, maintenance, and car insurance. But the $345 was enough to pay for all that and the monthly car payment. The money T & T, Inc. paid to her for the car allowance was not reportable on her personal tax return but she was responsible for keeping good records and reporting her mileage to the corporation on a consistent basis.

Achievement Awards
A corporation can give up to $400 a year for a nonqualified achievement award or up to $1,600 under a defined qualified plan. While the qualified plan requires a written plan that does not favor the top paid employees, the nonqualified plan has no specific guidelines. So Theresa gave herself a $400 award

for being T & T, Inc.'s best employee. It did not matter that she was the only employee. This was a tax free gift to her and a deduction for the corporation.

Travel Expenses

Theresa's network marketing group had fantastic annual meetings in desirable destinations. She could deduct her travel, lodging, transportation, and half her meals. Tony would have to pay his own travel and meals, but the rest was paid for by the business. One year the group held their meeting in Paris. Tony and Theresa had never been to Europe. Theresa had learned from her accountant that there were special rules for writing off foreign travel. But as long as there was a business purpose to the travel, it was for one week or less (not counting travel days), and Theresa spent 75 percent or more of the time involved in the business, she could write off her foreign travel. The trip to Paris was a memorable deduction for them.

Health Insurance

The corporation paid for Theresa's health, dental, and eye insurance, and for her dependents as well. In this way Tony could stop paying extra for dependent health coverage at work, saving the family $175 a month. T & T, Inc.'s health insurance plan also paid for disability insurance in case something happened to Theresa.

Group Term Life Insurance

T & T, Inc. provided each employee (Theresa) with $50,000 worth of term life insurance. This was a valuable benefit to Theresa and a deduction for the corporation.

Dependent Care

T & T, Inc. could pay up to $5,000 in dependent care services per employee. (The amount is $2,500 if you are married and filing separately.) This deduction is only available for dependents under the age of thirteen. (If you have children over age thirteen, a cafeteria plan—described below—can be used.) This deduction of $5,000 was valuable to Theresa because with all her work she needed help covering the children after school.

Cafeteria Plan

In order to maximize deductions for day care and term life insurance, Theresa looked into instituting a cafeteria plan. This is a benefits package that allows employees the choice of receiving cash or qualified benefits. A set amount is withheld from the employee's check, before payroll taxes. This amount is set aside for the employee to later use in the benefits cafeteria. Some can be used for day care, even for children over thirteen, some can be used for additional term life insurance, medical insurance, or medical expenses. Like a cafeteria, you get to select what you want.

It was also favorably noted by Theresa, as the employer and owner of T & T, Inc., that the monies put into a cafeteria plan were not subject to payroll taxes. Neither T & T, Inc., nor Theresa individually, had to pay their half of the 15.3 percent in payroll taxes to receive the significant benefits of the cafeteria plan.

Education/Dues/Subscriptions

Theresa had always wanted to finish her college degree. She only had ten units to go. With T & T, Inc. now able to deduct day care, she had the time to go to her local college again. And the beauty was, because her degree would improve the skills needed for her trade and business, her education expenses, including tuition and books, were deductible for T & T, Inc. By later hiring her children as employees, T & T, Inc. could set up an educational assistance plan and pay up to $5,000 per year of their education.

Theresa had also joined a Women in Business organization. She found it valuable to meet with other entrepreneurs and share ideas. As long as the organization's principal purpose was not simply to hold entertainment activities for its guests (like a country club), the dues and related expenses could be deducted. In this case, the group conducted professional seminars and workshops and so Theresa was justified in writing off the dues.

Theresa also loved reading magazines like *Inc.* and *Entrepreneur.* These were expenses that T & T, Inc. could write off.

Retirement Plans

Theresa learned that there were two types of retirement plans she could utilize. They were available to S corporations, LLCs, and sole proprietorships as well. But with a sole proprietorship there were significant disadvantages in that a sole proprietorship is a bad entity when it comes to retirement because:

(1) All retirement contributions are subject to self-employment taxes; and

(2) There is no ERISA (Employee Retirement Income Security Act) protection, and therefore no asset protection, in a sole proprietorship retirement plan.

A defined contribution plan allows for 15 percent of eligible compensation up to $35,000 (or more in later years) per year to be set aside for retirement. This is a deduction to the corporation and a benefit to Theresa.

A defined benefit plan allows contributions in excess of $140,000 based upon your salary. It is important to note that a defined benefit plan is a yearly requirement—your corporation, whether it had a good year or not, must put in a fixed amount of money in order to meet a defined benefit in the future. As a start-up Theresa did not favor such a requirement.

Because the defined contribution plan was more flexible and contributions could be based upon how well the corporation did in a given year, Theresa chose to set up an adjustable 401(k). If the corporation did well and her salary was $100,000 she could have T & T, Inc. set aside $15,000 for her retirement.

As well, if her defined contribution plan or defined benefit plan was qualified (meaning approved by the IRS under the ERISA rules), she had tremendous asset protection. A creditor cannot touch an ERISA—your retirement monies are safe.

Lower Tax Rate

One of the significant advantages of the C corporation is that it has a lower tax rate, only 15 percent on the first $50,000 in profits. Let's see how that differs from an S corporation scenario, assuming Theresa's individual tax rate is at 28 percent.

	T & T, Inc., a C Corporation	T & T, Inc., an S Corporation
Corporate profit	$50,000	$50,000
Corporate tax	7,500	—
Individual tax	—	14,000
Amount remaining	42,500	36,000
Difference	6,500	N/A

By flowing $50,000 in profits from an S corporation (or LLC) onto her tax return, Theresa pays $14,000 in taxes and has $36,000 remaining. She may keep that money herself or, as in many cases, may have to allow the corporation to use that money for future growth or expansion.

By using a C corporation, the tax rate is much lower and, in this case, the tax payments are $6,500 less than if using an S corporation. If Theresa needs to keep money in the corporation for growth or other needs, she will be better off using a C corporation. On the other hand, if the corporation is mature, consistently generated a profit, and Theresa wanted the money in her own account, an S corporation may make sense. Again, the only right answer is what works for Theresa (or you) according to the facts and needs of each case.

Conclusion

Both Theresa and Tony were very pleased with the way T & T, Inc. worked for them. They used the tax code to their advantage, freeing up Tony's salary for greater retirement and college savings and quality-of-life improvements.

--- **Rich Dad Tips** ---

- To fully maximize your C corporation and the available deductions it offers, consider adding a good accountant to your team.
- You may want to also consider going to the IRS website and obtaining Publication 334, "Tax Guide for Small Businesses," to learn more about the deductions you can take.

Chapter 3

How to Use an S Corporation Without Fear of Failure

For many readers you will consult with your accountant or attorney as to choice of entity and they will emphatically state:

S CORPORATION!

And you may check some more, perhaps asking some business owner friends and others in the know as to choice of entity, and they may be just as certain:

S CORPORATION!

So why not just form an S corporation? Well, you can. For many businesses it is the right choice. But you need to know the rules and how it operates differently from a C corporation.

Case No. 7—Burnham's Baked Hams

Jeanne, Elizabeth, and Bernie were ready to enter the baked ham business. They had done their homework and felt they knew their niche and could succeed in it. Elizabeth had done quite a bit of studying. Being cautious by nature she knew they had to form a corporation to protect themselves. Jeanne was more concerned about how the money flowed. If they were going to form a corporation it had to be an S corporation. She did not want to pay a double tax on profits and she did not want to pay self-employment taxes on profits above salaries. Bernie was a sunny optimist. He just wanted to be in business making money selling his delicious baked hams. He left the details to Jeanne and Elizabeth.

After incorporating they obtained their EIN (Employer Identification Number—their taxpayer ID number) from the IRS. With that they filed the Form 2553 within forty-five days of incorporating in order to qualify for S corporation status. They issued themselves each 100,000 shares and were one-third equal owners of Burnham's Baked Hams, Inc.

Right off the bat, in their first year of business, they were successful. Bernie baked a tasty baked ham. They each took a salary of $40,000 per year. Self-employment taxes were paid on those salaries. At the end of the year there was a profit of $120,000. They each received a dividend of another $40,000.

Because they were an S corporation, the $120,000 in profits was not taxed as a dividend as in a C corporation. Instead, it flowed through the corporation without tax to their individual tax returns. And unlike an LLC, where the flow-through would be subject to self-employment taxes, the dividends came to them free of Social Security and Medicare taxes.

Their S corporation was a beautiful thing. Normal taxes were paid on salaries and flow-through taxation for profits. Bernie was happy, as always, Jeanne was pleased to be getting her money, and even ever cautious Elizabeth was content.

As always, an S corporation can work wonderfully until you break some arcane rule that, bingo, automatically terminates your tax status.

Burnham's Baked Hams, Inc. was expanding rapidly. Bernie had negotiated a very large and favorable deal for distribution throughout Canada. In order to get the deal done, Basil Lee, a Toronto-based distributor, wanted to receive 5 percent of the company. Bernie and, surprisingly, prudent Elizabeth were for this arrangement. But Jeanne did not want Basil in the company. She did not like him or trust him. Still, the deal would be huge for their company. So a compromise was reached whereby the corporation would authorize two classes of stock—one class of common voting shares that could elect the board of directors and a second class of nonvoting preferred that would not elect any directors and thus have no say in management. Basil was then issued preferred shares equal to 5 percent of the total authorized shares (common and preferred together) but he had no power to control the company, which is how Jeanne wanted things.

Elizabeth had her own issues. She did not like holding the company shares in her own name. There were too many unethical potential creditors, too many vexatious potential litigants, just too many questionable people out there for her liking. She knew her views were justified and wanted to have the shares held by an irrevocable spendthrift trust where they would be safe from the claims of others. She formed an irrevocable trust to hold the shares and transferred them from her name to that of the trust.

Sometime thereafter the company received a notice from the IRS. Their S corporation status was terminated.

Why?

Because Burnham's Baked Hams, Inc. had the following:

(1) A non-U.S. shareholder (Basil the Canadian);
(2) More than one class of stock (preferred for Basil and common for the others); and
(3) A trust as a shareholder (Elizabeth's trust)

Any one of those three is enough to terminate S status. And that is how Jeanne, Elizabeth, and Bernie learned the problem with an S corporation. Things can be going along just fine when through some unforeseen transaction (a shareholder unwittingly sells to a nonresident alien, for example) you lose your tax status. And when that happens you become a C corporation and cannot be taxed as an S corporation for five years.

As it turned out, Burnham's Baked Hams, Inc. was better off as a C corporation. Basil's deal took the company into a much higher realm of revenue. It probably would not have happened if he was not a shareholder. As well, with more money coming in, the company needed to accumulate monies for even greater expansion. That would be tough to do with an S corporation, for one needs to allocate profits to flow through and at least pay taxes on that income. With corporate tax rates being lower, profits may be better used for growth. Further, with an S corporation, fringe benefits for shareholders owning greater than 2 percent of the company's stock must be included as income to the shareholder. A comprehensive and generous fringe benefits package had been developed for Jeanne, Elizabeth, Bernie, and now Basil. With a C corporation it could be deducted, as opposed to each of them paying tax on the value received in an S corporation.

Fortunately, the S corporation tax status termination did not hurt Burnham's Baked Hams, Inc.

As discussed, for certain businesses an S corporation is the right choice. You just need to be careful not to lose your tax status through inadvertence or a less than complete understanding of the rules. What follows is a more detailed and technical discussion of S corporations.

S Corporation Eligibility Requirements

- The corporation must be a corporation organized in any U.S. state but not one from outside the U.S.
- It must not be an ineligible corporation (certain types of businesses are not eligible).
- It must not have more than seventy-five shareholders.
- Only individuals, decedents' estates, estates of individuals in bankruptcy, and certain trusts may be shareholders. Corporations and many types of trusts may not be shareholders.
- No shareholder may be a nonresident alien. Only U.S. individuals may be shareholders.
- The corporation may have only one class of stock, but different voting rights are allowed.

Corporate Form

The primary advantage of S corporation status is that it allows businesses to operate in corporate form without paying income tax at the corporate level. The S corporation is a flow-through entity; it allows losses and other deductions to be taken at the shareholder level.

The primary disadvantage to S corporation status is its complexity. There are many technical rules that can serve as pitfalls for the unwary. S corporations have ownership and class-of-stock restrictions that are more burdensome than those of other entities. For instance, shareholder loans can create a second class of stock causing termination of S status.

Built-in Gains Tax

A corporation electing S corporation status is subject to the built-in gains tax. When an S corporation sells an asset it owned as a C corporation a tax is imposed equal to the highest rate for corporations on the unrealized gain (the difference between book value and market value) at the time of its Subchapter S election. The gain is subject to the corporate-level tax, and the same amount (minus the amount of tax paid by the corporation) is taxed to the shareholders. The built-in gains tax is applicable for ten years after the corporation has elected S corporation status.

Net Operating Loss

A C corporation with substantial loss carryovers that expects to start making a profit should usually not elect Subchapter S status until the loss carryovers are used up. While the corporation is an S corporation, the loss carryovers created by the C corporation cannot be deducted by either the corporation or its shareholders. There is a minor exception to this rule where the loss can be deducted against the built-in gains tax.

Losses can never flow through from a C corporation to its shareholders. By contrast, losses generally do pass through from an S corporation to its shareholders. However, the amount of such losses cannot exceed a shareholder's adjusted basis (the amount invested) in the corporation's stock and debt. Any loss in excess of basis carries forward for the benefit of the shareholder in question.

Federal Taxation

C corporations are taxed as separate entities. One disadvantage to a C corporation is that its earnings can be taxed twice—once when earned at the corporate level and again when distributed to shareholders as dividends. This double taxation often can be minimized if the entity pays out most or all of its earnings as deductible salary (the amount must be reasonable) or reasonable rent (where you own the building).

Because S corporations are pass-through entities, each owner is allocated a share of the entity's income and other tax attributes based on the owner's ownership interest. These items are then reported on the owner's individual return. When an S corporation distributes property, the owner-recipient generally recognizes gain only to the extent that the value of the property exceeds the owner's stock basis.

State Taxation

A C corporation can expect that state income tax laws will generally parallel federal laws. State income taxes may, however, affect the use of an S corporation in some states. Five states that tax income do not have laws that correspond to Subchapter S. The lack of such laws may produce unfavorable tax results (e.g., a double state tax on distributed income); a shareholder will pay tax on the income in the state where the income is earned and in his state of residence.

Rich Dad Tip

- Residents of the District of Columbia, Michigan, New Hampshire, New York City, and Tennessee should be cautious using S corporations. Their jurisdictions do not recognize S corporations, thus minimizing many of the benefits.

The state taxation issue adds considerable complexity to the personal tax returns of shareholders of an S corporation doing business in multiple states. As well, S corporation pass-through income will be taxable to shareholders living in states that impose state income taxes.

Compensation

Salaries paid to shareholders of S corporations and C corporations are deductible by the corporations and subject to FICA, Medicare, and other usual taxes associated with payroll. However, distributions of earnings from an S corporation are not subject to FICA and Medicare taxes. Therefore, unlike a C corporation where you attempt to keep salaries as high as possible, with an S corporation one tries to distribute greater profits directly to the shareholder.

And please note: An S corporation's income flows through to its shareholders whether it is actually distributed or not. (You can have phantom income when a gain is allocated to you with no cash to pay the taxes.)

Fringe Benefits

As we have discussed, a C corporation has the greatest ability to provide fringe benefits on a tax-favored basis. Such benefits can include life insurance (with limits), health insurance, certain death benefits, and meals and lodging in limited circumstances. In addition, contributions by the corporation to a qualified pension plan may also be deductible when made but not currently taxable. The corporation can also set up a cafeteria plan to let employees pick and choose fringe benefits. This flexibility is much greater than that afforded an S corporation.

In general, an S corporation may deduct the cost of providing the benefit, but any shareholder in an S corporation who owns at least 2 percent of the corporation's stock must include the value of such benefit in income. Thus, there is no real tax benefit to either the entity or the owners.

Sale or Exchange of Stock

The shareholders of a C corporation may qualify under Internal Revenue Code Section 1202 to exclude from income one half the gain on the sale or exchange of their stock. This section only applies to qualifying stock issued after the effective date of the Revenue Reconciliation Act of 1993. Thus, a qualifying taxpayer may pay an effective tax rate of 10 percent instead of 20 percent on a large gain. On the other hand, the shareholders of an S corporation do not qualify for the exclusion.

Passive Activity Losses

Under Internal Revenue Code Section 469, the limit on passive activity losses applies at the shareholder level in the case of an S corporation. An S shareholder generally can deduct a passive activity loss only against income from a passive activity. By contrast, a closely held C corporation generally can use a loss from a passive activity to offset other income (except for portfolio income). Thus, a corporation with both passive activity losses and active income may be better off as a C corporation than as an S corporation.

Tax Year

A newly electing S corporation generally must use either a calendar year or a year approved by the IRS. If the shareholders use calendar tax years, the S corporation generally will also have to use a calendar taxable year. The IRS generally allows a new S corporation to choose to use a corporate year ending in September, October, or November. Use of such a fiscal year results in some deferral of tax for calendar-year shareholders, but the IRS requires an interest-free deposit to offset this benefit. By contrast, C corporations can have a year end in whatever month they want.

Termination of S Election

When an S corporation terminates its election and converts to a C corporation, no gain or loss is realized upon the conversion. There is, however, one significant tax consequence. That is, the corporation is unable to elect to be an S corporation again for five years unless the IRS consents to the election.

If a corporation has not distributed all of its earnings to shareholders when it terminates its S election, it has a limited amount of time to distribute cash without the distribution being considered a dividend. The cash is then considered a distribution of earnings attributable to the time the S election was in effect, and thus, the shareholders are not taxed on its receipt if they have sufficient basis.

A similar rule applies if at the time the S election is terminated an S corporation shareholder has been unable to deduct his share of the corporation's losses because he does not have sufficient basis in his stock. If he receives sufficient basis during a specific period of time after termination of the S election, he can deduct his share of losses that had been carried forward. A shareholder may also deduct losses that were disallowed because of certain at-risk rules if he receives a sufficient at-risk amount during the period. Be sure to consult with your tax professional regarding these rules and their consequences.

What follows is another chart comparing the differences between C corporations and S Corporations. After taking all this in, and perhaps with the assistance of a professional advisor, you will be able to select the entity best suited for your particular purpose.

C Corporation vs. S Corporation

	C Corporation	*S Corporation*
Separate taxable entity	Yes	No
Taxation of income	Taxed to corporation. Shareholders taxed upon distribution of dividends.	Taxed directly to shareholders at their rates. If there is built-in gain the S corporation is taxed.
Allocation of profit and loss	Pro rata to number of shares unless varied by other class of stock	Pro rata to number of shares
Deduction of losses on owner's tax return	No. Deductible against corporate income.	Yes. Deductible by shareholders to the extent of basis in stock and loans from shareholder to corporation. Deductibility may be limited by passive loss and at-risk rules.
Fringe benefits	Shareholder-employees may receive tax-qualified fringe benefits without restriction	Owners of more than 2 percent of S corporation shares generally cannot receive tax-free benefits. Expenses for benefits are deductible in computing taxable income but amounts used to purchase benefits for more than 2 percent shareholders flow through as income to them.
Liquidation	Corporation and shareholders generally recognize gain or loss	Corporation recognizes gain or loss, which is taxed to shareholders
Character of income and loss	Not applicable	Character is passed through from entity
Maximum number of owners	No limit	Number of shareholders may not exceed 75
Trust may be an owner	Yes	Limited types of trusts may be shareholders
Corporation may be an owner	Yes	No. Only individuals, estates, and certain trusts may be shareholders.
Partnership may be an owner	Yes	No. Only individuals, estates, and certain trusts may be shareholders.
Nonresident alien may be an owner	Yes	No

	C Corporation	S Corporation
Basic ownership unit	Share	Share
Limited liability	Yes	Yes
Transferability of interest	Freely transferable, absent restrictions in stockholder agreement	Freely transferable, absent restrictions in stockholder agreement. However, a transfer to an ineligible party may result in termination of S corporation status.
Employment taxes	FICA and Medicare tax payable by the corporation and employees on wages and salaries	FICA and Medicare tax payable by the corporation and employees on wages and salaries. Distributions of earnings are not subject to FICA and Medicare.

Now that you appreciate the difference between good and bad entities, and have a feel for which one is best for your purposes, let's explore which is the best state for a good entity.

Chapter 4

Using Nevada Corporations to Your Maximum Advantage and the Benefits of Multiple Corporation Strategies

If you listen carefully, you will hear people in the know speak approvingly, even fondly, about Nevada corporations. They will describe how their Nevada corporation saves them money in taxes, maintains their privacy, and maximizes their asset protection strategies. They will describe how a Nevada corporation is flexible for their needs and yet protective against the outside world.

Can a Nevada corporation really accomplish all that?

Yes—and more.

To appreciate how so, it is important to understand a little bit about Nevada. Recently, Nevada has been the fastest growing state and Las Vegas one of the fastest growing cities. The state is diversifying its economic base away from its traditional reliance on gaming, mining, and ranching. In the Reno area certain divisions of companies such as Microsoft, Cisco, and Intuit as well as smaller high-tech ventures have located for the quality of life and taxation benefits. A group known as the Tech Alliance (www.newnevada.com) is attracting high-tech companies to the area.

It was not always this way.

From 1859, when silver and gold were first discovered at Virginia City, until the 1930s, Nevada was essentially controlled by California interests. The incredible fortune from Nevada's mineral wealth did not stay in or benefit Nevada but rather contributed to the development of San Francisco and other parts of California. For sixty years the California interests had their people elected as Nevada's governors and U.S. senators and representatives. (Some of them were even residents of California at the time they held their Nevada office.) The mining, railroad, and other interests in California viewed Nevada the same way Britain saw India—as a colony for the extraction of wealth.

This did not sit well with native Nevadans. And to this day there is strain running through Nevada's population that resents the interference of outside interests—be it from California or the federal government (which happens to own over 80 percent of all the land in Nevada, another source of friction between locals and outsiders). This collective sense is manifested in some of Nevada's laws. And so, from about 150 years of historical context, a unique Nevada corporate law has emerged. Importantly, you can use it to your advantage.

The first thing to know when it comes to Nevada's corporate laws is that Nevada protects the privacy of individuals. The state is the only one in the U.S. that does not share information on a corporation's shareholders with the IRS. Why? Because it conveniently does not collect such information. When asked by California's Franchise Tax Board—which is about 1,000 times more aggressive and obnoxious than the IRS—to provide them with bank records on certain Nevada corporations, Nevada banks, absent a Nevada court order, will refuse the request. Their duty is to their depositor, not the California tax authorities.

If you do not want to be identified on the public record as an officer or director of a Nevada corporation you do not have to be listed. Instead, you can use a nominee, a person other than yourself, to serve as the director and all officers, thus maintaining your privacy. Our firm provides an individual to serve in this capacity for $650 per year; other firms may charge more or less. But the important thing is that in this era of complete access to information via the Internet, your name will not appear on the public record.

What are the other benefits of a Nevada corporation?

Tax Free Status

Nevada has no state corporate or personal income tax. The state has no corporate shares tax and no franchise tax. Businesses save hundreds to millions of dollars per year by being incorporated in Nevada.

Corporate Flexibility

Directors, officers, and shareholders do not have to live or hold meetings in Nevada. Foreign nationals may own and operate Nevada corporations from outside the U.S. Telephone meetings may be conducted by persons from around the U.S.—or even the world. One person may be all of the directors and officers. Directors and/or officers need not be stockholders. Corporate bylaws can be expediently made or changed by directors. These and other favorable features of Nevada corporate law provide for great corporate flexibility and ease of maintenance.

Unique Corporate Structuring

Nevada corporate law allows for various classes of stock and debt, securities and voting restrictions, rights and preferences to be included in the articles and bylaws. Some very flexible arrangements can be made for your debt and equity holdings.

Favorable Capitalization

No minimum capital is required to incorporate. Shares may be issued for not only capital but for personal services, real estate, including leases and options, and personal property. A Nevada corporation may purchase, sell, hold, or transfer shares of its own stock. Nevada's corporate law features beneficial securities rules for the raising of capital.

Minimal Filings

The only annual filing required by the Nevada secretary of state is a list of the names and addresses of the officers and directors, along with a low annual fee of $85. (The first year's filing fee is $340.) There is a state business tax of $25 per employee per quarter. If you have no employees in Nevada, this tax is only $25 per year. No other corporate filings or monies are required by the state.

Low Annual Maintenance

The annual cost of maintaining a Nevada corporation is extremely low. Our firm charges $125 to serve as resident agent, and a minimal fee of $150 (or more depending upon time involved) for preparing the annual minutes of shareholder and director meetings. These services are required to maintain your corporate formality and avoid piercing the corporate veil and personal liability. For very little money your corporate records will be proper and up to date, thus providing peace of mind and security.

Complete Privacy

As mentioned, Nevada is the only state with no information-sharing agreement with the IRS. Not even Delaware offers such compelling privacy. As well, in Nevada shareholders are not a matter of public record and bearer shares may be issued—both of which allow for maximum anonymity and privacy. In addition, as mentioned, nominee officers and directors can be provided to further protect clients.

But What About Delaware?

You will always hear someone say that Delaware is the best state for incorporating. If you are a Fortune 500 company this is true. For massive corporate restructurings, takeovers, and proxy battles Delaware has a well-defined corporate law and specialized courts to deal promptly with such issues. But if you do not have over several billion dollars in annual revenues that advantage is not significant, not when compared to Nevada.

Let's look at the differences . . .

• Delaware imposes an 8.7 percent income tax on corporate profits earned in Delaware. Nevada is absolutely tax free. Delaware will prove costly if you anticipate corporate earnings. Nevada will not cost you one cent.

• Delaware shares information with the IRS. Only Nevada does not. With a Nevada corporation you are thus less likely to face an IRS audit, since there is no state tax information to trigger discrepancies and/or monitoring.

• Delaware has a franchise tax. Nevada does not. The Delaware tax is modest, but it unfortunately requires voluminous annual disclosures—such as dates of stockholder meetings, places of business outside of Delaware, and disclosure of the number and value of the shares of stock issued. This is not the privacy you need in your asset protection program. Nevada requires none of this information. Nevada only requires a current list of officers and directors. The stockholders are not a matter of public record in Nevada, nor does the state ask who they are. Stock may be held in bearer shares, further protecting shareholders.

- Delaware does not allow future services or an unsecured promissory note to serve as consideration for the issuance of stock, Nevada does.

- Nevada not only beats Delaware in privacy, but Nevada also offers corporate officers and directors far broader protection than does Delaware. Example: Articles of incorporation in Nevada may eliminate or limit the personal liability of officers and directors for claims resulting from breach of their fiduciary duty. This is true in all cases, other than those involving the improper payment of dividends. In contrast to Nevada, Delaware has a longer statute of limitations to sue when improper dividends are paid. It also provides fewer creative options for director indemnification. And while in Delaware the right of director indemnification is at the discretion of the court, it is an absolute right in Nevada.

- Nevada also allows creative financial arrangements to indemnify. Indemnification can be extended to any person serving the corporation who may incur liability. The corporation can make these arrangements regardless of its authority to indemnify. These financial arrangements include insurance in the form of trust funds, self-insurance, or granting directors a security interest or lien on corporate assets to guarantee indemnification. From an asset protection viewpoint, the absolute authority of corporate officers and directors to place liens against their own corporation for purposes of indemnification provides them near complete control over corporate assets. Unlike Delaware, and most other states, where such self-serving financial and legal arrangements are usually invalid, Nevada fully supports such protective arrangements. In fact, in Nevada, absent fraud, the decision of the board of directors concerning any financial arrangement is conclusive and is neither void nor voidable. This is not true in Delaware, nor in most other states. As such, Nevada is the superior state.

"Okay I'm sold," you say. "But how can I use a Nevada corporation to my benefit?"

Let's look at several ways.

Strategy One: Doing Business in Your State

For purposes of this discussion "Your State" refers to any state outside Nevada. Whether you have a dry cleaning business in California or a consulting business in Arizona, if you are doing business in and generating revenues in Your State you need to pay the applicable taxes there. Remember, it's legal and acceptable to avoid taxes. However, evading taxes is not something you want to do. The difference between avoidance and evasion is twenty years. So you pay the state taxes on money earned in your state.

How can a Nevada corporation help if you are only doing business in Your State?

First of all, by incorporating in Nevada you can take advantage of Nevada privacy and flexibility. For example, the Arizona consulting firm only does business in Arizona. They incorporate in Nevada and qualify to do business in Arizona. This means they go to the Arizona secretary of state with their Nevada corporate papers and pay the same fee a new business incorporating in Arizona would pay. In this way they are "qualified" as a Nevada corporation to operate as an Arizona corporation would.

The cost is minimal. On an annual basis you are essentially paying the extra cost of maintaining a Nevada corporation—$85 to the Nevada secretary of state and $125 for a resident agent in Nevada. You have to pay the same Arizona fees whether you are a Nevada or Arizona corporate entity.

So for a small extra amount every year you get the benefits of Nevada's corporate laws:

- No sharing of corporate information with the IRS
- Greater protections for officers and directors
- Flexibility in corporate management
- Flexibility in capitalization and corporate structuring
- Privacy

Because you have incorporated in Nevada, not in Your State, Nevada's corporate laws govern. And better yet, someday, you may choose to use Strategy Two below or you may just move your entire business to Nevada for the taxation, ease of doing business, and quality-of-life benefits. In those situations, you will not have to pay more money to reincorporate in Nevada and merge your state corporation into the new entity. You will already be home as it were.

Strategy Two: Doing Business in Your State and in Nevada

Case No. 8—Ken and Cindy

Ken and Cindy had a used car business in Your State. It was an S corporation called K & C Autos, Inc. They did a lot of advertising on local TV stations, spending over $100,000 per year. They needed to spend that much for screaming and yelling and doing foolish stunts to get people in the door to buy a used car.

Ken realized that if he had his own ad agency he could take the 15 percent agency commission as his own. Cindy realized that if they created a Nevada corporation to be the ad agency they could minimize their state taxes. They consulted with their accountant, who, being open-minded, agreed that several thousand dollars a year in taxes could be saved.

So Ken and Cindy formed K & C Advertising, Inc., a Nevada corporation. Ken continued to film his zany TV commercials with a handheld video camera as he always had. But they had K & C Advertising, not themselves or a local agency, place the advertising. For very little money they had a Nevada office set up. K & C Advertising did the ad placement and billing through a service from Nevada and all the banking and accounting was located and performed in Nevada.

As a result, when their used car lot spent $100,000 in local advertising, $15,000 went to their ad agency, K & C Advertising in Nevada. They did not want to use an S corporation because all profits would flow back to them in Your State and be taxed on their individual returns. So they had K & C Advertising, Inc. be a C corporation. They paid the small expenses to operate each year and put the rest into a retirement plan for their benefit. There were no federal corporate or individual taxes to pay at the end of the year and they were saving for retirement in tax free Nevada. Ken and Cindy spoke fondly of their Nevada corporation.

What kind of arrangements can be used to achieve this strategy? They are numerous:

- Research and development
- Marketing services
- Consulting services
- Sales agencies
- Equipment leasing
- Receivables factoring

By entering these arrangements you can legitimately upstream income from Your State to Nevada.

What are the advantages of upstreaming?

Expenses in Your State—Income in Nevada

By having Nevada, Inc. perform a legitimate service for Your State, Inc., Your State, Inc. has an expense to write off against its income, thus reducing taxable revenues. Nevada, Inc., on the other hand, has income. After all deductions are taken and a profit remains, taxes are paid to the IRS (at only 15 percent on the first $50,000 if they are a C corporation). Remember, there are no state taxes in Nevada. So just by shifting income from a taxable state to a no-tax state you are saving money.

What does the IRS think of this? They are okay with it. They get their money in corporate taxes in either event. (But see the discussion on controlled group status, below.)

Asset Protection

By using Nevada, Inc. to hold and lease assets to Your State, Inc. you can protect valuable corporate assets. Assuming Your State, Inc. is involved in a day-to-day business where it could be sued, by having all the good assets in Nevada, Inc. and leasing them to Your State, Inc., you have removed these assets from risk. If someone sues Your State, Inc. there is not much to get. All the valuable assets are in Nevada, Inc. Remember, segregating assets in separate entities away from risk is a cornerstone business strategy.

Lower Corporate Taxes

Subject to the controlled group rules (see below), two or more corporations may pay less in federal corporate taxes. First let's look at the corporate tax rates:

Corporate Tax Rates

Taxable Income Over	But Less Than	Tax Rate
$0	$50,000	15%
50,000	75,000	25%
75,000	100,000	34%
100,000	335,000	39%
335,000	10,000,000	34%

Assume Your State, Inc., a corporation, makes a $150,000 annual profit. Your federal corporate income tax is $41,750. What if you used two Nevada corporations in addition to Your State, Inc. and by upstreaming income each has a profit of one cent less than $50,000 each. The tax on each corporation is 15 percent, or $7,500 each. Instead of Your State, Inc. paying $41,750, the three corporations together pay only $22,500, a savings of $19,250.

The problem is, for all you may think or say about the IRS, they are not stupid people. They are not going to let you get out of paying that much in taxes that easily. Which is why in the cat-and-mouse game of finding loopholes and then closing them, the IRS came up with controlled group status.

WHAT IS CONTROLLED GROUP STATUS?

If you are found to be a controlled group you can lose your dual and multiple corporation benefits. And note, this is a complicated area so be sure to consult with your tax advisor for specific advice.

That said, the following applies:

A controlled group exists when:

1. Two people own more than 50 percent of each of two corporations. (For Ken and Cindy—half ownership of K & C Autos, Inc. and K & C Advertising, Inc. would result in controlled group status.)

2. A parent-subsidiary controlled group is where one corporation owns at least 80 percent of another corporation.

3. A brother-sister controlled group is where five or fewer persons (including individuals and trusts) own at least 80 percent of the shares of both corporations.

A controlled group does not exist when:

1. One spouse owns 100 percent of one corporation and the other spouse owns 100 percent of a second corporation. Each spouse maintains separate control of corporate assets and separate management control. (So if Ken owns 100 percent of K & C Autos, Inc. and Cindy owns 100 percent of K & C Advertising, Inc., they are okay.)

2. You own less than 50 percent of one corporation and your child over twenty-one years old owns the rest. You then own 100 percent of the second corporation.

3. You own less than 80 percent of the first corporation and an unrelated person owns the rest. You then own 100 percent of the second corporation.

It should be noted that controlled group status relates to the payment of taxes. If you want to own 100 percent of two corporations for asset protection purposes and are willing to pay any higher taxes the IRS will assess, you will be fine. In that case, even the IRS will approve of your asset protection strategies.

But it should also be noted that if two or more corporations are not controlled group entities you can take advantage of reduced corporate taxes. Again, please be sure to consult with your tax advisor before venturing into this arena.

Strategy Three: Doing Business in Your State and Borrowing Money from Nevada, Inc.

Case No. 9—John and Denise

John and Denise owned a crafts store in a busy local mall. They were incorporated as an S corporation in Your State under the name Neesette Crafts, Inc. They found that they needed credit at times to purchase inventory. They had the money to lend the company but wanted it protected. John was also aware that it was best to minimize their exposure by protecting and segregating whatever Neesette assets they could.

After consulting with their advisors they decided that the best thing to do was to combine both needs (credit and protection) into one strategy. Their plan was as follows:

Neesette Crafts, Inc.   ←—$50,000 Loan
Denise owns 100%   John's Nevada Inc.
                        Promissory Note/UCC-1 —→   John owns 100%

To avoid controlled group status, Denise owned and managed 100 percent of Neesette, Inc. And John owned and managed 100 percent of John's Nevada Inc., a newly formed Nevada C corporation.

Neesette, Inc. borrowed $50,000 from John's Nevada, Inc. and signed a promissory note promising to pay the money back with interest. The note was due on demand so that if trouble arose John's Nevada, Inc. could demand payment at any time. A security agreement was signed whereby all the assets of Neesette were used as collateral for the loan. To reflect this collateralization, a UCC-1 form detailing the secured assets was filed with the secretary of state in Your State and in Nevada, and with any county recorder's offices, if appropriate.

As long as no one else filed first, John's Nevada, Inc. had a priority over the assets of Neesette, Inc. The assets were encumbered, or subject to the claims of others. If a lawsuit is filed and judgment is rendered, the creditor cannot collect until the debt to John's Nevada, Inc. is first paid. This priority is true as against all creditors—except, of course, the IRS, which is first in line on all claims.

This was the perfect solution for John and Denise. They were able to lend money to Neesette, Inc. without tying it up. It could be demanded back at any time. And they had encumbered all the assets of Neesette, Inc., thus removing them from creditor claims. They felt much more secure about their business situation.

Concerns When Transferring Assets

There are two major issues that arise when you transfer or encumber property and assets.

FRAUDULENT CONVEYANCE

When property is transferred or encumbered it is effectively put out of the reach of a creditor. A problem arises when the transfer is accomplished with an identified creditor in mind. That is, if someone has a judgment against you, is in the process of suing you, or is even threatening to sue you, you cannot just start transferring assets to others to avoid the payment of a claim. Think about it: It would be too easy to avoid your debts if you could just give your assets away. So the courts and legislatures have come up with the concept of a "fraudulent conveyance" and they have given the courts the power to undo a transfer of property that is fraudulent and unjust.

Most states have passed the Uniform Fraudulent Transfer Act (UFTA). Under the UFTA, the term "creditor" means simply "a person who has a claim," even if that claim is disputed and is not yet reduced to judgment. If the court determines that a transfer was made with the intent to hinder, delay, or defraud a creditor, the transfer is subject a variety of legal challenges. The law requires the court to consider a variety of factors, some of which indicate the absence of fraudulent intent. These factors include whether:

• The transfer was to an insider (which includes a relative, a corporation in which the debtor is an officer, director, or a person in control, a partnership in which the debtor is a general partner, or an affiliate);

• The debtor retained possession or control over the property transferred;

• The transfer was disclosed or concealed;

• Before the transfer was made, the debtor had been sued or threatened with suit;

• The transfer was of substantially all of the debtor's assets;

• The debtor absconded;

• The debtor removed or concealed assets;

• The debtor received reasonably equivalent value as consideration for the transfer;

• The transfer rendered the debtor insolvent;

• The transfer occurred shortly before or shortly after a substantial debt was incurred; and

• The debtor transferred the essential asset of a business to a lienor who then transferred the assets to an insider.

A creditor who proves that a transfer was made with the requisite intent to hinder, delay, or defraud the creditor can request the court to void the transfer, enjoin future transfers, appoint a receiver, and/or satisfy the claim out of the transferred property.

How do you avoid a fraudulent conveyance issue?

By setting up your asset protection structures long before you ever get sued. For example, if John and Denise set up and implement their Nevada corporation, promissory note, and UCC-1 when they first get into business, a

creditor who they start doing business with a year later cannot say their structure was fraudulent. There was no intent to defraud the creditor—they did
not even *know* the creditor when their corporate structure was implemented.

The rule of thumb is to set up your asset protection when the seas are
calm. When there is clear sailing and no trouble ahead, you are perfectly
within your rights to structure your affairs to your advantage. When the seas
get rough, either your assets have been previously protected or they have
not. At that point it is too late for transfers.

MONEY LAUNDERING

A second concern when transferring assets involves the Money Laundering
Control Act.

This act makes it criminal for anyone to conduct or attempt to conduct
certain financial activities that involve the proceeds of unlawful activities.
The transfer of assets into a corporation, limited partnership, trust, or other
entity can constitute a financial activity within the scope of the act. The specified unlawful activities under the act consist primarily of drug trafficking offenses, financial misconduct, and environmental crimes.

Drug trafficking offenses include the manufacture, importation, sale, or
distribution of controlled substances; the commission of acts constituting a
continuing criminal enterprise; and transportation of drug paraphernalia.

Covered financial misconduct includes the concealment of assets from a
receiver, custodian, trustee, marshal, or other officer of the court, from creditors in a bankruptcy proceeding, or from the Federal Deposit Insurance
Corporation, the Resolution Trust Corporation, or a similar agency or person; the making of a fraudulent conveyance in contemplation of a
bankruptcy proceeding; bribery; the giving of commissions or gifts for the
procurement of loans; theft, embezzlement, or misapplication of bank funds
or funds of fraudulent bank or credit institution entries or loan or credit applications; and mail, wire, or bank fraud or bank or postal robbery or theft.

Environmental crimes include violations of the Federal Water Pollution
Control Act, the Ocean Dumping Act, the Safe Drinking Water Act, the Resources Conservation and Recovery Act, and similar federal statutes.

Other specified crimes include counterfeiting, espionage, kidnapping or
hostage taking, copyright infringement, entry of goods by means of false
statements, smuggling of goods into the United States, removing goods

from the custody of Customs, illegally exporting arms, and trading with U.S. enemies.

So by engaging in those activities, and then transferring the proceeds into another entity, you have compounded the claims against you.

How do you avoid a money laundering issue? Do not do it. There is too much money to be made in this world by engaging in legal activities. You really do not need the sleepless nights of criminal enterprise.

One Final Point on Maximizing Corporate Benefits

In putting together strategies to benefit you and your family, the courts allow flexibility in your arrangements. A classic example of this involves the payment of taxes.

> Anyone may so arrange his affairs that his taxes shall be as low as possible: he is not bound to choose that pattern which will best pay the Treasury; there is not even a patriotic duty to increase one's taxes. (Federal Judge Learned Hand, *Helvering v. Gregory*, 69 F.2d 809 (2d Circ. 1934))

This ruling was in turn confirmed by the U.S. Supreme Court:

> The legal right of the taxpayer to decrease the amount of what otherwise would be his taxes, or altogether avoid them, by means which the law permits, cannot be doubted. (*Gregory v. Helvering*, 293 U.S. 454 (1935))

And, as we have learned, the best state for legally reducing your tax obligation is Nevada.

Rich Dad Tips

- If any of the strategies you've read about in this chapter appeal to you, consider implementing them sooner rather than later.
- The reason for moving ahead now is simple. The longer you are in business the more potential claimants you will deal with. Protect yourself now and for the future.

Chapter 5

Organizational Steps for Forming a Corporation, Limited Liability Company, and Limited Partnership

Once you have decided to form a good entity you need to take certain organizational steps. Even if your professional advisor is going to prepare these documents for you the following is good to review and know. Further details on each individual state's corporate requirements are found in the Appendix.

Corporations

The first step in organizing a corporation is to prepare the articles of incorporation for filing with the secretary of state. While each state has its own rules and requirements (again, see Appendix), there are common requirements:

ARTICLES OF INCORPORATION

Corporate Name

Select a name that you can grow with and then check with the secretary of state (and trademark office, if appropriate) on name availability.

Purposes and Powers

Nevada and certain other jurisdictions allow the articles to state that the purpose of the corporation is to engage in any lawful activity for which a corporation may be organized. Others, such as Massachusetts, require that at least one specific purpose be stated in the articles of incorporation.

Board of Directors

Some states require that the names and addresses of the initial board of directors be listed.

Authorized Capital

The total number of shares the corporation is authorized to issue, the rights and preferences of each class, and the par value of the shares need to be included.

Duration

Because most states allow a corporation to continue indefinitely, the articles of incorporation will permit a perpetual duration.

BYLAWS

The bylaws of a corporation are the rules for the conduct of business affairs. While each version is different, they generally contain the following common provisions:

Meetings of Directors

The bylaws will set out what kind of notice requirements are needed to call meetings and the minimum number of annual meetings that are required.

Meetings of Shareholders

The date for the annual meeting will be fixed, along with requirements for calling special meetings.

Officers and Directors

The responsibilities of each officer and the director(s) will be set out in the bylaws, as will be the procedures for removing them.

Records and Reports

Procedures for inspection of the books by shareholders as may be required shall be set out in the bylaws.

Name and Address of Resident Agent

States require that a resident agent be designated. The real purpose of the resident agent is to receive the service of a summons and complaint (a lawsuit) in the state. So do not have someone serve as your resident agent who will not fully appreciate the importance of being sued and the need to answer a complaint promptly.

Rich Dad Tips

- The fact that each state requires that a corporation, LLC, or LP have a resident agent in that state underlines the importance of choosing a reliable agent.
- Do not have some mom-and-pop resident agent service perform this function. They may not be around in a year from now. In such a case, you could be sued, never receive a notice to defend yourself, and have a default judgment entered against your company.

Limited Liability Companies

The first step in organizing an LLC is to prepare and file the articles of organization. Each state's unique rules are found in my book *How to Use Limited Liability Companies and Limited Partnerships.* Again, there are common requirements:

ARTICLES OF ORGANIZATION

LLC Name

Check for name availability and consider separately protecting the name.

Purposes and Powers

As with corporations, many states allow a broad unlimited power to be stated.

Name and Address of Resident Agent

For the same purposes as a corporation, the resident agent and address are listed. Please note that, as with LPs and corporations, if you live in your state of organization you can serve as your own resident agent.

Manager- or Member-Managed

Unlike a corporation, either all of the members or just a manager(s) may run the LLC. Usually, this decision must be stated in the articles of organization.

OPERATING AGREEMENT

Like the bylaws of a corporation, the operating agreement provides the rules for operation of the LLC. Common provisions likely to be found are:

Managers

The number of managers, the term, election, and removal of managers will all be set out.

Restrictions on Transfer of Interests

Unlike shares of a corporation, the transfer of LLC membership interests is more complicated. The rules are set out in the operating agreement.

Distributions to Members; Profits and Losses

Distributions are governed by partnership law, unlike dividends in a corporation. The rules are more complex and are set out in the operating agreement.

Meetings

Many states leave the whole need for meetings up to the members. Any requirements should be set out in the operating agreement.

Charging Order

Although many states require creditors to follow the charging order procedure as a matter of state law, it is a good idea to include it in the operating agreement (see next chapter).

Limited Partnerships

To organize an LP most states require that a certificate of limited partnership be filed with the secretary of state. As mentioned with LLCs, the unique state requirements are found in my book *How to Use Limited Liability Companies and Limited Partnerships.* The following are common requirements:

CERTIFICATE OF LIMITED PARTNERSHIP

Limited Partnership Name

As with the other corporate entities, check on availability with the secretary of state and remember that there are separate trademark requirements (see Chapter 8).

General Character of Business

You need not be too specific in most states.

Name and Address of Resident Agent

Again, for the same reasons as with an LLC and corporation, choose a resident agent that will be in business next year.

Name and Address of General Partner

Some states also require the names and addresses of all limited partners.

Amounts of Contributions

Not all states require this and for good reason. Not many investors want it on the public record that they put $1 million into XYZ, L.P.

Duration

Many states limit a limited partnership to only thirty years' duration. You must specify a termination date.

Events of Termination/Dissolution

Some states require the certificate of limited partnership to state what triggers dissolution or termination.

LIMITED PARTNERSHIP AGREEMENT

The limited partnership agreement, like the LLC's operating agreement and a corporation's bylaws, sets out the road map for operations. Common provisions include:

Management by General Partner

The agreement will set out the duties, authority, and compensation of the general partner.

Limited Partners' Role

The rights, powers, and voting rights of the limited partners will be set out.

Restrictions on Transfers/Distributions to Partners

Like an LLC, partnerships can be fairly complex with regard to these issues. They should be set out in detail.

Events of Termination/Dissolution

Because limited partnerships generally have a fixed duration (e.g., thirty years), the provisions for termination and dissolution will be detailed.

Charging Order

As with LLCs, you may want to provide that a charging order is a creditor's exclusive remedy.

And we shall consider the benefits of a charging order in our next chapter . . .

Chapter 6

How a Charging Order Works to Your Advantage

The charging order procedure is a unique part of the asset protection offered by limited partnerships and limited liability companies. In most states, a judgment creditor—one who has sued and obtained a court judgment—may only obtain a charging order against an LP or LLC. This means that a creditor does not get title to the property owned by the LP or LLC but rather only the right to receive the interest holders' distributions.

An example helps explain the concept. Please note that we will use an LP for our case, but that an LLC would apply as well.

Case No. 10—Joe and Family

Joe had a thriving forklift sales and repair business. He had started as a sole proprietorship and had grown it over the last seven years. His accountant said it was definitely time to protect his now considerable assets, especially since he was thinking of investing in an unrelated and far riskier venture. Joe liked the idea of using a limited partnership. He wanted to maintain control as general partner and yet gift limited partnership interests to his children.

With the help of his accountant Joe understood that he did not want the liability as a general partner. So Joe's Management, Inc. was formed to be the general partner of Joe's Forklift, L.P. Joe's Management, Inc. had a 4 percent interest in the limited partnership. Because Joe may get sued in the new, un-related venture, he could not be the majority owner of Joe's Management, Inc. If he was a majority owner, a creditor could get at Joe's shares, assert control over Joe's Management, Inc., and, as general partner of Joe's Forklift, L.P., thwart the whole plan by making distributions from the LP as the creditor saw fit to satisfy his debt. It was best that he not give his spouse control of Joe's Management, Inc. since she may be found jointly liable with Joe for any debts if he is sued. So Joe gives 60 percent of Joe's Management, Inc. to his trusted adult son Paul. Joe is still the chairman, CEO, president, and all other officers of Joe's Management, Inc. He has overall authority for both Joe's Management, Inc. and as corporate general partner, over Joe's Forklift, L.P.

Once the forklift business is contributed to Joe's Forklift, L.P., Joe begins a gifting program of limited partnership interests. After two years, Joe, his sons, Paul, Scott, and Dave, each own limited partnership interests of 24 percent of Joe's Forklift, L.P. The remaining 4 percent is held by the general partner, Joe's Management, Inc. All was in place.

Joe had always wanted to own a sports bar. And against his wife's, his accountant's, and everyone else's advice, he and two others put $100,000 each into a business that was by any standard high-risk. Their town already had three sports bars and Joe's location was not prime. But Joe and the other investors wanted to do it and that was that. The three had used a corporation for the sports bar business but they needed a bank loan for another $500,000 to get the bar open. The bank, quite prudently, demanded and received personal guarantees for the loan. The three new owners obtained the loan, made the improvements, and opened in June.

Two weeks after the bar opened the baseball players and owners started feuding again. A week later the players went on strike before the owners locked them out. The owners cried that they had locked the players out first. And the players whined that they went on strike first. No one expected a World Series, and for the immediate future no games were to be played or televised. This was bad for business. The fans were once again disgusted. "Take me out to the . . ."—nah, forget it. Joe's Sports Bar closed within three months.

Because he was the most solvent of the three bar owners, the bank immediately proceeded against Joe. His only asset was his 24 percent limited partnership in Joe's Forklift, L.P.

The bank's exclusive recourse was to obtain a charging order against

Joe's interest, which meant that they could not just march into Joe's Forklift, L.P. and take 24 percent of the equipment, furniture, and receivables. They had to wait until the corporate general partner decided, in its sole discretion, to make a distribution to the limited partners. The bank then gets to stand in Joe's shoes and receive whatever is distributed.

Now remember, Joe is the CEO of Joe's Management, Inc. He does not own a majority of the shares because the bank, as creditor, could get ahold of the shares, vote themselves into control of Joe's Management, Inc., and decide, as corporate general partner, to make favorable distributions to Joe's Forklift, L.P. limited partners. With their charging order the bank would receive Joe's 24 percent of those distributions.

But as CEO of Joe's Management, Inc. without fear of being voted out, thanks to Paul's ownership, Joe can decide to not make any distributions. So the bank, as well as his other children, get nothing. And, because profits are required to flow through a partnership, Joe can allocate profits on a Form K-1 filing with the IRS but not provide any money to pay the taxes on the gain. This is what is known as phantom income, and it is frustrating for creditors.

Say each 24 percent limited partner receives a taxable gain of $100,000 and the taxes on such a gain are $20,000. Joe decides to hire each of his boys in the business and pays them enough in salary to cover their tax obligation. The only one without money to pay the taxes is the bank. Oh sure, they can pay the taxes—they're a bank. But for the privilege of trying to collect from Joe it is going to cost them $20,000 this year. And maybe $40,000 next year. And after the money flows out without any hope of coming in, the bank is ready to settle their claim for 10 cents (or less) on the dollar.

And that is what happened. Joe settled the bank's claim for $50,000 and listened to his wife and accountant from there on.

While each state is different, there are a number of procedural hoops that a judgment creditor must jump through to collect on a charging order. Some include:

- Litigating the case and securing a judgment against a limited partner
- Going back to court to obtain a charging order
- Applying to foreclose on the limited partners' limited partnership interest
- Appointing a receiver to receive limited partnership distributions

As discussed, the steps that a creditor must take are a very large incentive for settlement.

Some readers may question whether the charging order is really fair to the bank. They loaned the money, they have a judgment, and they should be able to collect. There are three issues that arise in a discussion of that point:

1. The California Court of Appeal in similar-fact situations agreed that the creditor should collect. See *Crocker National Bank v. Perroton*, 208 Cal. App.3d 1 (1989) and *Hellman v. Anderson*, 233 Cal. App.3d 840 (1991). The court noted that the original purpose of the charging order was to protect limited partners who were not debtors and to prevent the interruption of partnership business. They noted its intent was not to allow partners to avoid debts. As remedies, the court in one case ordered the partnership interest sold with the other partners' consent. In the second, where it was found the sale would not interrupt the partnership business, the sale was ordered without the other partners' consent.

This remedy is limited to California at this writing but could be adopted by other states in the future. While it is important to know and recognize this possibility, as discussed below in point three, it should not deter one from using an LP or LLC. (It should be noted that the Nevada legislature recently made the charging order the exclusive remedy for LLC and LP creditors, a victory for asset protection.)

2. In the case above, the bank conducted (or should have conducted) a due diligence investigation into Joe's financial condition. As long as Joe did not lie on his loan application—a Money Laundering Act violation—the bank should have known that his sole asset was a limited partnership interest that would be difficult to get at. If the bank had a problem with it the solution is simple: Do not lend Joe the money.

3. The advantage of the charging order is not that it hurts legitimate creditors but that it deters frivolous litigation. Although many attorneys are honorable people, as in any profession there are some unscrupulous lawyers out there. The notions of justice, civility, and fair play are lost on these people. They do not care about you or your family or the fact that you do good things in the community. They just want to win and they like to win by aggressively pursuing you and making your life miserable. These people are despised by their mothers. That's not enough for them to lose their law license. And with a system that rewards lawyers quite well for taking on larger

net worth individuals, you need to take every step you can to protect your assets as best you can. Be assured, lawyers and their staff have ways of finding out what assets you own. (It is incredible what you can learn about someone on the Internet.) So it is important to take steps to keep your name off public records, use entities that are not legally tied to you, and take ownership in a form that is difficult to reach.

The limited partnership or LLC interest is one of the best ways to hold ownership for the protection of assets. When the ambulance-chasing or Mercedes-chasing attorney sees that your assets are in LP or LLC form— or better yet sees no assets—he will think hard about pursuing a case against you. Any step taken to deter frivolous litigation can bring peace of mind. Again, assets held by an LP or LLC are an excellent step in the direction of asset protection. And speaking of protection, to maintain it you need to follow certain rules, which we'll discuss in the next chapter.

Rich Dad Tips

- The strategy in today's litigious environment is to segregate assets.
- Keep the operating entities—the ones that deal with the public—away from the asset-owning entities.
- Consider having the operating entities hold fewer assets and lease expensive assets from the asset-owning entities.
- Consult with your accountant to ensure that controlled group status issues are addressed.

Chapter 7

The Importance of Corporate Formalities

The benefits of a corporation, as you have learned, are significant. From the English Crown in the 1500s to the legislatures of all U.S. states and territories, all Canadian provinces, and all other states and countries based on English common law, the historical means for encouraging risk taking while personally protecting the risk taker has been the corporation.

But with every right comes a responsibility. In the corporate realm that means following certain very basic but necessary rules. These rules are generally known as "corporate formalities." By abusing or ignoring these formalities you can lose corporate protection and become personally liable for your business's debts and claims.

And keep in mind that these rules may apply to LLCs as well. As mentioned, while the LLC is a new entity and a body of law has not developed, one can easily foresee without squinting that an LLC's veil of limited liability will be allowed to be pierced. Already, Colorado statutorily allows for this with a law that states:

> In any case in which a party seeks to hold the members of a limited liability company personally responsible for the alleged improper actions of the limited liability company, the court shall apply the case law which interprets the conditions and circumstances under which

the corporate veil of a corporation may be pierced under Colorado law. (Colorado Revised Statutes Annotated, Section 7-80-107(1)).

For an LLC, a corporation—for any business no matter what form—it is prudent to follow the basic formalities.

Here are the simple rules:

1. *Annual Filings*. After filing your initial articles of incorporation you will need to file an annual report and pay an annual fee to your state. It is not difficult. In Nevada, for example, you send in a one-page list of officers and directors along with a check for $85 each year.

2. *Minutes of Meetings*. Most states require a corporation's shareholders and directors to meet once a year. It is good protection and proper corporate form to prepare minutes of these meetings. Our firm charges $150 per year to perform this service. Others may charge less. Or you can quite easily do it yourself.

3. *Corporate Notice*. It is very important that you let the world know you are operating as a corporation as opposed to as an individual, sole proprietorship, or other format. On your business cards, letterhead, invoices, company checks, brochures, and the like you must identify yourself as doing business as a corporation. Do not just use "XYZ" when you are "XYZ, Inc." You want the world to know you are a corporation. Likewise, all contracts should be signed by you as president of XYZ, Inc. Signing your name without your corporate officer designation can lead to personal liability.

4. *Separate Bank Account*. You cannot run a corporation's banking out of your own personal bank account. A corporation is a separate tax entity with its own tax identification number. You must maintain a separate and independent bank account at all times.

5. *Separate Tax Returns*. Because the corporation is a separate tax entity it is necessary to file a separate corporate tax return. Listing revenue and/or expenses on your personal tax return that properly belong on the corporate tax return is not a good idea.

Failure to follow these five simple rules can allow a creditor to pierce the corporate veil and seek personal liability. What does it take to pierce the corporate veil?

Case No. 11—Roger and Donny

Roger Morton and Donny Brooks were excited about their new business venture. This was going to be their dream, their business home run. They had been working for eighteen months to get it to this point. They were about to acquire the local territorial franchise rights to Burger Bell, the hottest new food franchise since Taco King. Roger was going to handle the construction of the first location through his own construction company and Donny was going to handle the business details.

In preparation for doing this business, eighteen months ago Donny had filed the articles of incorporation with his local secretary of state. He did not use an attorney for this or consult with an accountant. They were a start-up and they needed to save money. He had recalled that an organizational meeting was needed but forgot to get it done.

Donny did not know that a corporation, as a separate legal entity, needed to file a tax ID number (EIN—Employer Identification Number) request with the IRS. If he had gone to a bank to open a corporate bank account he would have learned this, as banks will not open corporate accounts without an EIN for the corporation. Instead, Donny just assumed that you could use your own personal bank account and sort out what was what later. Monies that he and Roger advanced to the company were deposited to his personal account. As things progressed he tried to keep up by putting the checks he wrote for the business and some of the receipts in a specially marked shoe box.

About six months ago Donny had received a letter from his secretary of state's office requesting the payment of the upcoming year's annual fees. The letter also said he needed to return the check with his list of officers and directors for the upcoming year. Donny did not really understand what was needed, and was too busy with other tasks he felt were more important to deal with the request.

Donny recalled hearing that when you received the request from the state it meant that it was time to hold the corporation's annual meeting of shareholders and directors. Again, he was too busy to deal with some archaic requirement. And besides, it was just he and Roger. They spoke every day. What did they possibly have to meet about?

Recently, Roger had sent over a contract for Donny to review. It was for hiring a telephone answering service to handle their overflow calls. Donny reviewed it, signed "Donny Brooks" on the signature line, and sent it back to the answering service.

All was proceeding well. Until a woman fell on the construction site. While Roger had some insurance through his construction company it was not enough. It was an unfortunate accident and the young woman's injuries were serious. Two weeks later Roger and Donny learned the meaning of piercing the corporate veil.

The corporate veil of limited liability as to individual shareholders can be pierced, or set aside, in cases where the shareholders fail to follow corporate formalities. When a shareholder conducts his business as though the corporation does not exist or is so careless in his dealings that the proper recognition of a separate corporate identity is ignored, personal liability to each shareholder may attach.

A piercing of the corporate veil can be devastating, as it was for Roger and Donny. The attorney for the young woman had absolutely no problem proving a complete lack of corporate formality. The evidence was:

- A corporation EIN was never obtained.
- No corporate bank account was ever opened.
- The corporate charter was revoked for failure to file the annual report and pay the annual fee.
- No organization or annual meetings of shareholders and directors were ever held.
- No corporate tax return was ever filed.
- In at least one contract Donny signed as an individual, not as an officer.

Roger and Donny were held personally liable for the young woman's injuries. Their franchise rights were withdrawn due to their financial condition, which was the filing of bankruptcy. All their work, efforts, and dreams were lost for the failure to take some very simple protective steps.

To avoid your corporation (or LLC) from ever being pierced you need to develop a mind-set of separateness. You are not the corporation. The corporation is not you. You will help the corporation by serving as an officer and/or director and holding its shares. In return, the corporation will help you with limited liability and other protections. This beneficial symbiotic relationship cannot last if separateness is not respected.

To maintain separateness, consider the following rules as guidance:

1. Never see corporate assets as your own. They are not. They belong to the corporation. Title is (or should be) held in the corporate name and you as an officer have a duty to administer these assets in the best interests of the corporation. The fact that you own 20 percent, 70 percent, or 100 percent of the corporation is of no consequence. You only own shares, not corporate assets. You are one step removed from ownership of the assets.

2. Never commingle corporate and personal assets or monies. Deposit all corporate monies into the corporate account. Putting corporate money into your personal account and later paying the corporation back is a bad idea. Using corporate funds to cover a personal obligation, even though you pay it back, is another bad idea.

3. Never divert corporate funds to noncorporate uses. Protestations of honest mistakes are useless. You have a duty to know what is right and wrong. If you have the slightest suspicion or twinge of guilt, do not do it. It is not worth the trouble, and it is not worth the consequences.

4. Never sell company stock without board authorization. You cannot be issuing stock without corporate management discussing it and approving it. To do otherwise is a clear securities law violation.

5. Never start out undercapitalized. In some states, including California, failure to properly capitalize the company can lead to a piercing of the corporate veil. If it is going to cost $50,000 to open your business, do not start signing corporate contracts and making obligations with vendors with only $500 in the bank.

6. Never go a year without holding an annual meeting. Minutes of annual meetings—documents proving you understand the difference between you and the corporation on a continuing basis—are an absolute must. The annual and consistent preparation of meeting minutes is worthy of greater discussion.

Minutes of Meetings

An excellent way to prevent having your corporate veil pierced is to type up and keep minutes of your board of directors and shareholder meetings. Besides that, in most states, it is a matter of state law that you hold these meetings anyway. And while the LP and LLC laws in most states do not require annual meetings, it is not a bad idea to hold them as well, if only to avoid future miscommunications and misunderstandings.

People frequently state how difficult it is to prepare annual meeting minutes. For some it is like going to the dentist.

Fear not! It is not that difficult.

What follows are samples of the minutes of first meeting of shareholders, the minutes of the board of directors' organizational meeting, as well as samples of the minutes of the annual meetings of shareholders and directors. You can use them to tailor meeting minutes to suit your needs. Or, if you still feel like you are about to sit in the dentist's chair, our firm or another service provider can do it for you. Our fee is $150 per year. (I guess that's better than going to the dentist.) The important thing is that they are prepared by someone on an annual basis to preserve your entity's limited liability protection.

Minutes of the First Meeting of Shareholders of XYZ, Inc.

Upon proper notice, the first meeting of XYZ, Inc. was held on _____, 200__. The meeting was called to order by Jack Smith, the incorporator, and the following shareholders, being a majority of the shareholders of the Corporation, were present:

Jack Smith
Jill Jones

Jack Smith acted as Secretary of the meeting.
There was presented to the meeting the following:

1. Copy of Certificate of Incorporation;
2. Copy of the Bylaws of the Corporation;
3. Resignation of the Incorporator;
4. Corporate certificate book; and
5. Corporate certificate ledger.

The Chairman noted that it was in order to consider electing a Board of Directors for the ensuing year. Upon nominations duly made, seconded, and unanimously carried, the following persons were elected as Directors of the Corporation, to serve for a period of one year and until such time as their successors are elected and qualify:

Jack Smith
Jill Jones

Upon motion duly made, seconded, and unanimously carried, it was

RESOLVED, that the items listed above have been examined by all shareholders, and are all approved and adopted, and that all acts taken and decisions reached as set forth in such documents be, and they hereby are, ratified and approved by the shareholders of the Corporation.

There being no further business to come before the meeting, upon motion duly made, seconded, and unanimously carried, it was adjourned.

_____
Jack Smith, Secretary

Organizational Minutes of the Board of Directors of XYZ, Inc.

The organization meeting of the Board of Directors of XYZ, Inc. was held on _____, 200__.

Jack Smith and Jill Jones constituting the total members of the initial Board of Directors of the Corporation, and a quorum, were present.

Jill Jones acted as Secretary of the meeting and Jack Smith acted as Chairman of the meeting.

The Chairman reported that the Articles of Incorporation had been filed with the Secretary of State of the State of _____. The Secretary was directed to insert a certified copy of the Articles in the minute books as part of these minutes.

The Secretary then presented the resignation of the incorporator. After reviewing the resignation of the incorporator, and upon motion duly made, seconded, and unanimously carried, it was:

RESOLVED, that the Board accept the resignation of the incorporator.

The Secretary submitted to the meeting a seal proposed for use as the corporate seal of the Corporation, along with a form of the stock certificate. After reviewing the seal and the stock certificate, and upon motion duly made, seconded, and unanimously carried, it was:

RESOLVED, that the form of the seal and the stock certificate submitted to this meeting are adopted and approved as the corporate seal and stock certificate of the Corporation. The Secretary of the Corporation is hereby authorized and directed to insert a copy of the stock certificate with these minutes, and to affix an impression of the seal on the margin of these minutes.

The Secretary then presented the proposed Code of Bylaws relating to the regulation of the business and affairs of the Corporation, its shareholders, Directors, and officers. After reviewing the proposed Code of Bylaws and upon motion duly made, seconded, and unanimously carried, it was:

RESOLVED, that the Bylaws presented to this meeting are adopted as the Bylaws of the Corporation, and the Secretary is directed to certify and insert the Bylaws into the minute book (containing the minutes of the proceedings of the Board of Directors and other relevant corporate documents).

The Chairman stated that the next order of business was the election of the officers as specified in the Bylaws. The Chairman called for nominations for officers to serve for one year or until their successors are elected or qualified. After discussion, the following persons were nominated and seconded to the following positions:

Jack Smith	President
Jill Jones	Secretary/Treasurer

The Chairman called for further nominations, but none were made. A voice vote was taken and since there was no opposition, the Chairman declared that the nominees are the duly elected officers of the Corporation to serve until the next annual Board meeting, or until their successors are elected and shall qualify.

The Chairman stated that the next order of business was to determine the compensation of the officers. After discussion and upon motion duly made, seconded, and unanimously carried, it was:

RESOLVED, that the salary of the corporate officers shall be (_____) or (determined at a later date).

The Chairman stated that the next order of business was to consider paying all expenses and reimbursing all persons for expenses paid or incurred in connection with the formation and organization of the Corporation. After discussion, upon motion duly made, seconded, and unanimously carried, it was:

RESOLVED, that the Treasurer of the Corporation be authorized and directed to pay all charges and expenses incident to the formation and organization of this Corporation and to reimburse all persons who have made any disbursements for such charges and expenses.

The Chairman stated the next order of business was to consider reimbursement to officers and Directors of the Corporation of travel and other expenses which such employees expend on behalf of the Corporation. After discussion and upon motion duly made, seconded, and unanimously carried, it was:

RESOLVED, that the Corporation shall reimburse each officer and Director for any reasonable necessary expenses which they incur in connection with the purposes of the Corporation and in furtherance of its business.

RESOLVED FURTHER, that it shall be the policy of this Corporation to reimburse each officer and Director or to pay directly on behalf of each officer or Director necessary and ordinary out-of-pocket expenses incidental to travel for all business activities of the Corporation requiring travel.

The Chairman stated that the next order of business was to consider an election under Section 248 of the Internal Revenue Code to amortize the organizational expense of the Corporation over a period of sixty (60) months, beginning with the first month of business of the Corporation. The Chairman explained that if the election was not made, the organizational expenses would constitute a nondeductible capital expenditure. After discussion, upon motion duly made, seconded, and unanimously carried, it was:

RESOLVED, that beginning with the month in which the Corporation begins business, the Corporation commence amortizing its organizational expense over a period of sixty (60) months in accordance with Section 248 of the Internal Revenue Code.

The Chairman stated that the next order of business was the designation of a depository for the funds of the Corporation. After discussion, upon motion duly made, seconded, and unanimously carried, it was:

RESOLVED, that _____ is designated as the depository for the general account of the Corporation, and all checks, drafts, and orders on any of the accounts with the depository may be signed by the following: Jack Smith or Jill Jones. The President, Secretary, and Treasurer are authorized and directed to execute any documents necessary to open and continue any accounts with the depository.

FURTHER RESOLVED, that the Secretary of this Corporation be, and hereby is, instructed to annex a copy of such documents to the minutes of this meeting.

The Chairman stated that the next order of business was to consider the designation of a Registered Agent and registered office of the Corporation in the State of _____. The Chairman stated that the Articles of Incorporation stated that _____ is the Registered Agent of the Corporation and the principal place of business is _____. Upon motion duly made, seconded, and unanimously adopted, it was:

RESOLVED, that _____ be, and hereby is, appointed Registered Agent for the Corporation in the State of _____. The office of the Registered Agent is to be located at _____.

After a discussion and upon motion duly made, seconded, and unanimously carried, it was:

RESOLVED, that _____ be retained as the Corporation's legal counsel.

The Chairman stated that the next order of business was to consider the issuance of capital stock of the Corporation pursuant to Section 1244 of the Internal Revenue Code. The Chairman stated that Section 1244 permits ordinary loss treatment, as opposed to capital loss treatment when the holder of Section 1244 stock either sells or exchanges such stock at a loss or when such stock becomes worthless. After discussion, upon motion duly made, seconded, and unanimously carried, it was:

RESOLVED, that the capital stock of the Corporation shall be issued pursuant to Section 1244 of the Internal Revenue Code. The Corporation is authorized to offer and issue its authorized common stock. Said stock shall be issued only for money and other property (other than stock or securities). The officers of the Corporation are authorized and empowered, and directed to perform, any and all acts necessary to carry out this plan and to qualify the stock offered and issued under it as Section 1244 stock as that term is defined in Section 1244 of the Internal Revenue Code and the Regulations thereunder.

The Chairman stated that the next order of business was to consider the issuance of shares of the capital stock of the Corporation. The Chairman stated that the following individuals offered to acquire a total of _____ shares of common stock of the Corporation, $_____ par value, in exchange for a total of $_____.

Name	No. of Shares
Jack Smith	_____
Jill Jones	_____

The Chairman further explained that the stock, upon issuance, is to be fully paid and nonassessable. After discussion, upon motion duly made, seconded, and unanimously carried, it was:

RESOLVED, that in consideration for the payment of _____ Dollars ($_____), the Corporation shall issue to Jack Smith _____ shares of the Corporation's fully paid, nonassessable common stock having $_____ par value per share.

RESOLVED, that in consideration for the payment of _____ Dollars ($_____), the Corporation shall issue to Jill Jones _____ shares of the Corporation's fully paid, nonassessable common stock having $_____ par value per share.

RESOLVED FURTHER, that the President or Secretary of this Corporation be, and they hereby are, authorized and empowered to execute any and all other instruments and certificates, and to do and perform all other acts and things necessary, or by them deemed desirable, to effectuate the purposes of the foregoing resolutions.

The Chairman stated that the next order of business was to consider the adoption of a fiscal year for the Corporation. The Chairman explained that the Corporation could elect to end its fiscal year during any calendar month. Upon motion duly made, seconded, and unanimously carried, the following resolution was adopted:

RESOLVED, That any one of the President, Secretary, or Treasurer of this Corporation is hereby authorized to select _____ fiscal year for the Corporation by filing of a tax return, other appropriate tax form, or by any other proper action.

The Chairman stated that the next order of business was to authorize certain corporate officers to execute and deliver deeds, conveyances, promissory notes, deeds of trust, mortgages, and other instruments necessary to accomplish the aims and purposes of this Corporation. After discussion, and upon motion duly made, seconded, and unanimously carried, it was:

RESOLVED, that the Officers of the Corporation, and only the Officers of this Corporation, be and they hereby are, authorized and empowered, for and on behalf of this Corporation, and as its corporate act and deed, at any time, or from time to time, to negotiate for and/or to enter into any lease, leases, mortgages, promissory notes, other agreement, or other agreements with any party or parties, containing such terms and conditions as said Officers may deem necessary or desirable in order to promote and fully effectuate the conduct, by this Corporation, of its business and/or businesses.

The Chairman stated that the next order of business was to establish a time for the regular meetings of the Board.

RESOLVED, that the meetings of the Board of Directors of this Corporation be held at the principal office of the Corporation, or at such other location as a majority of the Board may determine, from time to time, as may be called by the President, and that no further notice of such regular meetings need be given.

There being no further business to come before the meeting, upon motion duly made, seconded, and unanimously carried, the Chairman declared the meeting adjourned.

_____
Jill Jones, Secretary

APPROVED:

_____
Jack Smith, Chairman

Minutes of Annual Meeting of Shareholders of XYZ, Inc.

The Meeting of Shareholders of the above-named Corporation was held upon proper notice on _____, 200__, at _____, __:__. The meeting was called to order by the President, heretofore elected by the Board of Directors, and the following shareholders, being a majority of the shareholders of the Corporation, were present:

Jack Smith
Jill Jones

Jill Jones was elected temporary Secretary of the meeting and took Minutes of it for the corporate records.

A discussion was then held regarding the election of the Board of Directors for the coming year. As the current board had performed well in the previous year and wished to continue, upon motion duly made, seconded, and unanimously carried, it was:

RESOLVED, that the following persons are elected Directors for the forthcoming year:

Jack Smith
Jill Jones

Further discussion was held regarding the services rendered by the previous year's Board of Directors, up to and including today's date. Services had been well performed. As a result, upon motion duly made, seconded, and unanimously carried, it was:

RESOLVED, that the shareholders ratify the actions of the Board of Directors for the previous year.

There being no further business to come before the meeting, upon motion duly made, seconded, and unanimously carried, it was adjourned.

_____
Secretary

Minutes of Annual Meeting of Board of Directors of XYZ, Inc.

The annual meeting of the Board of Directors of XYZ, Inc., a Nevada corporation, was held upon proper notice on _____, 200__, immediately following the conclusion of the annual meeting of shareholders of the corporation.

Present in person or telephonically were the following directors:

Jack Smith
Jill Jones

The president called the meeting to order. The meeting then proceeded to elect officers to serve until the next annual directors meeting. The following nominations were made and seconded:

NAME	OFFICE
Jack Smith	President
Jill Jones	Secretary/Treasurer

There being no further nominations the foregoing persons were unanimously elected to the offices set forth opposite their respective names. Each of the officers so elected thereupon accepted the office to which he was elected as aforestated.

[Insert any specific corporate issues here.]

A discussion was then had regarding the actions taken in the preceding year on behalf of the company.

After further discussion it was:

RESOLVED, that the actions taken by the officers in the preceding year on behalf of the company were approved and ratified.

There being no further business, the meeting was adjourned.

_____
Secretary

Wasn't that easy. You just saved your home and your car and your bank account. Now your spouse won't leave you for screwing up and allowing the corporate veil to be pierced. Prepare the minutes. Follow the formalities.

Rich Dad Tips

- It is important to keep your minutes in a safe place. Obviously, losing or misplacing them does not fit into your protection strategy.
- Corporate minute books are binders for holding your meeting minutes as well as articles, bylaws, and other corporate documents. They generally cost about $75, and if they force you to be organized will be money well spent.

Again, please remember that minutes are your friends. By illustrating an appropriate level of duty to the corporation, they will protect officers and directors from litigation. The following list contains some of the items to be reviewed by the officers and directors and reflected in the minutes:

- Electing officers of the company;
- Amending the articles of incorporation;
- Amending the bylaws;
- Adopting a stock option plan;
- Approving the issuance of securities and granting warrants and options;
- Declaring stock splits or dividends;
- Entering into a buy-sell agreement (see Chapter 12);
- Entering into employment contracts with key employees;
- Approving contracts, leases, and other obligations;
- Borrowing significant sums and the granting of security in connection therewith;
- Acquiring other businesses;
- Buying or selling significant assets;
- Forming subsidiaries;
- Merging or reorganizing the company;
- Responses to tender offers;

- Resistance to proxy contests;
- Approval of proxy statements; and
- Taking other actions material to the business.

So fear not. The formalities are not that difficult. And it is certainly worth the protection. And once again, while we are still on the topic of protection . . .

Chapter 8

Protect Your Entity Name

A very important and often overlooked element in forming a corporation, LLC, or LP is choosing the right name.

What's in a name? A lot of headaches if you are not careful.

Case No. 12—Cathy and Peter

Cathy and Peter had decided to form a computer leasing business to be called CompuCo. When they called their Southeastern state's secretary of state to see if the name was available it was. They incorporated under the name CompuCo and started doing business. They thought the name issue was resolved by incorporating with the name they wanted.

But the name issue was far from over. Cathy and Peter were good businesspeople and their enterprise flourished. So much so that they started to attract the attention of other similar businesses. One was a large, well-financed company out of California's Silicon Valley. They were very interested in CompuCo's business because, of all things, their name was also CompuCo. And they held the federal trademark registration on the name.

CompuCo of California sent Cathy and Peter a cease-and-desist letter demanding that they stop using the name CompuCo. It was asserted, quite correctly, that with their federal trademark registration they owned all rights to the mark throughout the entire United States.

And because they were from Silicon Valley, where everything regarding intellectual property is important and litigated, CompuCo demanded that

Cathy and Peter pay them $500,000 for their infringement of the CompuCo name.

Cathy and Peter were devastated. They did not have that kind of money. They had only been using the name locally for sixteen months. How much damage could there be?

They promptly went to an attorney. After reviewing the case, the attorney explained that they had to immediately stop using the CompuCo name. He explained that a corporate name is just that—the ability to use the name without confusion in the secretary of state's office. It had nothing to do with conducting a business. For that you really need a trademark.

A trademark is any word, phrase, slogan, symbol, or design that is used to distinguish a product or service. Trademarks are usually a name or logo but they can be other distinguishing characteristics such as the shape of a container or the design and color of a label. Marks that designate services are sometimes called service marks but their legal function is the same.

The attorney stated that if you do not do a search to see if a trademark is available for your name, and someone else is using that name, you can run into big problems.

Still, he saw CompuCo of California's letter for what it was: protection of the mark. If a trademark owner learns of someone else using their mark he must take all steps to protect it—or lose his own rights to the mark. CompuCo had to send such a letter to protect themselves.

The lawyer called CompuCo and worked things out. Cathy and Peter promptly stopped using the name without the payment of additional monies and the matter was resolved.

But it cost them over $25,000 to create a new logo and change their name on all their brochures and advertising, as well as pay their attorney's fees. This money would not have been lost if they had done a proper trademark search and trademark filing in the first place.

In a competitive marketplace, few things are as valuable as instant customer recognition of your product or service. Businesses in the U.S. invest billions of dollars each year to establish their products or services in the minds of their customers. Trademarks are the primary means of establishing instant customer recognition.

Yet, trademarks can be stolen, lost, and weakened if they are not protected properly. Federal trademark registration is the strongest tool available for protecting trademarks. The benefits of federal trademark registration include:

- Protect customer recognition and goodwill developed in your mark.
- Protect your investment in advertising and promotions.
- Prevent conflicts with other companies that may use your name in the future.
- Reserve names that you intend to use in the future.
- Gain income from licensing the mark to others.
- Give constructive notice of ownership to all later users of the mark.
- Have the right to display the federal registration symbol ®.
- Gain the right to make the mark "incontestable" after five years of continuous use.
- Have a presumption of ownership if the mark ends up in litigation.
- Allow registrants to use the federal courts in a dispute.

Mark Searches

Before choosing a name for your business, product, or service, you must do a mark search. As with the CompuCo example, a comprehensive search before you have developed a market presence with an unacceptable name prevents costly and frustrating name changes later. If you choose a name that is being used by another company, you may be drawn into litigation and forced to change your mark. A mark search can help determine if the name you choose conflicts with any other company's mark.

Searches are also recommended before applying for trademark registration. A search can save a lot of time and money by detecting possible conflicts early.

A common mistake made by small companies is relying upon a state business name search performed by a state government. This is inadequate as a mark search because it is limited to that state's list of registered business names. You must do a search on a powerful computerized database that is much more comprehensive and can detect names used in all fifty states.

The Registration Process

The federal registration process begins with an application to the Patent and Trademark Office. Once filed, the application is examined by a trademark examiner. The examination process may include one or two written exchanges with the examiner. The examiner may reject the application or it may be approved immediately.

Once approved, the application is published for opposition. This allows another party to object to your application. However, most applications do not receive objections. If the mark is not opposed, the mark will be placed on the federal register.

The registration process generally takes one to two years.

Types of Applications

There are two kinds of applications: in-use and intent-to-use. If the mark is currently being used with a product or service in interstate commerce, an in-use application may be filed. If the mark is not currently being used in interstate commerce but the applicant has a bona fide intention to use it, an intent-to-use application may be filed.

An intent-to-use application allows the applicant to establish an early priority date. Even though the applicant is not using the mark, the applicant can claim priority over all those who were not using the mark before the date the application was filed. An intent-to-use application can be renewed every six months up to a maximum of three years.

Getting Started

In order to start the application process, the following information and specimens must be assembled:

• The name, address, and telephone number of the applicant. If the applicant is a corporation, you must include the state of incorporation.

• The exact spelling of the mark as it is used in your business. If the mark includes a logo, you will need a clear drawing of the logo that can be placed on a drawing page. The drawing must be clear enough to photocopy and it must be no larger than four inches by four inches. If the logo is not available in this form, trademark artists can make the proper drawings.

• A complete list of the goods or services the mark is or will be associated with. The list should be as comprehensive as possible.

• How the mark is used on the goods. For example, printed on the goods, printed on the labels attached to the goods, printed on packaging material, and so on.

- The first date of use of the mark anywhere and the first date of use of the mark in interstate commerce. Interstate commerce means selling the goods across state lines or in another country. No dates are needed for an intent-to-use application.

- Three specimens of the mark as it is used with the goods. Specimens of marks used on goods may be labels, boxes, pictures of the goods, or the goods themselves if they are flat. Specimens of service marks may be promotional materials such as brochures or advertisements. All three of the specimens may be the same. No specimens are needed for intent-to-use applications.

Costs

The Patent and Trademark Office currently charges a $325 fee for each trademark application. Our firm charges $650 for a name and trademark search and $325 for preparing the application. Subsequent prosecution of the application, if necessary, is billed at an hourly rate. Other law firms or trademark services may charge more or less than the amounts quoted above.

Rich Dad Tips

- Consider trademarking your name and slogans as you would an improvement to your house.
- Just as a newly remodeled kitchen can increase the value of your house by two times the amount spent on the remodeling, trademarks can also increase your company's value in a similar way.

Licensing

A trademark owner has the right to sell or license his trademark. This may be an attractive option to trademark owners who have an underutilized mark with special appeal. Be sure to seek specialized assistance in negotiating and drafting license and assignment agreements. For an excellent review of the entire intellectual property landscape see *Protecting Your #1 Asset* by Michael Lechter.

And so, you have a great company name. It is trademarked and now you need help . . .

Chapter 9

Raising Money

You have prepared your business plan, you have assembled your business team, you have decided on your business entity—now you need money.

What do you do?

You can sell an ownership interest in your company. In a corporation you sell stock, in a limited partnership you sell limited partnership interests, in a limited liability company you sell membership interests. But you must be careful. Raising money for your business can be tricky. In fact, if you do it the wrong way you can land in jail. That is why it is important to read and understand this section. It is not rocket science. Look at all the businesses around you. A goodly number of them sold stock or limited partnership interests or membership interests to get into business. It can be done and it is done every day.

You can do it too. We'll show you how in our next case.

First, some background information.

Securities rules and regulations involve both federal and state law. The United States Securities and Exchange Commission (the SEC) was founded in the wake of an extraordinary number of false or misleading projects to separate naive investors from their money (think of the classic stories of people buying ownership interests in the Brooklyn Bridge, retirement paradises that proved to be Florida swamps, or interests in stage shows that, as in Mel Brooks's movie *The Producers*, amounted to an aggregate of 500 percent ownership). The SEC's approach to these problems was to require a company to provide:

(1) "Adequate full disclosure" to potential investors about the business history;

(2) Reasonable projections that are clearly noted as being speculative or "forward-looking"; and

(3) Serious discussion and warnings about the risks of investment.

That may sound hefty, but it is really not when you compare it to the seriously debated alternative, which was for the government to actually review the investment to determine if it was a good deal. How would they know? The last thing anyone wants in a free marketplace is for the government to decide what we can invest in. Not when they keep telling us that with a 2 percent annual return Social Security is a really good deal. So, instead, although you have to give investors a good bit of information, the SEC has prudently said, once you've done so, it's the investor's own choice and risk. They protect widows and orphans, not idiots.

Although many states follow the federal government's disclosure method, many others have gone with the alternative approach: You not only have to prove to the state government that you have provided full disclosure, but you must also give the government good reason to think it's a good investment for its citizens. This is called the "merit review" approach, and it creates tremendous burdens of time and effort to meet such high standards. And again, how can these states even begin to judge what is a good investment or not? No one is sure, but they define it as their duty to do so.

Merit Review States

If your company is making an offering of securities under a rule other than Regulation D, Rule 506, then the transaction and required disclosure materials prepared in connection with your offering will likely become subject to a merit review by several (perhaps even all) states into which you are intending to sell securities. Under a merit review, your transaction and disclosure materials are not only scrutinized by each state securities agency for accuracy, level of disclosure, and compliance with state legislation, but also as to whether the transaction(s) your company is proposing to undertake with the monies raised from the private placement offering has merit as a viable business proposition. In practical fact, this can be a lengthy and extraordinarily expensive endeavor.

Currently, states that conduct a full, or substantial, merit review of private placement offerings *not* made under Regulation D, Rule 506, of the Securities Act of 1933, as amended, are as follows:

Alabama	Kentucky	New Mexico
Alaska	Maine	New York
Arizona	Massachusetts	Ohio
Arkansas	Michigan	Oklahoma
California	Minnesota	Oregon
Florida	Mississippi	Tennessee
Hawaii	Missouri	Washington
Indiana	Nebraska	West Virginia
Kansas	New Hampshire	

It is important, therefore, to consider how best to deal with potential subscribers from these states, and whether conducting a private placement offering under a rule or regulation other than Rule 506 is desirable. It may be that the cost of having a merit review conducted on your company's private placement memorandum outweighs the subscription funds to be received.

Keep this in mind as we go along, for you may want to consider the burdens of an offering to investors within a state based on the standard of review. When you start looking for serious outside financing, the time and costs of a merit review offering are going to become very important for you to consider.

To begin with, however, let's just look at getting off the ground with something called founders' shares. There are two reasons for issuing these:

First, to get shares in the hands of the founders for a very low price, sometimes at the par value or founders' price of $0.001 (one tenth of one cent per share). If you are going to receive shares early on as a founder, if you are going to take a start-up risk, you want to pay as little as possible for your reward. The cost of one million shares at a founders' price of $0.001 is only $1,000. Even at one cent a share that rises to $10,000 for a million shares. Not everyone wants—or should—pay that amount. You are much better off only putting in $1,000 and seeing where the company goes.

Please note, you cannot sell stock for less than the par value amount. You have to pay at least $0.001 per share. Also note that when you take stock for services (organizing, managing, or promoting the company at the outset), you must pay taxes on the value received. So if you take one million shares at $0.001 for your services, you have an income tax obligation based on $1,000 of income; that is far better than having to pay taxes on the receipt of one million shares at one cent per share, or $10,000.

The second reason for using founders' shares is to create a stable group of interests that will hold enough control to prevent later investors from easily upsetting the ownership, management, and future of the business.

How do founders' interests sit in each of our good entities?

Limited Partnership

In a limited partnership, actual control of the operations of the business will be in the hands of the general partner; and, as discussed earlier, the very nature of an LP is that it limits liability for limited partners so long as they have no actual role in running the business. Thus, here you need mainly be concerned that if there will be more than one general partner, you'll want to have firm agreements as to who manages what, how voting control works, and how profit distribution is to be allocated among general partners in addition to allocation of profits among limited partners. Generally speaking, think of a good friendship where you still memorialize the important things in writing. Because limited partners are not "in control" but only entitled to their allotted profits and rights upon dissolution, the founders' interest issue is not a crucial one.

Limited Liability Company

It's different with a limited liability company. The articles of organization and operating agreement create an entity that is rather more democratic. Membership has its privileges. Whatever the capital contribution, you'll need to separately establish the value of the membership interest received in exchange for it. Because LLCs typically involve a small group of investors with a common mission, the founders' interest issue relates to essentially all original membership interests. Members are entitled to vote and approve major decisions not delegated to a managing member, so in terms of control consider the number and percentage of weight that multiple members will be able to swing in spite of the fact that you may be the managing member.

Sometimes LLCs organize so that a group of members with a controlling percentage for voting purposes operate collectively as managing members. You can also create mandatory buy-back provisions or rights of first refusal by the LLC or its members when a member wants to sell their interest so that you can increase your control and prevent unwanted investors from getting into the group. Thus, for an LLC, the most important founders' considerations are making sure you have the right group of individuals and providing that management and membership interests are well protected. This must be balanced against being so possessive that you deter any future investors from wanting to join in.

Corporations

For corporations, the concept of founders' shares is well established. These shares are created partly as a block of shares that will retain a fair level of voting control over the corporation, especially in its early and nonpublic years. The last thing a founders' group may want is for the first-round money guys to have immediate control. That can happen after a few rounds of funding; but not at the start.

Founders' shares are also a reward for investing what is often far more valuable at the inception of a corporation than money—the blood, sweat, and tears that will create a great business because of the founders' skills and dedication, in spite of a significant uncertainty of later reward.

As such, both reasons for issuing founders' shares are satisfied by issuing a substantial percentage of what will be the corporation's expected total number of outstanding shares after several rounds of funding.

However, although you'll be tempted to keep a tight grip on voting control, know that you'll eventually have to surrender some of it, especially if you want to become a public corporation. Both underwriters and general investors tend to steer away from public companies with highly concentrated control. On the other hand, at this stage it is best to keep a tight grip on things. It's a common tactic for early venture capitalists to offer what (to a fledgling business) seems like a staggering sum of money but require a huge percentage of stock. Often little further money follows, fault is found with existing management, and directors and the block of shares in the hands of the venture capitalists may be enough to grab your company right out from under your feet before it's six months old. Hence the term "vulture capitalists."

Early-round private offering investors may be up to the same thing, so keep an eye on the percentage of control you'll need and how much other stock you can sell to well-trusted initial investors and later in private offerings without putting your company's future in unknown hands.

Next, you'll almost certainly need start-up capital—seed money—with which to get the business off and running and making money of its own, and that's way more than you've likely got in the bank. Most commonly, before incurring the great expense of (and finding the right kinds of investors for) a full-blown offering of stock, the initial round of raising capital is from so-called angel investors: friends, family, old business acquaintances, your college roommate, and others. These are not quite the same as your founders. These people are risking a lot of cold hard cash. Accordingly, they are often rewarded by getting their shares at a price much lower than you'll be asking for in a regular offering.

Let's look at a case involving a company that may some day go public.

Case No. 13—Z Tech

Robert, Sam, and Tom had a phenomenal idea that they had patented. Because they had a patent they now had a technology. And by owning a technology they absolutely had to use some derivation of the word "technology" in their corporate name.

Thus, Z Tech, Inc. was born and formed as a corporation.

The next step was to issue stock to founders and to raise money to commercially exploit their technology.

The three agreed that they did not want to lose control initially. They knew their business and their technology. If done properly it would be a once-in-a-lifetime opportunity. A huge and satisfying score for all of them. If handled poorly, they would have to keep working for the rest of their lives.

Z Tech, Inc. was incorporated in Nevada with a total of 20 million common shares and 5 million preferred shares authorized.

The total of 25 million shares each at a par value of $.001 per share, or a par value capitalization of $25,000, was a suitable amount of shares to be authorized for the company's future growth. Please note that the par value of shares is an antiquated concept not worth discussing. All you need to know at a cocktail party is that:

1. You cannot sell stock or grant founders' shares for less than par value.
2. Par value is an antiquated concept not worth discussing.

Robert, Sam, and Tom agreed that they would each take 20 percent of the common shares, or 4 million shares each. Their contribution was valued at $4,000 each. While they could have received shares for services rendered (and paid tax on it), the three decided that the company needed the money and each paid $4,000 for their 4 million shares, which equaled $0.001 per share.

By each taking 20 percent of the authorized common shares they would have 60 percent control when all 20 million common shares were issued. As it was, with only 12 million shares issued, they each owned 33⅓ percent of all issued shares. Their current one-third ownership would be diluted or reduced as more shares were sold, which, of course, they needed to do to get the business going. But they would still maintain control of the company once all 20 million common shares were sold and until the 5 million nonvoting preferred shares were converted to voting common shares.

They had authorized the preferred shares for future flexibility. They were nonvoting so the three could issue them without worrying about losing control. If they were later converted to voting common shares and all shares were issued they could lose control. By holding only 12 million shares out of 25 million issued they could be voted out. But remember, their angel investors would have some shares and presumably they would side with them in a shareholder dispute. However, you can never know.

Once Robert, Sam, and Tom issued themselves their founders' shares they were ready to issue shares to their angels. Robert's mom, Ethel, was willing to invest $10,000 at the right price. Sam's brother, Lenny, was willing to invest $10,000 if he could get options, and Tom's best friend, Mason, was willing to invest whatever Tom needed just because. The three founders figured that they needed a total of $50,000 to get Z Tech, Inc. going. They had already together put in $12,000, so $38,000 more was needed fairly soon.

The $50,000 would take care of initial expenses and cover reduced monthly expenses for six months. They would not take salaries in order to conserve money. After they had proven their concept they would need $1 million to really pursue their business.

So the task was to figure out what to charge per share in the angel round and what to charge per share in the first round of funding. They wanted to benefit their angels with a low share price but also provide an attractive incentive for the $1 million investors.

Robert, Sam, and Tom figured it was fair to set the angel round at 5 cents per share and the first round at 25 cents per share. Once these rounds were completed their shareholders would be as follows:

Approximate Time	Raise	Name	Shares	Price per share	Amount raised
Day one	Founder	Robert	4,000,000	$.001	$4,000
	Founder	Sam	4,000,000	.001	4,000
	Founder	Tom	4,000,000	.001	4,000
Day ten	Angel	Ethel	200,000	.05	10,000
	Angel	Lenny	200,000	.05	10,000
	Angel	Mason	360,000	.05	18,000
Six months after angel round	1st Round	Investor	4,000,000	.25	1,000,000
		Total	16,760,000	—	$1,050,000

It should be noted that if Lenny was granted stock options to purchase, for example, 100,000 more shares for 10 cents a share within two years, the same exact options would have been granted to the other angel investors. You must give all the investors in one round the exact same deal. You cannot change prices or any other terms within any round. If one gets options, they all get options. Everyone gets the same deal. Not only is this the law but as a very practical matter it keeps your shareholders happy. No one wants to find out he paid the same price as the next guy but did not get the options.

Also, in terms of prices, you should try not to go down in share price between offerings as a nonpublic company. When you are a public company and trading on an exchange the price will freely go up and down every day. But when the company is not public the share price is set by the founders or management. Unless there is a legitimate economic reason to do so, it is bad practice, and unfair to the shareholders, to set the price high in one round and low in the next. Put yourself in the shoes of your shareholders and ask yourself if you think it is fair. Not when your are the one who paid $1.00 a share for stock now selling for 5 cents a share.

Likewise, under the securities laws you cannot conduct multiple offerings of the same stock at the same time. And you should not conduct offerings of stock one right after the other. The SEC prefers to see a six-month quiet, nonselling period between offerings. Consult your legal advisor as to the importance of these and other securities rules.

Robert, Sam, and Tom wanted to follow the securities laws. So when they granted Lenny his stock options they gave the same deal to Ethel and Mason. As well, when they stopped selling the angel round, they waited six months to go after their first round of funding.

They hired securities counsel to guide them through this complicated process. Z Tech, Inc. impressed its early investors, kept its promises and its books in order, and without too much delay was given permission by the SEC to do an initial public offering. Robert, Sam, and Tom became very wealthy.

LP and LLC Investor Rounds

LPs and LLCs are not usually associated with the funding of numerous rounds of investors. Because corporations are vehicles for going public, rounds of increasing share prices are more common. As well, LPs and LLCs do not offer the complete free transferability of interests, making a public market difficult.

Likewise, later contributors to LPs and LLCs are treated much the same as earlier partners or members. As a flow-through entity you are buying, for example, 10 percent of the LP or LLC for the flow-through of money, not for the appreciation of your interest. Investors in both need to think in terms of long-term investment and the attraction of consistent returns once the business begins realizing profits. The drill in an LP or LLC investment is not to bring in more investors at higher prices but to increase the profits on your percentage ownership of the entity.

How to Bring Investors In

The first step for bringing in investors is, no matter how thin it may be as yet, provide each one with a copy of your business plan. Also, give each potential investor copies of the required documents verifying the appropriate business and legal organization of the entity (articles of incorporation, bylaws, certification of the secretary of state, as applicable).

Included should be a realistic financial statement of the business, showing the costs to get it going, the minimum and maximum amounts you are expecting to raise, and fair projections showing where the business will be, both at its low-end and high-end estimates, in the next six months, a year, and so on. Remember, the further out you project, the less reliable these forward-looking statements will be. Make sure to state just that: (1) These projections are not verifiable or reliable; (2) They are provided with the warning that they may not be reached; and (3) The whole business may not even succeed.

You may not like the sound of that, but think back to the Brooklyn Bridge and Florida swamp examples. Potential investors have a right to know these significant material things, to be reminded of the risks that go along with faith, and to be warned about putting too much faith in dreams of the future. They could actually lose their whole investment!

Earlier, the full-disclosure and merit review requirements that governments impose on those who sell interests to investors were discussed. At the very least, under either standard, you have to tell them all the risks you can think of. Try to trust that people will appreciate your candor about this; they may even be more inclined to invest if they know you have your feet on the ground and are studying all possibilities with a clear head. Thus, not only are such disclosures required, but they could actually help you get prudent investors. And to be sure, a sophisticated investor who has read an investment prospectus or two will just gloss over the risks and warnings. They're in every one.

Finally, create a subscription agreement. This is a formal document listing the materials given to the potential investor. It states that the investor has reviewed them and has had an opportunity to ask questions and review any other requested materials that you could reasonably furnish them. It affirms that they are aware of the risks of the investment, but states they have chosen to make the investment based on their own informed decision. Include a place to state the amount of the investment and what they are to receive in return, such as common or preferred stock.

Make sure the investor manually signs and dates the subscription agreement and gives the document to you along with payment. Finally, place a statement at the end by which the business accepts the subscription, and sign and date that in the capacity of your official corporate position. Make a photocopy of the fully executed subscription agreement and a copy of their check for them to keep with their other important documents. Now, and only now, can you take the check to the bank and deposit it in the business's account. As soon as possible, a certificate should be issued to each partner or member, indicating the business's name, the investor's name, the date of the issuance, and the type and amount of shares now owned by the investor. The stock certificate should be treated like handling a bar of gold. Be careful.

Fill out and spell everything exactly as it should be, and sign and date it just before delivering it to the new owner. Don't skimp on the postage if sending it through the mail either. Pay a bit extra and send it certified, return receipt requested. Take the same care with each certificate and number them consecutively. Finally, keep a careful ledger recording the consecutive certificate numbers, investor names, issuance dates, payments for investment, and the type and amount of stock interest for each investor.

Your state may require that you file this information, fill out additional forms, perhaps receive advance approval by the state regarding the form and perhaps the content of investment documentation, and you'll quite likely be required to pay a fee. Check with your state and/or securities attorney for the most recent approval and filing requirements in advance of any offering, as such requirements frequently change in a number of states.

If you have investors from more than one state, include in your documents, especially the subscription agreement, that the offering is being conducted pursuant to the exemption of Rule 506 under Regulation D of the Securities Act of 1933, as amended.

Rule 506 allows you to sell securities interstate without having to register them or get approval with the Securities and Exchange Commission. Better still, Rule 506 offerings preempt the varying laws of all fifty states; therefore, in every applicable state, even in merit review states, the most the state can require of you is a fairly simple form to file along with a filing fee. They can't demand that you fulfill any other requirements. Within fifteen days after you accept a subscription agreement from your first investor in the offering, you'll just need to file a copy of Form D with the Securities and Exchange Commission—and there's no fee. And think about a nice side effect of the timing for filing the form: It needs to be filed within fifteen days after the first investment—file it immediately after the first one and you need only provide the information with respect to that single investor. That will save you a bundle of time trying to fill in information for everyone else. The SEC doesn't require—or even want—you to amend or add to Form D. Just make sure you do it on time. Meeting deadlines will become increasingly important for your business and its securities status. You don't want to start off looking ill-prepared and unprofessional.

There are three other significant points about Rule 506 that you should note. First, for purposes of federal law, the offering may have no more than thirty-five nonaccredited investors (for the moment, think basically million-aires versus nonmillionaires). Second, and related, is that in any given six-month period from the time an offering ends, the number of nonaccredited investors will be counted in the aggregate if you have more than one offering that is essentially similar in nature during the succeeding six months (this is called the integration rule). Thus, you need to be careful about the total number of nonaccredited investors that you may have now and in any initial private placement offering.

For the friends and family round at present, many, if not all, will probably be nonaccredited. So consider that although you need the cash to get the business going, don't exhaust all thirty-five allowed nonaccredited investors or have so many that it would hobble your next-round offering with the burden of having to find almost all accredited investors to sell enough stock at the higher price. Although the typical angel investor offering involves a small number of people, keep in the back of your mind that the money raised will have to last at least a good six months from the time it ends before you can initiate another offering without worrying about oversubscribing to nonaccredited investors. Also, your state may have even lower allowable limits on the number of nonaccredited investors you can have within that state. Nevada only allows twenty-five nonaccredited Nevada residents as investors, which means any of the ten more allowed by federal law would have to come from another state. Be sure to check about state regulation of nonaccredited investors as well.

There's a pretty good reason for this limit. Accredited investors can afford—at least in theory—to lose all the money invested without suffering extreme consequences in their personal lives. Nonaccredited investors are taking a bigger risk, and the government doesn't want you to rely on the aid of too many people who may not be as able to afford the risks of investing. Otherwise, they'd start to feel an increasing obligation to review and authorize your offering materials. To allow young businesses the opportunity to raise funds without too much government oversight, delays, and costs, this exemption from registration was created. So remember that the SEC is firm about the thirty-five nonaccredited investor limit and the six-month integration rule. These are at the heart of allowing this exemption, so be careful to live up to the spirit and letter of the law.

You'll need to explain to investors how they are classified, so here's a basic definition of accredited investors and a suggested definition for the types of people who could best afford the risk although not accredited:

An accredited investor is defined in Regulation D to include:

- A natural person (United States citizen or permanent resident—*i.e.*, not an entity of any kind) whose individual net worth (excluding home, home furnishings, and automobiles), or joint net worth with such person's spouse, exceeds $1 million at the time of purchase;
- A natural person who has an individual income in excess of $200,000 in each of the two most recent years or joint income with that person's spouse in excess of $300,000 in each of those years and who reasonably expects to reach the same income level in the current year;
- A business entity, not formed for the specific purpose of acquiring the units offered, with total assets in excess of $5 million; or
- An entity in which all of the equity owners are accredited investors.

A nonaccredited investor is an investor who does not meet the income and asset test set out above. While there is no minimum income and asset test for a nonaccredited investor, it is a good idea, when considering offering securities to nonaccredited investors, to establish a minimum income threshold, for example, a yearly taxable income of $40,000 or more. In addition, certain states may impose different or additional suitability standards, which may be more restrictive.

Under Rule 506, the company may accept subscriptions from no more than thirty-five nonaccredited investors in total, per private placement offering. Remember also to consider states' laws when calculating the number of nonaccredited investors. As an example, Nevada only allows twenty-five per offering.

A crucial point to remember, however, is that the level of disclosure is significantly higher when nonaccredited investors are being solicited. A full private placement memorandum must be prepared, using the specific disclosure guidelines and headings promulgated by the SEC; and in addition, audited financial statements, no more than three months old, must be included with the private placement memorandum. Where a company can demonstrate significant hardship or expense in preparing a full set of audited financial statements, it is permissible to provide nonaccredited investors with an audited balance sheet only, but again, no more than three months old.

The third and final significant point about this exempt form of seeking investments is that when offering securities to nonaccredited investors under Rule 506, you are required to provide them with audited statements for some of the financial material. An audit, even a limited one like this, is going to be costly. A very few CPAs and accounting firms (and not the big ones) may consider receiving shares at least as partial compensation in exchange for their services, but this is not an option when being audited. The auditor cannot have an ownership interest in the company, which would obviously create conflict-of-interest problems. So you may need to set something aside from the outset for auditing expenses and, if possible, arrange to have part of the payment to be made to the auditor from proceeds of the offering.

Another important point to know: Unless you conduct a registered public offering (which you won't be doing in the early stages), there are restrictions on an investor's ability to transfer their interests to another. This is usually referred to as a Rule 144 restriction. Under Rule 144 of the Securities Act, no shares can be sold by an investor for one full year from the time they purchase their shares. During the second year, they are limited to selling shares equaling no more than 1 percent of the entire "public float" of the company's securities during any given three-month period. The public float means anyone other than people in controlling positions within the company, owners of 10 percent or more of the company's securities (a position known as a "beneficial owner"), and any affiliate of the company (i.e., another entity controlled by your company, in common control of your company, or in common control with your company over another company). After the second year, those investors whose shares are within the definition of the public float will have all restrictions on transfer lifted and the stock becomes fully marketable.

Shareholders not part of the public float remain subject to the 1 percent limit provision for so long as they remain in the positions that prevent them from being regarded as within the public float. If they cease to be in such positions, after three months from the time they meet the public float definition, they will then be treated as any other member in the public float.

So, on the certificates you issue, include a restrictive legend prominently on the front so that the corporation can show it has notified each investor of the Rule 144 restriction and has made sure anyone seeing the certificate will be alerted to the limitations on transfer. After the second year, you can replace restricted certificates with ones that have no restrictive legends. The following is such a legend commonly used:

> The securities covered hereby have not been registered under the Securities Act of 1933, as amended ("Act"), and may not be offered or sold within the United States or to or for the account or the benefit of U.S. Persons (i) as part of their distribution at any time or (ii) otherwise until one year after the later of the commencement of the offering of such securities or the closing date of the sale and transfer thereof, except in either case in accordance with Rule 144 under the Act. Terms used above have the meaning given to them by Rule 144.

Make sure you also discuss these restrictions within the documentation you give potential investors, and especially make a point of it (and the investor's understanding and acceptance of it) on the subscription agreement.

All this may seem like a lot of work at first, but after reviewing this material you'll find it isn't as overwhelming as it may appear at first glance. However, there's one more significant thing to make a point of right now, and this is really important: Skip or screw up any part of the several previous paragraphs on conducting an offering, and you may very easily find yourself in a great deal of trouble with the federal or state government—or both. From this point on, you're playing with other people's money, and obligations like the above will exist with every step of your business's existence.

It is important to again review the process for designating a lower price per share for angel investors than what you will be hoping to sell shares for in future offerings, as it requires a bit of advance calculation.

Think of the total number of shares you will want to have issued and outstanding after your first major private placement offering. Also think of the total funds you will need to raise including from that offering. Now backtrack and figure in the percentage of founders' shares needed to keep some solid control over the stability of the corporation, your board of directors, and initial officers. Subtract that from the total shares, and the rest is available for the angels, the first major private offering down the road in six months, and some extra stock for a few other purposes.

Again, a good rule of thumb for the angel investor offering is to pour enough money into the coffers to get the corporation fully operational, to meet its initial goals, and to get revenue streams up and generating enough money to keep you afloat by the end of six months. That's a goal, but prepare in case revenues don't prove as fast and large as you'd hoped in that amount of time. You may also have to put off some projects for the time being, for almost certainly in six months you won't be able to do everything you hope for, although you can make reasonable projections for getting the business into shape and looking good for future investors. Also, recall the six-month integration limit for Rule 506, so put a short fuse as to when the angel investor offering will end, for it's from that time that the six-month integration rule will count. You'll probably need a good number of nonaccredited investors in the next offering, so try to get enough angel investor money to last through till then, cover the costs of the next offering (generally in the range of $10,000 for a first major private placement), and be able to take on another full thirty-five nonaccredited investors next time. Again, keep in mind that some states have lower limits on the number of their residents that can invest in a private placement.

Quite often, new businesses find themselves unable to generate enough capital through stock offerings alone. At this point, you may want to think about figuring in loans to help you get going. Without a strong background, bank loans are going to be tough to obtain, but you may wish to request information from the Small Business Administration, which can sometimes be a useful resource for ideas. You may simply have to sign promissory notes for loans and agree to sizable interest payments. Here, if possible, you may be able to create a promissory note that allows for an election of repayment either in cash or the company's securities in an effort to prove the company's worth to the creditor and issue stock rather than paying back large sums of money for a still fledgling business.

In any case with loans, try to get as much time and the lowest monthly payments you can. No matter how well you plan, finances are always tight for new businesses. You don't want to add creditors beating at the door to the other matters you'll need to devote your time and attention to. There is also a lending counterpart to private and public offerings, called a convertible debenture, but like those later equity offerings, structuring and marketing a convertible debenture offering is a costly and complicated process that is probably best left for debt financing as the company reaches a more mature stage.

In all issuances of shares, you'll need to hold a meeting of the board of directors during which the matters are discussed, the general elements of the offering are set forth, resolutions authorizing the same are given, and a resolution is passed directing the officers to take all necessary action to proceed.

At this point, you may be able to do much of this work without having to retain corporate and securities attorneys to put together the materials for founders and angels, but if you find yourself unsure, it's best to pay the money and have a professional make certain everything is done right. A few thousand dollars now might prevent you from the headaches of rescissions, lawsuits, state and federal investigations and fines—virtually any and all of which will cost a lot more than a good attorney helping you at the start.

Which leads us to the next stage of securities. You've got your paperwork in order, a good business and financial plan, a solid set of founders, reliable officers and directors (or partners/managing members, as the case may be), and some much needed financing from the angels who've gotten you off the ground. It's now time for a reality check: If you don't retain legal counsel from now on, you could quickly find yourself sliding along the edge of disaster. No longer will it be Aunt Mabel's money and faith in you. No, now you are entering a world of investors who expect strong business judgment, serious answers to their concerns, and a reliable probability that their money will grow if invested with you.

There are also a good number of sharks in this sea who are smelling for newcomers. They are ready to seize on any sign of uncertainty, hesitation, or inexperience, both in business and finance, either to get a high return for little investment or even to wrest control of the company right out from under you (recall the brief earlier mention of certain less scrupulous venture/vulture capitalists). Don't fall into the fear that everyone will be out to get you, but be realistic. From now on you're going to need lawyers—competent corporate counsel for objective assistance with the business, securities counsel to assist you with future, more complicated financing strategies, and both for maintaining protection of the corporation. Forget the lawyer jokes. A good corporate/securities lawyer is about to become among your business's most trusted friends.

Let's move on to your first private placement offering. This is going to require a good deal of time and effort, so begin preparing at least a couple of months before you hope to begin the offering. As stated earlier, a private placement generally costs something in the range of $10,000. Some law firms will only require a retainer of a few thousand dollars in a trust account to begin with and will draw the remainder of the bill from the proceeds of the offering if it seems probable that you'll raise significant sums to not only pay legal fees, but also to emerge with a large amount of money to support the company's short-term future plans over the next several months to a year. Not all attorneys are willing or able to defer payment, though, so be prepared with funds to cover legal counsel, accounting requirements, and printing fees.

One of the best ways to hold down the legal costs of the offering is to knock yourself out drafting and redrafting your business plan so that it flows smoothly and coherently, in a well-ordered outline, presenting a fair and accurate picture of the company, its results to date, and its hopes for the future. If you do so, your securities attorney will not have to spend days or weeks drafting this material, but rather will be able to adjust the language into "securities-speak," add additional legal legends, warnings, and discussions around your business plan, and thus be able to focus this costly attention on fine detail instead of doing the basics you could have done for yourself.

Taking the time to review and revise your business plan at regular intervals is also simply good business practice. It forces you to take a hard look at where things are, how well you are meeting expectations, what plans seem to work and what may need to be revised or dropped, and how to structure future activity and ever more realistic financial statements and planning.

There are strict limits about announcing, advertising, or paying anyone for seeking investors in private placements. Remember the key word: private. There can be no general solicitation of investors; in fact, it's important to keep knowledge of the offering very quiet and limited to those who need to know. Telling others can lead to problems of "attempting to create a market for securities," which is a big bad thing for both the SEC and most state purposes. This becomes of extreme significance at the point where shares become less restricted or unrestricted or publicly trading. People go to prison for insider trading. Even at an early stage, inside information is something to really guard against allowing to travel beyond those persons directly and of necessity involved in the offering. Accordingly, don't even mention it on your Web site, if you have one; individually number each private placement memorandum (the document you'll prepare with your securities attorney and accountants that houses the securities-oriented business plan, financials, other exhibits, and the subscription agreement); and require return of all materials should a potential investor choose not to subscribe. Keep a list of the private placement memorandums by consecutive number, who they are delivered to, and note the date of their return or the receipt of a subscription agreement.

But how do you find the investors in the first place? You'll need to demonstrate, if ever asked, that potential investors have some sort of prior relationship whereby they know who you are and inquired of their own volition if they may receive materials to consider investing in an offering of your stock. In fact, the subscription agreement will ask the potential investor to state how they found out about the offering. Sounds strange, right? How do you get someone to ask about an offering if you can't tell them it exists? For practical purposes, preexisting relationships are the main safeguard. The potential investor knows about and has been watching your company with interest. They have an inkling that an opportunity to invest may be coming soon, and they ask you—in writing!—for investment information when available. A fun new wrinkle in this process has entered the securities world with the advent of the Internet. You can't announce the offering, but someone who frequents your Web site may e-mail you (without being asked or encouraged to do so) and request information about investment opportunities. If there were ever a reason for not deleting an e-mail and keeping a hard copy in a safe place, this is it.

This limitation of not initiating new investor contacts, but rather only responding to potential investors who aren't informed of the offering itself in advance, is certainly frustrating to imagine. But consider how, if things have gone well, the growth and demonstrated early success of your company will lend a hand. A lot more people can inquire of their own accord now than you would have had reason to expect earlier on. You will have met them personally, sold them your product or service, and they may have even seen a mention of your company in the business section of the newspaper.

In fact, many people interested in investment opportunities make it a practice to keep an eye out for promising young businesses, and they frequently network themselves with other spheres of investors who find and observe young businesses for potential investment opportunities at a lower price by getting in early.

In addition, even with little or no idea that you're preparing for another offering, your own staff and prior investors may be familiarizing additional people among their own family, friends, and other acquaintances about the existence and status of your company. But remember they must keep a lid on any inside information such as a big contract that may be signed soon or even the preparation of the offering itself. Without you instigating direct interest in an offering, these people may be asked by others who are becoming familiar with your business through them to give them general company contact information to look into the possibility of investing someday themselves. And that's acceptable, so long as the potential new investor initiates the interest and your personnel and prior investors aren't suggesting the merits of an investment or directly encouraging someone to subscribe. They just provide a link—the offering, when it comes, will do the selling for itself.

There's one other method available for others to bring in potential investors, but be very careful and use it sparingly, if at all. A small finder's fee can be paid for introductions of potential offerees who are acquainted with current investors. The finder is very limited in acceptable action, however; he may only simply mention to the acquaintance that he's invested in the company and, if requested, can pass the potential investor's name and phone number or address along to the company. He can't do anything else that could even hint at being a sales pitch. He just passes along the contact information to the company, which does all the rest of the work without further involvement of any kind by the finder. The finder's name is simply added to the information records of private placement memorandums being sent out on request. If the person later chooses to subscribe, the finder may receive a fee for the introduction.

This fee is usually kept very small, a set figure or share equaling 1 percent to 3 percent of the amount invested. Finder's fees as high as 10 percent to licensed broker-dealers have been held allowable in some SEC opinions, but it's best not to get close to the edge.

There is no real limit on the number of private placement offerings that may be held. However, keep in mind the integration problems of thirty-five (or fewer in certain states) nonaccredited investors in any six-month period, and remember that every time you issue authorized shares the present ownership percentage of current shareholders (including the founders!) will be proportionately diluted, so don't go overboard.

Let's say it's been a few years, and things are going well for the company. Perhaps the timing is right to employ the last tool of securities to be discussed in this book: going public. In fact, things had better be going really well. For starters, there are minimum threshold requirements that differ depending on what system, market, or exchange you want to become public on. In general, this decision will be based upon your asset value, the number of shareholders and the value of their shares, and the company's overall strategy.

Nasdaq SmallCap Listing Requirements

The Nasdaq SmallCap exchange (NSC) is designed for companies with a limited operating history and a lower asset base than those heading to the Nasdaq National Market. Both the NSC and the National Market are distinct tiers of the Nasdaq.

In order to list on the NSC, a company must meet one or more of the following initial requirements (it must thereafter meet maintenance requirements, set out further below):

INITIAL LISTING REQUIREMENTS

- It must have net tangible assets (total assets less total liabilities) of $4 million; OR
- It must have at least one year of operating history, and have had a net income during that year of $750,000, or, where it has been in operation for more than one year, it must meet the net income requirement of $750,000 for two out of the last three completed fiscal years; OR
- Where a company has less than one year's operating history, it must have its initial market capitalization (i.e., its initial public offering) for a minimum $50 million.

ADDITIONAL LISTING REQUIREMENTS

Assuming the initial requirements to file a listing application are met, at the conclusion of a company's IPO, it must then meet the following additional requirements:

- A minimum public float of one million shares must be held by out-siders (i.e., not officers or directors [directly or indirectly] or beneficial [10 percent or more company ownership] shareholders);

- The market value of the minimum public float must be $5 million;

- The company must engage a minimum of three market makers to regulate the market for its securities (a market maker is defined as an independent dealer who actively competes with other independent dealers for investors' orders, and uses their own capital to buy and sell Nasdaq securities). The purpose of market makers is to help establish a market for a company's securities, and then to ensure a continuous and orderly market (i.e., to protect against share dumping and wild swings);

- The company must have a minimum number of shareholders of 300, each of whom must hold at least a round lot (a round lot is defined as a block of 100 or more shares);

- The company must have at least a one-year history of operations, or, failing that, must attain the market capitalization of $50 million set out above; and

- The company must conduct ongoing corporate governance in accordance with Nasdaq policies. Corporate governance is the overall term for the requirement for public companies to disseminate certain information to the public on an ongoing basis. This includes, but is not limited to, the distribution of annual and interim reports, establishment of an audit committee, holding of annual shareholder meetings, solicitation of proxies, quorum requirements, obtaining shareholder approval for certain transactions, ensuring timely release of press releases, and ensuring that the company remains in good corporate standing (i.e., maintaining the appropriate number of directors, audit committee members, and other requirements).

POST-LISTING REQUIREMENTS TO MAINTAIN NASDAQ SMALLCAP LISTING

Once a company has completed its initial public offering and begins trading on the NSC, it must then continue to meet the continued listing requirements as follows:

- Retain an asset base of at least $2 million; OR
- Retain market capitalization of at least $35 million; OR
- Meet continuing net income requirement of $500,000 per year;

AND

- Maintain a public float of 500,000 shares, having a market value of $1 million;
- Maintain a minimum share price of $1.00 per share;
- Continue to engage two or more market makers;
- Maintain 300 public shareholders; and
- Maintain all corporate government requirements.

Accordingly, the most straightforward NSC listing application would feature a company that had been in business for at least one year and had $4 million in assets. This company would need to do an IPO for a minimum one million shares at $5.00 per share, and would have to sell that offering to at least 300 arm's length public shareholders, who would each be required to purchase at least 100 shares. The 300 public shareholders must be at arm's length to the company, they may not be officers, directors, or insiders of the company, nor may they be shareholders already holding 10 percent or more of the company's shares (although an arm's length investor may *purchase* 10 percent or more under the IPO).

Therefore, a newly formed company with assets of less than $4 million would have to do an IPO for a minimum of 10 million shares at $5.00 per share, to make the market capitalization requirement of $50 million. Again, it would be required to sell the offering to at least 300 shareholders, each of whom must purchase at least a round lot.

Nasdaq National Market Listing Requirements

The Nasdaq National Market exchange (NNM) is the top tier of the Nasdaq and is designed for companies with significant revenues and asset bases.

The listing requirements for the NNM are set out in three standards. Companies must be able to meet one or more of the standards in order to list on the NNM, and following their listing must be able to meet ongoing maintenance requirements. We have set out the listing and maintenance standards below:

Nasdaq National Market Requirements

Requirements	Initial Listing			Continued Listing	
	Standard 1	Standard 2	Standard 3	Standard 1	Standard 2
Net tangible assets	$6 million	$18 million	N/A	$4 million	N/A
Market capitalization	N/A	N/A	$75 million or	N/A	$50 million or
Total assets	N/A	N/A	$75 million AND		$50 million AND
Total revenue	N/A	N/A	$75 million		$50 million
Pretax income (in latest fiscal year or 2 of last 3 fiscal years)	$1 million	N/A	N/A	N/A	N/A
Public float (shares)	1.1 million	1.1 million	1.1 million	750,000	1.1 million
Operating history	N/A	2 years	N/A	N/A	N/A
Market value of public float	$8 million	$18 million	$20 million	$5 million	$15 million
Minimum bid price	$5	$5	$5	$1	$1
Shareholders (round lot shareholders)	400	400	400	400	400
Market makers	3	3	4	2	4
Corporate governance	Yes	Yes	Yes	Yes	Yes

Note:

- *Net tangible assets* means total assets less total liabilities.
- *Market capitalization* means the amount to be raised under the initial public offering.
- *Public float* means shares held by outsiders, that is, not officers or directors (directly or indirectly) or beneficial (10 percent or more company ownership) shareholders.
- *Round lot shareholders* are shareholders holding a block of 100 shares or more.
- *Market makers* are defined as independent dealers who actively compete with other independent dealers for investors' orders, and use their own capital to buy and sell Nasdaq securities.
- *Corporate governance* is the overall term for the requirement for public companies to disseminate certain information to the public on an ongoing basis, and they must do so in accordance with NASDAQ policies.

OTC Bulletin Board Listing Requirements

As the OTC (over the counter) is not a formal exchange, it does not have formal listing requirements as you would find at the Nasdaq or New York Stock Exchange. It does, however, require that companies meet and maintain certain eligibility requirements.

The OTC Bulletin Board is a quotation service, which is regulated and run by a branch of the National Association of Securities Dealers, Inc. (NASD), a quasi-independent body that regulates the nation's securites exchanges, including Nasdaq. The OTC is not a formal exchange or listing service, as you may understand the term. It is, rather, a virtual network of market makers whereby unlisted companies, or foreign companies listed on non-U.S. stock exchanges, may find a market for their stock.

REGISTRATION WITH THE SECURITIES AND EXCHANGE COMMISSION

The first requirement is that your company be registered with the SEC. This is done by filing a registration statement with them, and, following acceptance of your registration, making quarterly filings of unaudited financial statements, and yearly filings of audited financial statements and annual reports.

There are three main types of registration forms, being Form 10 (any domestic company), Form 10SB (small businesses, under $25 million in assets), or Form 20F (for foreign issuers). You are not making a public offering of your company's securities by filing a registration statement (that is done by filing a proper prospectus or other offering document), but merely introducing yourself, your business, and your company to the SEC. Therefore, a registration statement is fairly limited in the amount of disclosure it must contain and relatively easy to prepare.

FINDING A SPONSORING MARKET MAKER

As indicated earlier, market makers are broker-dealers of securities. Market makers are also members who have purchased an ownership share in one or more stock exchanges in the U.S. (or throughout the world). In fact, historically speaking, stock exchanges were originally conceived as a convenient place for these broker-dealers to meet and exchange information). And, as all stock exchanges are owned and operated by their members, you can see why sponsorship by a member is required on any exchange.

Although the OTC is not a formal exchange, it is still owned and operated by a group of market makers. As such, you must have at least one market maker agree to sponsor your company onto the OTC before you will be allowed to have your company's securities quoted on it.

AND, AFTER SPONSORSHIP?

After your company has found an agreeable market maker, it is fairly straightforward. The market maker prepares and files a listing application on behalf of your company, and, upon acceptance by the OTC, your company is assigned a trading symbol and quotation of your company's securities may now begin. However, please note that your company must continue to make at least the quarterly and yearly financial statement filings, as well as its annual report filing, in order to remain eligible for quotation on the OTC.

New York Stock Exchange Listing Requirements

The New York Stock Exchange (NYSE) is perhaps the most prestigious stock exchange in the world, and certainly within North America. Due to the significant listing and maintenance requirements, companies listing on the NYSE tend to be well-funded, mature companies, with significant asset bases and revenues. It is also not for the faint of heart, as the listing and maintenance fees are prodigious.

Companies seeking a listing on the NYSE must first go through an eligibility review process. The NYSE holds absolute control over this process, and reviews each company applying on its own merits to determine whether the NYSE feels it is a suitable listing candidate. The NYSE can amend its standard listing criteria and impose additional listing considerations as it sees fit, on a case-by-case basis. Accordingly, even if your company meets the NYSE minimum listing requirements, it does not guarantee that the NYSE will accept your application and deem you eligible to submit a listing application.

The minimum listing requirements are as set out below.* Assuming that the company meets these, and that the NYSE grants you eligibility status, the company may then prepare and file its listing application.

---

*Of course, if your company has this much money, you probably don't need to be reading this book, but it's good to think of the future of your business in the most optimistic of terms possible, so we have included the information.

Shareholder base	2,000 arm's length shareholders, each holding a round lot of 100 shares; OR
	2,000 arm's length shareholders, and average monthly trading volume of 100,000 shares per month for the preceding 6 months; OR
	500 arm's length shareholders, together with an average monthly trading volume of 1 million shares per month for the preceding 12 months; AND
	A public float of 1.1 million shares.
Market capitalization (i.e., value of public float)	$60 million existing or for IPOs where the company is a spin-off or otherwise affiliated, and $100 million for all other types of companies. For IPO listings, requires written commitment from underwriters guaranteeing minimum market value will be met.
Pretax earnings	*Alternative No. 1*
	$2.5 million in latest fiscal year, plus $2 million for preceding 2 years; OR
	$6.5 million aggregate during past 3 years, of which $4.5 million must have been earned in the last year and profitability achieved in each of the preceding 2 years.

These amounts must be liquid and free of all debt, acquisition costs, and other financial obligations (in other words, after all is said and done, this is what needs to be in the bank).

Alternative No. 2

$500 million in market capitalization and $200 million in revenues during the preceding 12 months, plus net cash flow of $25 million aggregate over the past 3 years, with each year being profitable.

Alternative No. 3

$1 billion in market capitalization and minimum $100 million revenue during preceding 12 months.

Affiliated company standard (parent company is already listed)	$500 million in market capitalization, 12 months' operational history, parent company must be in good standing and must retain control of affiliated company.

Things had better be going well for the company because the price tag is staggering. Merely getting a listing under the Securities Exchange Act of 1934, as amended, will cost anywhere from $20,000 to $50,000. And that alone does nothing more than create a public marketplace for whatever securities are no longer subject to Rule 144 restrictions. It may not even do that: In late 1999 the SEC released a no-action letter suggesting that small businesses going public under the Exchange Act without also separately itemizing and registering securities under the Securities Act (another $20,000 or so) won't be able to rely on the belief that such securities will be regarded as freely trading under many circumstances even though technical compliance with meeting Rule 144 requirements to cease restrictions may have been met.

You'll also need to keep in mind that once you become public, you'll have a minimum of four quarterly status filings to make each year to the SEC. These are expensive and time-consuming to produce, and the requirements and deadlines for filing are strictly enforced. The market or exchange may also have its own requirements for periodic reporting that you'd have to contend with and pay for.

So before taking the plunge, be sure you'll be able to afford not only the large initial expense, but also the ongoing costs of being a public company. It's a big move—as you're about to see.

It's true that many of the elements of private placements discussed above are also used here, most notably polishing a very sophisticated business plan and audited financial statements that will form the basis of your prospectus (the public company counterpart to a private placement memorandum). But the degree of care and expertise becomes dramatically more important and subject to far greater scrutiny than any securities activity you've done before. At this point, you absolutely cannot expect to accomplish this without the aid of a number of experienced professionals: a significant accounting firm for the audit, a qualified and experienced financial printer through which filings with the SEC will be electronically transmitted and prospectuses printed, and the guidance of knowledgeable corporate and securities attorneys.

Additional information will be added after the end of the prospectus in accordance with SEC filing and reporting requirements. Together, this material and the prospectus are called a registration statement. Depending on the type of business, its size, and the type and size of the offering, a variety of forms can be used and your securities attorney will determine the one most appropriate. But for your purposes, they all require variations of the same theme you'll have gotten used to with your private placements: full disclosure of every material fact and risk, and forward-looking statements (boldly identified as such) to the extent that a reasonable investor will know everything they could possibly need to know, both good and bad, to be able to determine whether the investment seems sound and appropriate for their purposes. Actually, there will be two registrations taking place, one under the Securities Act and one under the Exchange Act, but much of the material is treated together. The people who will market your securities, which we'll discuss in a moment, often handle much of the Exchange Act compliance activity as well as play a large role in filing the appropriate market or exchange applications.

In all public offerings, but especially in the case of an initial public offering, you should be prepared to expect extreme scrutiny to be undertaken by examiners at the SEC. This time, the work has to be more extensive and perfectly professional than even your best private placement writing. And in spite of the quality you achieve, you can still be certain to receive several comment letters from your assigned SEC examiner requiring answers to questions, clarification of certain issues, and redrafting or additional drafting to an amended registration statement. This process can take several months, and it is not uncommon to receive several comment letters and to find yourself drafting several successive amended registration statements. Not only will this be time-consuming and burdensome for the professionals assisting you, but frequently the officers, directors, and other company executives themselves will suddenly, in addition to their other tasks, be working very long hours, including weekends, trying to comply with new SEC requests as they flood in. It takes lots of time and lots of money. Keep this in mind when you hear the sirens sing the praises of public offerings.

A thought about the SEC examiner. You may feel like they're being nitpicky and overdemanding, but actually your SEC examiner is one of the best friends you've got. Their mission is to make certain you provide full and adequate disclosure about the company and its offering. Not their own preferences, and not with a view to the relative merits of your business and the investment potential of your stock. They're just getting you to look long and hard at what you do and what you should know, and to make certain you'll be able to get it across clearly to your potential investors. Following their guidance, you'll end up with an objective professional assessment that you've said everything you need to—and an assurance like that has real teeth when the SEC says you've made adequate disclosures. It will be hard for anyone to complain or seek legal recourse against you—providing you told the truth and tested your mettle fully with your SEC examiner. So in the midst of all the work, try to keep this in mind through the process of getting your registration statement approved: The SEC examiner, with a wealth of experience and expertise in studying new entries of businesses on their way into the public market, is there to assist you to do it right and will help you help yourself prevent trouble from coming up later.

You'll also be entering into the world of market makers, the professionals who will find a market and actually go out and sell your stock once your registration statement gets its final approval. Preliminary work to that end usually takes place during the SEC review, but, much like in the earlier situation of finding investors who have to find you first, this is also a delicate art in which no sales are actually made; presentations of the company's business, current status, and proposed offering (often called road shows) simply lay out limited available information, and your preliminary prospectus (called a red herring), in its present "pre-effective" form, includes a prominent legend down the left side of the front cover warning that it's not final and is not an offer to sell securities.

Also at this point, inside information scrutiny goes into high gear. The SEC will be keeping an eye on your company. Absolutely no one is to know information they don't absolutely have to know to do their job. Before the deal is done, the market makers are also going to want what are called lockup agreements from your current shareholders—a document by which the shareholder agrees not to trade his or her shares for a period of time while the offering is being conducted. This is to help the market maker keep control over the volume and price of shares in the marketplace to ensure stability and as strong a market of investors willing to purchase the stock at the market maker's price as possible.

If your company is strong and reliable with proven revenue and probable growth, you may attract the attention of a major underwriter or underwriting syndicate. Moreover, if you qualify by their standards, you probably won't have to go door-to-door trying to get them: They'll know who you are already and will compete with one another to entice you into engaging them as your lead underwriter.

The big boys generally will only consider you if you can qualify for listing on something like the Nasdaq National Market and if they believe your company can command results for them to be able to sell a good $20 million of stock, at least. On the other hand, on this higher plane, the underwriters will agree to a "firm commitment" offering, meaning they actually buy all the stock in the offering from you, payment in full, as soon as SEC approval is obtained, at a price a bit below what they think will be a resale price sufficiently attractive so that they can sell all of the stock. They keep the difference and, with their reputation at stake, will do everything they can to make the company and its stock as realistically attractive as possible.

The underwriters will work closely with you, and they and their own attorneys (who, by tradition, they get to select but you get to pay for—in addition to your own attorneys) will most likely be a harmonious group. The idea is to get the deal to work, so the haughty and inflexible types tend not to travel in this crowd. The most common points about which major underwriters will be more demanding include an almost certain requirement that you hire a Top Five accounting firm for the audit. Remember, they have their reputation to consider.

They will also expect that their concerns about the content and style of the prospectus be taken as seriously as your own, which begins with a first "all hands meeting" where, after everyone involved has studied the first draft of the registration statement, they gather together (it needs to be a big room because everyone who will play a role in this offering will want to be there) and work slowly and steadily, often word by word, through the material—raising questions, revising language, grammar, and punctuation, and critiquing every element of every item—often continuing for fifteen to twenty hours at a stretch. In this setting you need to guard against alterations that may help sell the stock but put the company into the predicament of having too much to live up to in the future.

Regardless of all the good news they came back with from analysts and road shows, at the end, on the day before the stock is to go on the market, a very different tone will arise in the closing meeting between the company's leaders and the lead underwriter's top representatives. This scene—quite a sight to witness and also quite predictable—will almost always be certain to reduce into a fight by the underwriters to drive their purchase price down as low as possible, both to make sure they can sell every share and to maximize their profit margin. Think of it: Just as the final SEC imprimatur is being placed on the final prospectus, the underwriters will grow somber and "unsure" of their ability to sell the shares. This is the moment where you'll really need to be at your sharpest. You are swimming with sharks.

Consider three things to ponder as you prepare yourself for the closing meeting. First, you're on your own in there—really (by long tradition, the lawyers, the accountants, and everyone else stay out of the room—usually even out of the building—except for you and the other senior executives of the company), so prepare in advance with all the potential ammunition you'll need. It will be a time to think on your feet, and you can be sure of meeting stern disapproval if you dare leave the room to consult with others.

Second, the meeting will go on forever. The longer it runs, the more tired you get, and as the clock ticks further toward the moment when the stock is to be listed and traded, the more pressure you'll be under to "just do it!" But don't let the grip around your neck tighten easily—stay cool.

Third, though hard to believe after all the work the underwriters have done before this moment, they still haven't legally committed themselves to anything. Until every detail is agreed to and they've signed the formal underwriting agreement at the conclusion of the closing meeting, they can get up and walk out the door with no obligations whatsoever, so expect them to use this to their advantage and know that you'll be doing some tricky negotiating to get what you want without watching them walk.

But all that's in the future. For an excellent overview of the whole process, see *How Your Company Can Raise Money to Grow and Go Public,* by Robert Paul Turner. And for now, start working on that business plan. And in doing so make sure you have the right management . . .

Chapter 10

Know Who Your Directors and Officers Are!

You are raising money and things are looking bright. Until one of your big potential investors tells you that your management team consists of some well-known bad apples. He can't invest with them on board. And, he can't invest in you for allowing them in without having done a prudent background check.

You are devastated, but you've learned a huge lesson. You must know who your directors and officers really are.

What Are Directors and Officers and What Powers Do They Have?

As quick background, directors are individual persons appointed by the company's shareholders on a yearly basis at the annual shareholder meeting. Officers are positions such as president, secretary, treasurer, vice president, chief financial officer, and chief operating officer. They are appointed by the directors at the annual directors meeting (which follows immediately after the annual shareholder meeting).

Rich Dad Tips

- If you are going to run your own corporation you don't need to fill all the positions listed above. In Nevada, for example, one person can be the president, secretary, treasurer, and sole director.
- Even if it is just you running the company, you need to be mindful of and follow the duties listed below.

The directors of the company and, to a lesser extent, the officers hold an enormous amount of power and control over the actions of your business. They are responsible for the control and direction of the company. They can call meetings among themselves, sign contracts binding the company to various obligations, conduct purchases and sales of various assets, and incur debts in the name of your company. Directors can appoint and terminate the officers at any time, on a majority vote of the directors. Directors can also regulate the sale and transfer of the company's shares, including the price for purchases and sales, and they can control the company's bank account, including who may or may not sign checks. With that kind of power, investors are not going to turn money over to a board made up of bad apples.

FIDUCIARY DUTY AND INDEMNIFICATION

In almost every jurisdiction, language is written into the governing corporation law which imposes a "fiduciary duty" on directors and officers to act at all times in the best interest of a company and its shareholders. This means that the directors and officers must act for the good of the company as a whole, as opposed to their own individual interests. They have a higher duty than themselves. Failure to follow this higher duty can result in personal liability.

To mitigate the risks involved with fiduciary duty, directors and officers may be indemnified against personal lawsuits brought by your shareholders or by third parties who have contracted with the company. Indemnification provisions in some states must be included in the articles; in other states, they must be in the bylaws. If a director or officer is personally sued for their acts on behalf of the company, an indemnification will allow them to seek reimbursement from the company for any claims and/or legal defense costs. As long as the acts in question do not involve an improper personal benefit or willful misconduct, indemnification may be appropriate. The irony for the company is that, while poor business judgment and bad decisions made by your directors and officers may not necessarily be breaches of fiduciary duty, they may have the effect of landing your company in a world of trouble, including lawsuits, liens, and debts. The company, through its indemnification, may then have no recourse against these decision makers, unless it goes to court to hold the directors judicially liable to the company.

Of course, indemnification only applies where directors and officers uphold their fiduciary duty. Where they do not—where directors mislead or commit fraud (for example, convincing the shareholders to sell all or a significant portion of the company's assets to what appears to be a separate company, but which is actually controlled by one or more of your own directors)—they may be found to have breached their fiduciary duty. Indemnification does not cover wanton or willful (bad) conduct or improper personal benefit.

Let's further explore the duties of directors:

DUTY OF CARE

A director owes the company a duty of care. He must do what a prudent person would do with regard to their own business. There are several ways to breach the duty of care:

- *Nonfeasance (doing nothing).* With nonfeasance, a director is only liable if the breach of duty causes a loss. For example, if the director was an expert and the loss was caused by their lack of expertise, there would be a breach in the duty of care.
- *Misfeasance (doing something that loses money).* A director is not liable for misfeasance if he was prudent in his business judgment. This is referred to as the "business judgment rule." When determining whether a director used his best business judgment, you must inquire whether he or she carefully reviewed the course of action, sought out other options, and arrived at a decision supported by commonsense business judgment. If so, there is no breach of duty of care.

DUTY OF LOYALTY

A director must act in good faith and with a reasonable belief that what he does is in the company's best interest. There are several ways in which a director can breach his loyalty:

- *Interested Director Transactions.* In an interested director transaction, a director or one of his relatives enters into a deal with the company such as a sale of property or a loan. An interested director transaction will be set aside unless the director can show either: (i) that the deal was fair to the company; or (ii) that disclosure was made and approval obtained from a majority of disinterested directors.

- *Competing Venture.* A director breaches his duty of loyalty if he competes directly and unfairly with the company. For example, a director cannot be on the board of a beauty school and start his own beauty school without independent board approval.

- *Corporate Opportunity.* A director breaches his duty of loyalty if he usurps a business opportunity from the company. A corporate opportunity is anything the company would be interested in pursuing. Before taking the opportunity himself, a director must inform the board and wait for the board to turn the opportunity down before proceeding. A company can be awarded damages for loss of a corporate opportunity, or a company can make the director sell the property to the company.

WHICH DIRECTORS CAN BE HELD LIABLE?

The general rule states that a director is presumed to have concurred with the board's action unless their dissent is noted in writing in the corporate minutes or in a registered letter to the company's corporate secretary. There are some exceptions:

- Directors absent from the meeting in which the action was approved or undertaken are usually not liable.

- Liability may be limited by a good faith reliance on any of the following: (i) financial statements by auditors; (ii) book value of assets; or (iii) an opinion of a competent employee or professional.

You should also know about one trick Nevada law allows in this regard. If the articles of incorporation limit the director's control over the company or the manner in which he or she exercises his powers, the company may use such language as a defense against any shareholder or third party.

DIRECTORS AND OFFICERS LIABILITY INSURANCE

Because of the risks associated with director or officer liability, many qualified professionals with assets to lose will insist that the company obtain directors and officers (D&O) liability insurance before they will agree to serve. In order to get the good apples, you're likely going to have to get a D&O policy.

These policies differ widely, so be sure to consult with an insurance or other professional to make certain of your coverage. D&O insurance is not the easiest to obtain and the premiums may be high, in part because of the large claims associated with securities litigation. Insurers will look to the financial history and stability of the company, the background and reputation of the directors and officers, and a number of other factors.

Because insurance companies are well known for drafting fine-print requirements that get them out of covering a claim, you must be careful to follow their rules. For example, the notice provisions requiring notification within the policy period to a designated agent must be followed to the letter.

Another key element to consider when negotiating D&O coverage is the definition of the terms "fraud" and "dishonesty of the insured." In many cases, insurance companies will want to exclude such coverage, whereas those possibilities are the exact risks that the company is seeking to cover.

Another way an insurance company will deny coverage is by requiring that the directors and officers be listed by name on the policy. If someone leaves the company, their replacement name must be immediately placed onto the policy. While this requirement may easily be forgotten in the crush of daily business, failure to do so can mean that your new director or officer is not insured. In addition, if you are a new director or officer relying on D&O protection, ask for a copy of the policy with your name on it as an insured.

Finally, some policies will seek to not cover a company that is in bankruptcy. Of course, this is when the directors and officers need coverage the most. Be sure to negotiate that coverage to your satisfaction.

That final point raises an issue I sometimes see with clients who are about to serve on a board of directors or become an officer of a company. Generally, these people are cautious but many are lulled by the fact that the company will indemnify them. It must be noted that unless the company has money, indemnification is an empty promise. If the company is broke or bankrupt, it's not going to indemnify you for anything. You're on your own. So, unless there is a solid D&O policy in place or, in a start-up, no-money situation you are thoroughly involved in the company and see no immediate risk of being sued, be very careful. The company that indemnifies you may be giving you the sleeves off its vest.

Back to our main point: How will the backgrounds of your directors and officers affect potential investors and existing shareholders?

All potential investors into any type of company, be it a public, trading company with thousands of shareholders, or a private company with three shareholders, are entitled to receive certain information about the company and its directors, officers, and other management before investing. Included in this information requirement is the right to know whether any of these individuals have any criminal convictions, have been or are presently bankrupt, and whether they have been disciplined by the Securities and Exchange Commission or any state or other securities regulatory body for violation of securities laws. As you can imagine, this type of information can have a serious impact on potential investors and your ability to raise equity funds. Where this information is not provided to an investor prior to making the decision to invest in your company, the result can be financial penalties assessed by various securities regulatory authorities, as well as civil or even criminal proceedings being taken against your company for fraud and failure to disclose required information.

So, what does this all mean to you? That it is in your best interest to have some knowledge of the background and personal history of your directors and officers. In some jurisdictions, the local governing corporation law helps you by setting out certain requirements directors must meet. These requirements usually disallow individuals with criminal convictions or who are an undischarged bankrupt (that is, someone currently in bankruptcy) from acting as directors or officers. In other jurisdictions, directors' requirements are little more than having a pulse.

Therefore, where corporation law does not adequately protect your company, you need to take your own affirmative steps. One suggestion is to have all directors and officers complete and sign a questionnaire when they are elected or appointed, which requires them to disclose relevant information and attest to its truth. With this, if there is a problem stemming from information that a director or officer did not disclose, you have a much better chance of successfully proving that your company made reasonable effort to protect itself and its investors and shareholders, and deflect liability directly onto that individual director or officer (fiduciary duty, anyone?).

We have included a "consent to act as a director," which also contains a brief questionnaire covering the most troublesome issues, at the end of this chapter. You can modify this to suit your particular business endeavor, and you should, as a good point of practice, have directors and officers sign a new one every year following election or reelection, just to make sure your company stays current.

Consent to Act As a Director and Conflict-of-Interest Check

TO: _____(the "Company")

AND TO: The Board of Directors Thereof

I HEREBY CONSENT to act as director of the Company if appointed or elected, and to my reappointment or reelection from time to time unless and until this consent shall be revoked by me in writing, this consent to be effective from the date hereof.

Please answer the following questions. If your answer to any of these questions is "yes," please provide details on a separate sheet.

	Yes	No
(a) I am under the age of 18 years.	☐	☐
(b) I have been found to be incapable of managing my own affairs by reason of mental infirmity.	☐	☐
(c) I am an undischarged bankrupt.	☐	☐

During the preceding 5 years I have:

	Yes	No
(a) filed for personal bankruptcy or a company that I have been associated with as an officer or director has filed for bankruptcy.	☐	☐
(b) been convicted of a criminal offense (excluding traffic violations and other minor offenses) or am the subject of any such pending action, inside or outside the United States.	☐	☐
(c) been or currently am subject to any order, judgment, or decree (which has not been subsequently reversed, suspended, or vacated) of any court of competent jurisdiction permanently or temporarily enjoining, barring, suspending, or otherwise limiting my involvement in any type of business, securities, or banking activities.	☐	☐
(d) been found by a court of competent jurisdiction (in a civil action), the Securities and Exchange Commission, any state securities agency, or the Commodity Futures Trading Commission to have violated a federal or state securities or commodities law or regulation (which judgment has not been reversed, suspended, or vacated).	☐	☐

During the preceding 5 years, I have acted as a Director or Officer of the following reporting* and/or nonreporting domestic or foreign companies:

Company Name	Position(s) Held	Period of Service To:From	Reporting Y / N

During the preceding 5 years, I (or a company I am associated with) have entered into the following agreements with the Company, whereby I receive a direct or indirect benefit (including employment agreements, stock purchase agreements, incentive stock option agreements, etc.):

_____

_____

_____

I HEREBY UNDERTAKE to promptly notify the Company in the event of any change in my status.

DATED at _____, the _____ day of _____, 200___.

_____

(signature)

_____

(address)

*A reporting company is a company that files periodic financial and management reports with the Securities and Exchange Commission or other foreign securities regulatory agencies.

Consent to Act as a Director

If you answered "Yes" to any of the questions on page 1
(i.e., undischarged bankruptcies, felony convictions, or sanctions
by the SEC or any state securities authority), please provide details below.

_____

_____

_____

_____

_____

_____

_____

_____

_____

_____

_____

_____

_____

Chapter 11

How to Deal with All of the Employee Issues

You have a business plan and management team in place. Your angel round of financing has been placed and you have interest in your first round of funding. Now you need to hire employees.

There are four main issues to consider in this area. First, at the very start, you have to decide whether to hire employees or use independent contractors (be careful). Second, when hiring employees, you need to be familiar with what is involved in an employment agreement. Third, there are employment law issues you need to know. And finally, you need to decide what employee benefits you can offer.

Employee vs. Independent Contractor—Which Is Better?

Now that your company is incorporated and you're ready to begin operating, the next step is to think about employees, and how to fit them inside your business with the minimal amount of headache.

First up: Should you hire employees or engage independent contractors?

You know what it means to be an employee. Chances are you've probably been one. But once you step over to the employer side of the working relationship, it's a whole new ball game.

As an employee, your responsibilities include things like showing up for work on time, performing the duties assigned to you, and generally giving an honest day's work for an honest day's pay.

As an employer, however, you have to think about things like: payroll, remitting state and federal taxes, workers compensation premiums, health care plans and benefits, pension and 401(k) benefits, salary and performance reviews, paid holiday and overtime, vehicle allowances, sick and holiday time, assuming liability for certain acts of your employees (if they cause an accident driving the company van to make a delivery, guess who gets sued), severance pay, and on and on. Oftentimes this is going to effectively mean you either roll up your sleeves, train yourself, and go to it, or, alternatively, you bring someone in to do this for you. However, as a small start-up business, bringing someone in to manage your employee administration may not be economically possible. After all, you're just beginning and your efforts really need to be on growing your business.

The alternative is to turn away from a traditional employer-employee relationship to one of business—independent contractor. There are advantages and disadvantages to this type of scenario.

An independent contractor is just as it sounds. A contractor is someone who is contracted to perform services for someone else under a written agreement. The "independent" part of independent contractor means that you, as a party to a service contract, pay this individual a flat fee based on whatever terms you negotiate, and they assume all responsibility for their own taxes, health care premiums, workers compensation, and unemployment insurance. An independent contractor is specifically designated by law to *not* be an employee, and so your company takes on none of the obligations, liabilities, or responsibilities associated with traditional employer-employee relationships. You can also write specific indemnification clauses into your service contract, whereby you offset liability arising from certain acts of an independent contractor from attaching to your company. In many cases, people who are working as independent contractors have formed their own companies, in which case you would hire that company, and, by association, its employee(s), to perform whatever functions you agree to.

The drawback to this type of relationship comes mainly from IRS treatment of independent contractor relationships. Even though you and this individual have contracted out of the traditional employer-employee responsibilities and obligations, as far as the IRS is concerned, if an individual fits into certain criteria, then they are deemed to be an employee, regardless of contractual arrangements. In practical terms, this means that where an independent contractor fails to remit their taxes and statutory deductions out of the flat fee that you have negotiated to pay them, the IRS can and will come looking to you to make good if they consider the independent contractor to be classifiable as an employee.

An idea of the criteria used by the IRS to determine whether employee or independent contractor status is appropriate follows:

Employee	*Independent Contractor*
• Works for you (the employer) 100 percent of their time, at least during the length of time it takes to achieve a specific goal.	• Works for you (the business owner) on a part-time basis, and may also be working for other companies or individuals at the same time.
• Hours and days of work are scheduled by you.	• Is given a goal and a deadline, but no specific schedule is set.
• Is trained by you, and must perform work in a particular fashion, sequence, or method.	• Is responsible only for the attainment of a goal, without specific requirements on how the goal must be achieved.
• Is provided with tools and materials, and must work on your premises.	• Provides own tools and materials, and may work from home, own location, or anywhere else.
• Must perform the work personally.	• May hire assistants or subcontractors to accomplish the goal.
• Is paid hourly, weekly, or monthly.	• Is paid on a per-project, commission basis, or invoices you for time worked.
	• Holds their own business licenses, permits, and other necessary legal requirements.

So, in order to make the argument that you are contracting with individuals on an independent contractor basis, you must ensure that, at a minimum, you enter into an independent contractor service agreement, and that independent contractors all submit invoices to your company to cover work they perform. If your contract with these individuals contains most or all of the points mentioned above, then you stand a better chance of successfully arguing that you are not an employer.

A sample independent contractor service agreement may be found at the end of this chapter, as well as a sample employment agreement.

Employment Agreements and Considerations

Employment agreements will likely feature prominently in a start-up company's business plan, especially in connection with your key management or technical employees.

Traditionally, there are two types of employment groups associated with start-up companies: regular employees and key employees. Regular employees work under you, or other management, have a minor to moderate level of responsibility, and are paid accordingly. On the other hand, key employees are those you need to get your business plan off the ground. They are highly skilled in either technology or business operations and are essential to your company. They are likely to receive a considerable amount of money for their services, or, in many start-up companies where cash is not available, they receive a large allocation of founders' shares in return for all or a part of their contributions. The relationship of key employees to your company is probably closer to that of a business partner or founder than it is to that of regular employees. Regular employees may also receive a stock allocation or option to purchase stock in your company, but it is usually a considerably smaller amount than that granted to your key employees.

For new companies, the use of carefully crafted employment agreements may be the only way that you can attract the talent you need to get your business off the ground. Highly knowledgeable individuals possessing extremely marketable skills have likely invested their own time and money to obtain those skills and knowledge, and will be looking to secure their own future and ensure fair compensation for their services. In these instances, it is quite likely that they will be looking for a significant stock allocation in addition to financial compensation.

Having employment agreements in place with your company's key employees may also be a condition of attracting venture capital. Prospective investors, especially those from whom you are seeking a large capital investment, will be looking to see that you have secured the talent required to put your business plan into effect. A new company with a great idea, but which is relying on a single person to put this idea into effect, and the single person in question is not under contract or obligated to stay with your company in any way, is not an attractive proposition for a potential investor.

A carefully crafted employment agreement can secure other things besides guaranteed service and peace of mind for investors. Through the use of confidentiality and noncompetition clauses, your company can be protected from employees selling your valuable information and processes to a competitor, or worse, breaking away to form a new company to compete directly with your company, based on ideas developed with your company and marketed at your company's existing customer base. Through the use of ownership clauses, you can ensure that the software or products you are paying people to develop for you remain your company's property.

Even in cases where you don't have any employees, and the bright shining idea that is your company is you, an employment agreement can still be desirable, or necessary. Remember, investors are investing in your company, not you personally, and, by investing in your company, are also purchasing a degree of control over how your company operates. Therefore, they will want some type of assurance that the products or technology you are developing belong to the company, and not to you. Another point to consider is how you are to be paid for your efforts. Having an agreed-upon amount that you will receive for the products and services you are contributing to your company is, again, reassuring to potential investors. It would not be prudent to invest in a company in which there was no guarantee that the products or services, which attracted such an investment in the first place, could not be removed at any time. It would be equally imprudent to invest in a company where there was no method to control what funds went to company development and what funds went into someone's pocket.

Who Should Sign an Employment Agreement?

As set out above, it is desirable to enter into employment agreements with all of your company's key employees. These should include (but are not limited to) yourself and your partners or other founders of your company, scientific personnel, software and hardware developers, financial officers, accountants, lawyers (if your company has in-house counsel), and sales managers (particularly those with in-depth knowledge of and significant contacts in your company's target industry).

What Should Go into an Employment Agreement?

What goes into an employment agreement will depend on whom your company is contracting with. However, there are certain basic elements that should be contained in every employment agreement.

JOB TITLE AND SCOPE OF DUTIES

What is this individual going to do for your company and how specific do you need to be?

Although a job title may on the face of it be fairly easy to apply, when considering what the scope of someone's duties will be, you must consider how specifically those duties should be set out, and whether you need to leave some room for a job to change and grow. A checklist of powers and duties traditionally assigned to various corporate officers is found in the materials at the end of this chapter. But be careful in relying upon only one format, and think through the powers and duties as they apply to your own situation. If the job title's scope is too narrow, the risk is that you will constantly be renegotiating your company's employment agreements, particularly in a start-up situation where the chances of positions expanding beyond their original scope are high. If the scope is too broad, however, the risk comes when you try to narrow the scope at a future date, particularly where you are looking to remove certain responsibilities from an employee. An employee who disagrees with having responsibilities removed may argue that the legal concept of constructive dismissal applies and take legal action against your company. ("Constructive dismissal" means making unilateral—i.e., one-sided—changes to an employee's position, duties, or wages—usually involving reduction or removal—that fundamentally alter his or her job.) Alternatively, an employee in this situation may argue that your company has breached the employment agreement and, by doing so, has nullified the entire agreement, including the portions relating to confidentiality and noncompetition. It is always a good idea to include in any employment agreement a clause that states that a company's board of directors is the final policymaker and may choose to amend employment duties as they see fit to best benefit the company as a whole.

Where the employment agreement being created is for you, as the founder, additional consideration needs to be given to ensure that you do not lose control over your company to incoming investors. You may wish to consider including a clause limiting the amount by which your position can be changed by the board of directors. You may also wish to establish a separate shareholder agreement with these individuals, which would cover other facets of your relationship with these investors, including control issues, veto powers, and so forth, and use that shareholder agreement to ensure that you do not wind up in a situation where you lose shareholder control over your company and then are terminated from your position within the company, effectively removing you entirely from the operation.

TERM OF THE EMPLOYMENT AGREEMENT

There are several ways to approach the idea of how long an employment agreement should last. With certain key employees, it may be best to limit the term of the employment agreement to a specific time, in which a specific project or goal is to be achieved. Alternatively, you may wish to make the employment agreement renewable annually or biannualy, depending on your company's specific requirements. Where you anticipate the employment relationship as being long-term and continuous, you may wish to allow for that in the employment agreement. You may also elect to add a clause to the agreement whereby the employment agreement is for an initial term of one year, and automatically renews for additional one-year terms until terminated by your company or the employee. It is generally preferable to have key employees contracted for a longer term, as opposed to a month-by-month basis, as, again, your company is trying to promote an image of stability to investors.

HOURS OF EMPLOY

In addition to setting out the job title and scope of duties, it is also important to note in the employment agreement that while an individual is working for your company, they are to devote their full time and attention to carrying out those duties. Again, you need to guard against becoming too narrow—for example, scientific and high-tech employees will oftentimes be involved in conferences and seminars, writing papers, and information exchanges with other members of their scientific community. If employees are not permitted time for these other opportunities, the risk exists that their knowledge will become stagnant and of less value to your company. On the other hand, an employee who is never at work isn't much help either. You need to consider where balance will be achieved, and tailor the employment agreement to each individual situation. You may wish to consider a clause limiting the amount of time that may be spent on these outside activities, or that attendance or participation in certain activities must be subject to prior consent by your company. This is particularly important in the case of part-time or consulting employees, who may work for several other organizations simultaneously. The more organizations an employee is working for simultaneously, the more difficult it becomes to properly ensure that your company's trade secrets, proprietary processes, and methods are not being transferred or modified to suit these other organizations.

PAID EMPLOYMENT EXPENSES, INCLUDING TRAVEL AND RELOCATION

If you are anticipating that an employment position with your company may require travel and/or relocation, it is important that this be addressed in the employment agreement. A proper schedule and method of reimbursement must be set out, and adhered to by both sides. If receipts and documentation are to be required for reimbursement, this must be made clear.

SALARY AND OTHER BENEFITS

In addition to the monetary portion of an employee's salary, there may be other benefits to consider such as stock allocations or options to purchase stock in the future, medical and dental health plans, pension plans, profit-sharing arrangements, or paid vehicle allowances. It is a good idea, particularly in a start-up situation, where your company does not have significant cash on hand to pay large salaries, and is depending on stock allocations and options, to tie these to continuing service by employees, or upon milestones reached. A more detailed discussion on employee benefits is set out later in this chapter.

KEY MAN LIFE INSURANCE

It may be to the benefit of your company to consider life insurance on key employees, particularly in the case of a founders' employment agreement. Under such a policy, the company may be designated as beneficiary, or you may wish to consider having your company's investors as beneficiaries where the insured person is irreplaceable and your company not likely to succeed without them. Where such a clause is requested, though, you must ensure that the employee in question agrees to undergo any required medical examinations and perform such acts and sign any documents required to put such a policy into place.

ASSIGNABILITY

Any employment agreement should contain a clause allowing your company to assign the employment agreement to an affiliate, associate, subsidiary, or successor company to your company. You do not want to be in a situation where your company is being purchased by another company but a key employee whose services are essential to your company refuses to work for the successor company.

CONFIDENTIALITY AND NONCOMPETITION

As discussed earlier, it is vital for start-up companies to protect their intellectual property, patents, trade secrets, products, methods of production, and business model from being either provided to existing competitors, or from being poached by your own employees into new spin-off operations. An employment agreement should be fairly specific as to what is considered confidential information, and should also set out a clause whereby an employee acknowledges that breaching this confidentiality clause could leave him or her open to prosecution by your company.

Noncompetition, on the other hand, must be tailored a bit more specifically. For example, hiring a software engineer to write a certain piece of software for your company does not mean that this person may realistically be barred from ever writing another piece of software for another company, even if that company is in a similar business venture. What your company may be able to do, however, is set a reasonable time and/or geographical limit before that individual is permitted to engage in conduct that could be seen as in competition to yours, either directly, by creating their own start-up business, or indirectly, by working for a competitor, and potentially utilizing all of the knowledge gained at your company to assist the competition. It is important, however, when considering this provision to obtain proper legal advice on what is considered reasonable and what is considered excessive. Most courts hold that, as a matter of public policy, it is good for society for people to work. And so the courts are not fond of employers who try to limit, in draconian fashion, future activities of employees. For example, a requirement whereby a former employee is not permitted to engage in their profession for several years following termination of their employment with your company, or where they are not permitted to work in your company's state and six surrounding states, will likely be overturned by a court, and may even result in penalties being assessed against your company. You cannot prevent an employee from practicing his trade, especially where knowledge and skills have been obtained over a lengthy time prior to employment with your company. You can, however, seek to minimize, to a reasonable degree, what that employee can do with the knowledge gained *during* their employment with your company.

DEVELOPMENT AND OWNERSHIP OF INVENTIONS, TRADE SECRETS, AND NEW BUSINESS IDEAS

Again, as set out above, where your company is engaging individuals to help it develop a business, expand on an idea, and create new products, services, or ideas for your company, it is important that all parties be clear on who owns what. An employment agreement should have a section requiring an employee to acknowledge that ideas, inventions, and improvements created by that employee which (1) relate to your company's existing, proposed, or contemplated business, or actual or anticipated research; (2) result from work done by the employee, using your company's equipment, including software platforms; and (3) result from the employee's access to your company's trade secrets, assets, information, and so on, belong to the company, and not the employee. You should also follow up this clause with a clause requiring an employee to specifically assign all of his or her right, title, and interest in and to such idea, invention, or improvement to your company.

TERMINATION

It's going to happen, sooner or later. The best way to protect your company from future wrongful dismissal lawsuits is to set out a termination clause, identifying the circumstances under which an employee can be terminated, how much notice is required, or what appropriate payment in lieu of notice will be. In this clause, you should set out a "neutral termination" section, whereby either you or the employee can choose to terminate the employment relationship for no cause, by providing each other with sufficient written notice. A section allowing for "natural termination" should also be included, whereby either party can choose not to renew the employment agreement following the completion of its term. There should also be a "for cause termination," in which you set out specifically what is unacceptable conduct and what will result in immediate termination or termination on sufficient notice. It is also a good idea to set out a section dealing with what would constitute a breach of the employment agreement by your company, which should typically be limited to failure to pay salary.

Where the employment agreement is being drafted to cover you, as a founder, you may wish to include other events that would constitute a breach by your company, including fundamental changes to your job responsibilities and functions mandated by the board of directors that would constitute constructive dismissal.

In situations where stock allocations have been made, or more particularly, in situations where options to purchase stock have not been exercised, or have not entirely vested, it must be made clear what happens to unexercised or unvested portions. ("Vesting" is the term used to describe how ownership of shares is transferred in a situation where a stock grant is made over a period of time. For example, a yearly allocation of 120 shares per year, vesting on a monthly basis, would mean that ten shares per month would vest into an employee's name. Accordingly, should this employee leave after six months, a total of sixty shares would have vested in his name, and he would lose his entitlement to the remaining sixty shares). In addition, you may wish to consider a clause whereby all stock sold to an employee during the course of their employment is subject to repurchase by your company, at a favorable price, or at the purchase price. A repurchase clause is found most commonly in privately held company situations, where it is in a company's best interests to have shares held by as few shareholders as possible. You may also wish to consider a repurchase formula in employment agreements entered into between you, as a founder, with your company, particularly in instances where you are being bought out by investors. Alternatively, if your company is considering going public, then you, as founder, may wish to add a clause allowing you to retain your shareholdings and liquidate them into the public market following the completion of the going-public process. It may be advantageous to you to try and tie a stock repurchase formula to a noncompete clause in a founder employment agreement.

Another point for a founder to consider including in an employment agreement is a requirement for a valuation of your company's business to be performed prior to investors seeking to buy out your interest and terminate your working relationship with your company. Having a valuation conducted by a third party ensures that your shareholding and contribution may be fairly valued, and you get fully compensated for the time and effort you have put into building your company.

A sample founder/key employee employment agreement is found in the materials at the end of this chapter in addition to the sample employment agreement and independent contractor service agreement (discussed later in this chapter).

Employment Law Primer

We talked briefly in the "Employment Agreements and Considerations" section above about certain things your company should and shouldn't do in order to avoid being the subject of a wrongful or constructive dismissal lawsuit by former employees. The following is a very brief primer on fundamental employment law concepts to give you an idea of what exactly you are getting yourself into. As with everything else in this book, this section is not meant to take the place of proper legal advice, nor is it overly detailed. It is meant simply to cover the major laws in place surrounding the employer-employee relationship.

THE FAIR LABOR STANDARDS ACT (FLSA)

This is a federal-level law, which governs things like minimum wage, equal pay, overtime, child labor, and what records a company is required to keep regarding its employees. The FLSA covers companies who engage in commerce, production of goods for sale, handling, selling, or moving of goods with a minimum gross sale value of $500,000 (whether or not the goods were manufactured by them). The FLSA also covers all companies, regardless of what they do, if such companies engage in interstate commerce, which is essentially meant as a catch-all category, as it is very unlikely that a company would be able to purchase all of its raw materials and supplies, make sales, and conduct advertising and marketing strictly within its state boundaries.

Assuming that the FLSA applies to your company, minimum wage requirements will apply. The minimum wage is set by the federal government from time to time. As of this writing it is $5.15 per hour. If you are operating a business where employees receive tips, you may claim that up to 50 percent of their minimum wages may be paid by way of the tips they receive, but you must be able to prove that overall, wages and tips included, your employees receive at least the minimum wage.

Overtime is also payable, once an employee has worked more than forty hours in a workweek. Overtime is traditionally calculated to be 1.5 times the employee's regular wage, but there are exceptions to this rule, depending on the employee's specific classification. Before modifying the traditional 1.5 calculation, it is best to contact the U.S. Department of Labor to determine whether you have any employees who can be reclassified at a lower rate.

With respect to coffee and lunch breaks, the rule of thumb is, where the break is twenty minutes or less in length, the time is considered to be on the clock, and payable by the company. On the other hand, meal breaks of thirty minutes or longer in length are not considered payable, as long as the employees are relieved of all duties during this time, and are not required to remain on the job and eat at their desks or workstations.

The FLSA also provides that employees receive a Form W-2 on a yearly basis, which is a record of hours worked, wages received, and statutory deductions made. So good record keeping is essential, as you must be able to produce these records, complete and intact, should the Department of Labor come looking.

Child labor laws are strictly regulated under the FLSA. Children under the age of sixteen are generally prohibited from being employed, although there is an exception for children of a business owner. In addition, children are prohibited from performing hazardous work such as mining, or from being around hazardous work sites, such as heavy manufacturing or machining, transportation, warehousing, or construction.

THE CIVIL RIGHTS ACT OF 1964 (CRA)

The CRA is another federal law, which guards employees from being the target of discriminatory practices by an employer, including discrimination based on race, color, gender, religion, or national origin. A subsection of the CRA deals with the treatment of pregnant women in the workplace, prohibiting employers from using someone's pregnancy as a reason to deny her a job, or removing her from a job at a certain stage of pregnancy, unless that employee is physically unable to perform the work due to her pregnancy.

Sexual harassment is covered under the CRA, requiring an employer to provide a safe, harassment-free workplace. The CRA also provides for protection from retaliation by an employer against an employee who raises a complaint, as well as protection for any other employees assisting an employee with a discrimination complaint.

AGE DISCRIMINATION AND EMPLOYMENT ACT (ADEA)

As employment law has advanced significantly through the past few decades, the ADEA was written to cover those individuals who were found to not be covered by the CRA. Prior to the enactment of the ADEA, age had never been considered an applicable factor upon which to base a claim of discrimination. However, massive changes in the workplace led to situations where qualified individuals were denied employment because younger, cheaper, and *less qualified* help was available, or, individuals over a certain age were prohibited from applying for certain positions that had been reserved for younger individuals. The ADEA provides that companies may not discriminate against individuals in either hiring or firing, where age is a motivating factor. In addition, the ADEA also provides that a company generally may not force a person to retire, although there are certain compulsory retirement provisions applicable to executives who are sixty-five years or older and have held an executive-level position for a minimum of two years preceding their retirement.

AMERICANS WITH DISABILITIES ACT (ADA)

Another entry into the employment law forum is the ADA. Under the ADA, individuals with disabilities such as blindness, deafness, speech impediments, cerebral palsy, epilepsy, muscular dystrophy, multiple sclerosis, AIDS, cancer, heart disease, diabetes, mental retardation, and emotional illness are protected from discriminatory hiring and firing practices by employers. However, in order to rely on the ADA, disabled persons must be able to show that they are qualified as well as physically capable of performing the work required, or would be capable of performing it with reasonable accommodations and adjustments by an employer (e.g., installing ramps for wheelchair access). On the other hand, where an employer can show that employing the individual in question would be enormously costly, in terms of modifications required, to the point where the cost of hiring the employee would far outstrip the value of the work to be performed, then an exemption to the ADA may be available.

THE OCCUPATIONAL SAFETY AND HEALTH ACT (OSHA)

The OSHA was enacted to protect employees from being forcibly exposed to harmful substances while working. While the OSHA is not applicable to businesses with standard office environments, it is applicable to industries such as manufacturing, restaurant, agriculture, medical by-products and waste, and the like. Employers are required to provide a safe and healthy working environment, and to minimize the risk to their employees, through the use of protective equipment such as masks or breathing apparatus, or through the design of the workplace itself, e.g., proper installation of exhaust/ventilation systems.

WORKERS COMPENSATION

Even with the best efforts on the part of an employer and its employees, accidents in the workplace can and do happen. Workers compensation is designed to protect employees from being impoverished due to their inability to work following a work-related accident. It requires an employer to take certain steps, which include (a) obtaining an insurance policy to cover workplace accidents (the most popular method of complying with workers compensation requirements); or (b) establishing individual self-insurance funds, either on an employer-by-employer basis, or in collective groups of employers. Employers who do not have adequate workers compensation coverage may find themselves the subject of a lawsuit if an employee is left unprotected following a workplace-related accident.

As workers compensation is not applicable to independent contractors or subcontractors, it is important to be clear, when preparing any sort of employment agreement or independent contractor service agreement, regarding what the exact status of the would-be employee will be. Courts do not look favorably upon employers who attempt to reclassify employees as independent contractors to avoid paying workers compensation benefits.

THE EMPLOYEE POLYGRAPH PROTECTION ACT OF 1988 (EPPA)

An act for every situation, a situation for every act. Under the provisions of the EPPA, subjecting job applicants and employees to lie detector testing, although a novel way of interviewing, is illegal, unless it falls under a specialized exemption, for example, employees who will be dealing with certain controlled substances.

THE ELECTRONIC COMMUNICATIONS PRIVACY ACT OF 1986 (ECPA)

Wiretapping or other monitoring of an employee's conversations and actions while on the job is illegal without the express consent of the employee. So, for situations where you will want to visually monitor employees (as in banks or jewelry stores), or monitor by telephone (telemarketing, customer service, and so on), you will need to clearly explain what you are doing and obtain their consent ahead of time.

THE FAMILY AND MEDICAL LEAVE ACT (FMLA)

Under the provisions of the FMLA, employees may take up to twelve weeks per year of unpaid leave for medical reasons or to deal with family problems. The act covers employees seeking leave for childbirth or adoption, caring for an immediate family member with a serious health condition, or being unable to work due to a serious health condition. Employees are required to provide thirty days' notice prior to taking leave under the FMLA, although obviously this will not always be possible, given the nature of the family or medical emergency.

Again, we remind you, this is a brief overview to introduce you to certain employment-related issues that may arise in your company. It is not, nor is it intended to be, complete or to replace proper legal advice and assistance.

Employee Benefit Plans

An employee benefit plan can be a crucial element in attracting the talent that your company needs to grow and thrive. Oftentimes in the case of start-up companies, there is limited cash flow, and so a degree of flexibility and creativity is called for to make up for this.

Employee benefits may be broadly defined into two distinct areas—traditional benefits, such as health and dental plans, pension plans, vacation and sick allowances; and equity benefits, such as stock option grants, incentive stock option plans, profit sharing formulas, and performance bonuses. When considering how to implement employee benefit plans, it may be to your company's advantage to consider two separate plans, one covering the traditional benefits, which will be available to all employees, and the second one covering equity benefits, which may be available to select employees only.

The following is a brief overview of elements to consider including in your company's employee benefit plan. We have divided these elements into the traditional and equity sections, as discussed above. Because of the various tax implications involved in many elements of an employee benefit plan, we recommend that you not attempt to implement one into your company without individual legal and financial advice from your lawyers and accountants.

Traditional Benefits

HEALTH INSURANCE PLANS

Health insurance plans may be purchased through most insurance companies, in varying levels of coverage. Elements of a health insurance plan may include HMO coverage, dental and vision coverage, short-term and long-term disability coverage, life insurance, prescription reimbursement, cafeteria-style medical plans, and emergency hospitalization coverage. The levels and complexity of packages offered vary widely, and will require some time and effort on your part to review and consider the most appropriate plan for your company. Monthly premiums for coverage may be paid wholly by your company, or apportioned to some degree between your company and its employees.

The costs of implementing health insurance plans are tax deductible for your company, and are tax deductible for most employees as well. Where group insurance is included in a health insurance plan, however, it becomes subject to government regulation.

TAX-QUALIFIED RETIREMENT PLANS

A tax-qualified retirement plan is an employer-funded plan, whereby the company makes contributions on behalf of its employees, usually to a separate entity that then manages and invests the funds. The payments by the company into the plan are tax deductible at the time of payment, and do not become taxable until the employee withdraws the funds, at which time the employee is responsible for payment of the taxes. While from a taxation point of view this type of plan is attractive to a company, due to the tax deductible status of the contributions, it is subject to detailed government regulations, review, and continued monitoring by both the IRS and the Department of Labor.

SECTION 401(K) PLAN

A Section 401(k) plan allows for employees participating in certain tax-qualified retirement profit sharing or stock bonus plans to elect whether to receive company contributions in cash or to have them paid into a tax-qualified plan. Monies or shares paid into an employee's Section 401(k) plan are tax deferred until withdrawal, and are then taxed at a normal rate. In addition, a company may also negotiate with employees to enter into a salary reduction agreement, whereby an employee elects to have yearly salary raises, bonuses, and other compensation paid directly into their Section 401(k) plan, thus decreasing their taxable income.

SUPPLEMENTAL COMPENSATION BENEFITS

These are additional benefits from which employees may make a selection, with their premium rates being adjusted accordingly, based on the benefits they select. Supplemental compensation benefits may include things like interest-free loans, company car (for use on company business only), financial or retirement planning and counseling, or fitness or other club memberships.

Equity-Based Benefits

Equity shares are one of the most attractive benefits a start-up company is able to offer. Where your company has a sound business idea and a likelihood of success, the chances are good that your company's shares will increase in value, perhaps significantly. Therefore, a person receiving a share allocation as a part of their compensation potentially stands to make a profit from the sale of their shares in the future, or, alternatively, stands to benefit from shareholder dividends realized from the profits of your company. While the chances of success and profitability are not guaranteed, the potential to make significant profit is there, and, ultimately, may be higher than the employee would have received had they been receiving straight, market-value cash compensation for their services.

Equity compensation can take many forms, including outright grants of stock, grants of incentive stock options (the grant of a right to purchase stock in the future), phantom stock (see below), and stock appreciation rights (SARs). In many instances, equity stock granted using one or more of these methods may be subject to special capital gains treatment, and can therefore minimize the tax impact on employees.

STOCK PURCHASE PLANS

The simplest of all methods to provide employees with equity stock, a stock purchase plan provides a method whereby employees may purchase shares in your company, either at market value or at a discount. It is important, however, from a psychological and motivational viewpoint, to keep some type of link between employment performance and the stock purchase plan, for example, by offering employees interest-free loans to purchase stock. It is in your company's best interests to encourage a sense of motivation and participation among employees, as opposed to being merely passive shareholders. In addition, to provide incentive for your company's employees to stay with your company, you may wish to consider imposing a vesting schedule on all stock purchases. A vesting schedule provides that an employee must remain employed for a designated period in order to receive full ownership rights to all of the stock purchased. Where an employee ceases employment with a company prior to completing the agreed-upon vesting period, they must then sell a portion of their purchased shares back to the company, on a pro rata basis, or, they may have to forgo receiving future allotments of shares due to their termination. By using a vesting schedule, your company can maintain a tighter shareholder base, as well as provide an incentive for employees to remain with your company.

INCENTIVE STOCK OPTION PLAN

An incentive stock option plan is similar to a stock purchase plan, except that instead of actually purchasing stock, employees are granted a right to purchase stock during a set period of time, usually at a discounted price from the current market value. Employees may, therefore, choose whether or not to exercise all or a part of their option, depending on the market value of the company's shares, or other factors. Exercise of an incentive stock option is not mandatory. In addition, depending on the type of plan initiated, there may be no tax consequences to the employee until the option is actually exercised and the stock purchased.

There are two types of stock option plans, "statutory" and "nonstatutory," which differ mainly in tax treatment. Statutory plans must follow various government guidelines, and generally provide for the option granted to be taxed at the time of grant, but at a lower taxation rate than would otherwise be paid. Nonstatutory plans do not incur tax at the time of grant, but rather at the time the employee actually exercises the option. However, no discounted tax rate is available using a nonstatutory plan.

Generally speaking, options must be granted on an inclusive basis, that is, every time an option grant is made, it must be made to all eligible employees, and not a select few. However, the number of shares granted to employees may differ on an employee-by-employee basis, in keeping with various levels of compensation, or other previously established criteria.

PHANTOM STOCK AND STOCK APPRECIATION RIGHTS

Phantom stock is actually a deferred bonus arrangement that is intended to give an employee the economic advantage (but not the tax advantage) of stock ownership in a company if the stock appreciates, while avoiding the disadvantages should the stock depreciate. An employee is typically given a grant of stock, which is noted on the company's records, but not actually issued. This grant is monitored as would be a share position, and the employee is eligible to receive dividends and stock splits. Upon an agreed date, the amount of phantom stock is valued, usually based upon the market value of the company's shares at the time of the valuation, and the employee is then paid the equivalent value in cash, stock, or some combination of both. Payment may be made over a lengthy period of time, allowing for tax to be adjusted accordingly, and with corresponding tax credits to be granted to a company.

One advantage to using a phantom stock plan over an incentive stock option plan is that employees are not required to pay into the plan to receive a benefit. Furthermore, if an employee chooses to be paid out by way of cash, there is no dilution to the company's issued and outstanding share capital. Even if an employee chooses to be paid out in stock, this payout will still be in stock that has been previously accounted for in the company's financial statements, and will still cause no further dilution to the company's issued and outstanding share capital.

A disadvantage to using a phantom stock plan is that there are various accounting consequences, which could add to a company's yearly accounting costs. For example, fluctuating company earnings will lead to fluctuating values of the phantom stock, which will require adjustments to a company's net earnings.

Stock appreciation rights are similar to phantom stock. An SAR grant to an employee gives that employee the right to receive the value by which that SAR grant appreciates, from the time of the grant, to the time of exercise. Therefore, if you grant an SAR to an employee in the amount of 100 shares at $1.00 per share, for a total value of $100, and at the time the employee exercises their SAR grant the company's shares are worth $5.00 per share, the employee is entitled to receive the difference, namely $400.

SARs have no tax consequences to either the company or the employee upon their grant. Upon exercise, however, an employee will pay tax on the monies received, and the company will receive a corresponding tax credit.

SARs are subject to the same accounting-related disadvantage as phantom stock plans, in that fluctuations in a company's income will create fluctuations in the value of the SARs and additional accounting adjustments being required to the company's financial statements.

Rich Dad Tips

- In a small-company setting do not even mention the possibility of setting up a stock option or other benefit plan if you do not intend to offer one.
- Your employees will hold you to such a promise and will only be angered—perhaps to the point of litigation—if such a plan is not implemented.

The foregoing is a very brief overview of elements to consider when contemplating an employee benefits plan, and is not meant to substitute in any way for proper legal and financial advice. Prior to implementing any sort of employee benefit plan into your company, you should first make sure that you have discussed all elements to be included with your legal and financial advisors.

Following is a list of skills and qualities that are required and/or desirable in all of your corporate management, and particularly in your company's CEO and president:

- Managerial skills, including group management; motivational, organizational, and delegation skills; ability to develop, direct and control staff; strategic and analytical thinking, problem solving, and creativity; technical expertise
- Social and communication skills, including verbal and written communications, presentation, negotiation, cooperation, listening, and empathy
- Personal qualities such as enthusiasm, initiative, drive for achievement and results, as well as being self-motivated, stress-tolerant, and a calculated risk taker

Guideline of Powers and Duties and Required or Desirable Skills for Various Corporate Officer Positions

Chief Executive Officer

- Has general supervision over the company
- Presides at all corporate meetings
- Is often also the chairman of the board
- Has the power to sign all corporate documents, share certificates, and other instruments except, where by law, the president must sign
- Is often made an ex officio member of all standing committees

President

- May also be the chief executive officer
- May substitute for the chairman of the board in his or her absence
- Power is limited to matters that arise within the ordinary course of business and are in the best interests of the company, including, but not limited to: calling special meetings of shareholders; fixing compensation paid to officers; appointing and removing officers; setting out the duties of subordinate officers
- Has implicit powers with respect to carrying out authorized acts on behalf of the company
- Has authority to perform any act that the directors authorize and ratify, unless powers are restricted in the company's charter, articles, or bylaws
- Unauthorized legal acts may be ratified subsequently by the directors

Vice President

- Acts as assistant to the president
- Is often assigned an important role in corporate administration

- Assumes president's power and duties and acts in his or her place in the event of president's absence, death, or incapacity (but, in some cases, will require prior approval of the directors to carry out certain acts)
- Has no other powers by virtue of the office; without express or implied authority, cannot manage or bind the company
- Designated by seniority in situations where a company has multiple vice presidents

Corporate Secretary

- Keeps corporate books and has charge of corporate seal (if company has one)
- Has additional powers (assigned by president or directors), which may include: preparing shareholder lists for annual meetings; maintaining and recording entries in stock ledger; signing corporate documents and instruments
- Authority determined primarily by character of corporate business and relative powers of other officers
- Powers may overlap with those of treasurer, controller, or auditor

Treasurer

- Usual powers include: care, custody, and maintenance of corporate funds and securities; maintenance of books of accounts and records; preparation of financial statements; disbursement of corporate funds
- Has powers delegated to it by directors, committees, or by direction of president/CEO
- Is often appointed to finance committee and as advisor to other officers in financial matters

General Manager

- Has authority to perform acts necessary in the usual and ordinary course of company's business
- Specific functions vary with size and nature of business, and as delegated by directors, committees, or president/CEO
- Authority may be limited to general management over specific portions of the business, such as manufacturing or sales

Controller

- Is chief accounting officer with powers including, but not limited to: maintenance and audit of company's financial records; preparation of financial statements; supervision of company accounting practices
- Works with audit committee, outside auditors, creditors, and corporate counsel

Assistant Officers

- Perform specific duties assigned by directors and other senior officers
- May substitute for senior officers during absences (in order of seniority)

Founder/Key Employee Employment Agreement

THIS EMPLOYMENT AGREEMENT (the "Agreement") is made as of _____,
   200__
BETWEEN:

   [YOUR COMPANY], a [state of incorporation] Corporation with a registered
   office address at [address—you can also use your business address]

   (the "Company")

                                                OF THE FIRST PART
   AND:

   [INDIVIDUAL NAME], an individual, who resides at [Address]

   (the "Founder/Key Employee")

                                                OF THE SECOND PART
                           WHEREAS:

(a) [Founder only]The Company, the Founder, and [Names of Investors] (the
    "Investors") have executed a Subscription Agreement and a Stockholders
    Agreement (the "Stockholders Agreement"), each dated [date], pursuant
    to which, amongst other things, the Investors purchased for the amount of
    [amount], a total of [number of shares or securities purchased] of the Com-
    pany and the Founder purchased [number of shares owned by Founder]
    shares of Common Stock, par value of $[found in your Articles of Incorpo-
    ration, usually minimal, e.g., $0.001 or $0.01] per share;

(b) The Company is in the business of _____ (the "Business")
    and the [Founder/Key Employee] is acknowledged as a leading expert in
    the Business;

(c) [Founder only]The parties acknowledge that the Founder's knowledge and
    experience are unique and essential to the Business and that certain of the
    Company's investors (the "Investors") have been induced to invest in the
    Company by reason of the Founder's knowledge and experience;

(d) The Company wishes to formalize its agreement with the [Founder/Key
    Employee] as to his provision of services and knowledge to the Company,
    by engaging the services of the [Founder/Key Employee] as its [Job Title,
    i.e. President, Chief Executive Officer, etc.], and the [Founder/Key Em-
    ployee] has agreed to be engaged by the Company in this fashion;

NOW, THEREFORE, in consideration of the mutual promises, covenants, terms,
and conditions herein, and for other good and valuable consideration, the receipt
and sufficiency of which are hereby acknowledged by the parties, the parties agree
as follows:

1. Agreement to Employ. The Company agrees to employ the [Founder/Key Employee] as its [Job Title] and the [Founder/Key Employee] agrees to be employed in this capacity, upon the terms and conditions hereinafter set forth.

2. Term. This Agreement shall commence on the date hereof and shall terminate as of the earlier of:

   (a) [six months, one year, five years, etc.] (the "Initial Term") unless either the Founder or the Company notifies the other that he or it elects to extend the term hereof for an additional [number of years of Term extension] (the "Renewal Period"), such notice to be given within ninety (90) days before the end of the Initial Term hereof or within ninety (90) days before the end of each successive Renewal Period;

   (b) the death of the [Founder/Key Employee]; or

   (c) thirty (30) days after notice is given by one party to the other after a material breach of this Agreement, by either party; or

   (d) [for Founder] thirty (30) days after notice is given by one party to the other after a material breach of this Agreement [or of the Stockholders Agreement], by either party.

   The exercise of the right of the Company or the [Key Employee] to terminate this Agreement pursuant to subsection 2(c) shall not abrogate the rights and remedies of the terminating party in respect of the breach giving rise to such termination. The Company shall only be deemed to have materially breached this Agreement and the terms of the Founder's employment if it fails to comply with Section 3 hereof or the proviso in the second sentence of Section 4 hereof in all material respects.

   [or, for Founder] The exercise of the right of the Company or the [Founder] to terminate this Agreement pursuant to subsection 2(c) shall not abrogate the rights and remedies of the terminating party in respect of the breach giving rise to such termination. The Company shall only be deemed to have materially breached this Agreement and the terms of the [Founder's] employment if it fails to comply with Section 3 hereof or the proviso in the second sentence of Section 4 hereof in all material respects.

3. Compensation. For all services rendered under this Agreement:

   (a) (i) the Company shall pay the [Founder/Key Employee] a base salary of [amount], per annum, in equal monthly or semimonthly installments. Such salary shall be reviewed and adjusted annually, on the anniversary date of this Agreement during the Initial Term, or on the yearly anniversary date of each successive Renewal Term, to accommodate any change in the cost-of-living index for the region as compiled by the Department of Labor. The Board of Directors shall review, on an annual basis, the [Founder/Key Employee]'s salary with a view to increasing it if, in the sole judgment of the Board of Directors, the earnings of the Company or the services of the Founder merit such increases;

(ii) if the [Founder/Key Employee] has been disabled for a period of at least [how long?] consecutive days, the Company may elect, upon notice to the [Founder/Key Employee], to pay the [Founder/Key Employee] [how much?] of the compensation the [Founder/Key Employee] would otherwise be entitled to pursuant to clause (i) above and shall thereupon have no further obligation under Section 3(d) or (e) hereof. Disability shall mean the [Founder/Key Employee]'s inability, due to sickness or injury, to perform effectively their duties hereunder.

(b) During the Initial Term, the [Founder/Key Employee] shall be entitled to incentive compensation, payable by the Company within thirty (30) days after delivery to the [Founder/Key Employee] (which delivery shall be no later than [how long?] months after the end of each fiscal year of the Company) of the Company's annual audited financial statements, as follows:

(i) [percentage of gross/net profits attained by the Company] or (ii) formula or accomplishments agreed to between the parties];

subject to a yearly maximum limit of incentive compensation of [how much?] per annum.

(c) If this Agreement is terminated or the Company notifies the [Founder/Key Employee] in respect of the disability provision set out in 3(a)(ii) above, incentive compensation in respect of the fiscal year of such termination or in which such notice is given shall be computed as if such termination had not occurred and the [Founder/Key Employee] shall be paid an amount equal to the product of the incentive compensation to which they would otherwise have been entitled, multiplied by a fraction having a numerator equal to the number of days in such year preceding the date of termination and a denominator equal to 365; provided that the [Founder/Key Employee] shall not be entitled to any amounts pursuant to this Section 3(c) if this Agreement is terminated pursuant to Section 2(c) prior to the date of payment of such amount.

(d) During the term of this Agreement, the [Founder/Key Employee] shall be entitled to participate in any employee benefit plans or programs of the Company, if any, to the extent that his tenure, salary, age, health, and other qualifications make him eligible to participate, subject to the rules and regulations applicable thereto. Such additional benefits shall include, subject to the approval of the Board of Directors, full medical, dental, and income insurance, [how many?] weeks of paid vacation, and qualified pension and profit sharing plans.

(e) The Company will furnish the [Founder/Key Employee], without cost to him, a Company-owned or -leased automobile of the make and model authorized by the Company's policy, and life insurance in the amount of at least [how much?].

(f) The [Founder/Key Employee] shall be entitled to reimbursement of all expenses incurred by him in the performance of his duties, subject to the presenting of appropriate receipts and documentary evidence in accordance with the Company's policy.

4. Duties. So long as the Company has not notified the [Key Employee] of termination pursuant to Section 3(a)(ii) above, the [Key Employee] is engaged initially with the title and functions of [Job Title, i.e., President and Chief Executive Officer] of the Company and, subject to the direction of the Board of Directors, shall perform and discharge well and faithfully the duties which may be assigned to him from time to time by the Company in connection with the conduct of its business. Nothing herein shall preclude the Board of Directors of the Company from changing the [Key Employee]'s title and duties, if such Board has concluded, in its reasonable judgment, that such change is in the Company's best interest. If the [Key Employee] is elected or appointed a director or officer of the Company or any subsidiary thereof during the term of this Agreement, the [Key Employee] will serve in such capacity without additional compensation.

4. [or, for Founder] Duties. So long as the Company has not notified the [Founder] of termination pursuant to Section 2 above, the [Founder] is engaged initially with the title and functions of [Job Title, e.g., President and Chief Executive Officer] of the Company and, subject to the direction of the Board of Directors, shall perform and discharge well and faithfully the duties which may be assigned to him from time to time by the Company in connection with the conduct of its business. Nothing herein shall preclude the Board of Directors of the Company from changing the [Founder]'s title and duties, if such Board has concluded, in its reasonable judgment, that such change is in the Company's best interest; PROVIDED HOWEVER, that at all times during the term of this Agreement, the [Founder] shall be employed as a senior executive of the Company with appropriate and commensurate compensation, title, rank, and status. If the Founder is elected or appointed a director or officer of the Company or any subsidiary thereof during the term of this Agreement, the [Founder] will serve in such capacity without additional compensation.

5. Extent of Service. So long as the Company has not notified the [Founder/Key Employee] of termination pursuant to Section 2 above, the [Founder/

Key Employee] shall devote his entire time, attention, and energies to the business of the Company and shall not, during the term of this Agreement, be engaged (whether or not during normal business hours) in any other business or professional activity, whether or not such activity is pursued for gain, profit or other pecuniary advantage; but this shall not be construed as preventing the [Founder/Key Employee] from:

(a) investing his personal assets in businesses which do not compete with the Company in such form or manner as will not require any services on the part of the [Founder/Key Employee] in the operation or the affairs of the companies in which such investments are made and in which his participation is solely that of an investor;

(b) purchasing securities in any corporation whose securities are regularly traded PROVIDED THAT such purchase shall not result in his collectively owning beneficially at any time, five percent (5%) or more of the equity securities of any corporation engaged in a business competitive to that of the Company; and

(c) participating in conferences, preparing or publishing papers or books, or teaching, so long as the Board of Directors approves of such activities prior to the [Founder/Key Employee]'s engaging in them. Prior to commencing any activity described herein, the [Founder/Key Employee] shall inform the Board of Directors of the Company in writing of any such activity.

6. Disclosure of Information.

(a) The [Founder/Key Employee] represents and warrants to the Company that Exhibit "A" hereto sets forth:

(i) all rights, in respect of the [Founder/Key Employee]'s engaging in any business activity (whether or not for profit), of former employers, clients, principals, partners, or others with whom or for whom the [Founder/Key Employee] has performed services since [when?]; and

(ii) all of the business activities (whether or not for profit) of the [Founder/Key Employee] applicable to periods after the time such services were performed.

(b) The [Founder/Key Employee] recognizes and acknowledges that the Company's trade secrets and proprietary information and processes, as they may exist from time to time, are valuable, special, and unique assets of the Company's business, access to and knowledge of which are essential to the performance of the [Founder/Key Employee]'s duties hereunder. The [Founder/Key Employee] will not, during or after the term of their employment by the Company, in whole or in part, disclose such secrets, information, or processes to any person, firm, corporation, association, or other entity for any reason or purpose whatsoever, nor shall the [Founder/Key Employee] make use of any such property for his own purposes or for the benefit of any person, firm, corporation, or other entity (except the Company) under any circumstances during or after the term of his employment, provided that after the term of his employment these restrictions shall not apply to such secrets, information, and processes which are then in the public domain (provided that the [Founder/Key Employee] was not responsible, directly or indirectly, for such secrets, information, or processes entering the public domain without the Company's consent). The [Founder/Key Employee] agrees to hold as the Company's property, all memoranda, books, papers, letters, formulas, and other data and all copies thereof and therefrom, in any way relating to the Company's businesses and affairs, whether made by him or otherwise coming into his possession, and on termination of his employment, or on demand of the Company, at any time, to deliver the same to the Company.

7. Inventions. The [Founder/Key Employee] hereby sells, transfers, and assigns to the Company or to any person or entity designated by the Company, all of the right, title, and interest of the [Founder/Key Employee] in and to all inventions, ideas, disclosures, and improvements, whether patented or unpatented, and copyrightable material, made or conceived by the [Founder/Key Employee], solely or jointly, or in whole or in part, during or before the term hereof (but after [date]) which:

   (a) relate to methods, apparatus, designs, products, processes, or devices sold, leased, used, or under construction or development by the Company or any subsidiary; or

   (b) otherwise relate to or pertain to the business, functions, or operations of the Company or any subsidiary; or

   (c) [optional] arise in whole or in part from the efforts of the [Founder/Key Employee] during the term hereof.

   The [Founder/Key Employee] shall communicate promptly and disclose to the Company, in such form as the Company requests, all information, details, and data pertaining to the aforementioned inventions, ideas, disclosures, and improvements; and, whether during the term hereof or thereafter, the [Founder/Key Employee] shall execute and deliver to the Company such formal transfers and assignments and such other papers and documents as may be required of the Founder to permit the Company or any person or entity designated by the Company to file and prosecute the patent applications and, as to copyrightable material, to obtain copyright thereon. Any invention by the [Founder/Key Employee] within [how many?] year(s) following the termination of this Agreement shall be deemed to fall within the provisions of this section unless provided by the [Founder/Key Employee] to have been first conceived and made following such termination.

8. Covenant not to Compete.

(a) During the term hereof and, unless this Agreement is terminated pursuant to Section 2(d) hereof, for a period of [how long?] year(s) thereafter, the [Founder/Key Employee] shall not compete, directly or indirectly, with the Company, interfere with, disrupt, or attempt to disrupt the relationship, contractual or otherwise, between the Company and any customer, client, supplier, consultant, or employee of the Company, including, without limitation, employing or being an investor (representing more than five percent (5%) equity interest) in, or officer, director, or consultant to, any person or entity which employs any former key or technical employee, whose employment with the Company was terminated after the date which is one year prior to the date of termination of the [Founder/Key Employee]'s employment therewith. An activity competitive with an activity engaged in by the Company shall include becoming an employee, officer, consultant, or director of, or being an investor in, or owner of, an entity or person engaged in the business then engaged in by the Company.

(b) It is the desire and intent of the parties that the provisions of this Section shall be enforced to the fullest extent permissible under the laws and public policies applied in each jurisdiction in which enforcement is sought. Accordingly, if any particular portion of this section shall be adjudicated to be invalid or unenforceable, this Section shall be deemed amended to delete therefrom the portion thus adjudicated to be invalid or unenforceable, such deletion to apply only with respect to the operation of this Section in the particular jurisdiction in which such adjudication is made.

(c) Nothing in this Section shall reduce or abrogate the [Founder/Key Employee]'s obligations during the term of this Agreement under Sections 4 and 5 hereof.

9. Remedies.

(a) The parties hereto acknowledge that the damages suffered by the Company and the Investors from the [Founder/Key Employee]'s breach of this Agreement by his continued neglect of his duties in Section 4 or 5 is not ascertainable. Accordingly, if the [Founder/Key Employee] breaches Section 4 or 5 hereof by continuously neglecting his duties in either of said sections, the Company and the Investors (in proportion to the ownership of the Company's securities) shall be entitled to liquidated damages from the [Founder/Key Employee] in the amount of $_____.

(b) If there is a breach or threatened breach of the provisions of Sections 5, 6(b), 7 or 8 of this Agreement, the Company shall be entitled to an injunction restraining the [Founder/Key Employee] from such breach.

Nothing herein shall be construed as prohibiting the Company from pursuing any other remedies for such breach or threatened breach.

(c) If this Agreement is terminated pursuant to Section 2(d) hereof, the [Founder/Key Employee] shall not be required to mitigate damages otherwise obtainable from the Company hereunder.

10. Insurance. The Company may, at its election and for its benefit, insure the [Founder/Key Employee] against accidental loss or death and the [Founder/Key Employee] shall submit to such physical examination and supply such information as may be required in connection therewith.

11.　Relocation/Location of Performance.

(a) The parties acknowledge that the [Founder/Key Employee] [is/may be] required to change his place of residence to perform his obligations under this Agreement. The Company agrees that, should relocation become necessary, it shall pay all of the costs and expenses of the [Founder/Key Employee] and his family connected with such relocation, including reasonable moving and travel expenses and reasonable temporary dwelling costs (for a period not to exceed 60 days), [and costs associated with purchasing and selling a permanent place of residence], all such expenses not to exceed [how much?].

(b) The [Founder/Key Employee]'s services will be formed in the [where?] area. The [Founder/Key Employee]'s performance hereunder shall be within such area or its environs. The parties acknowledge, however, that the [Founder/Key Employee] may be required to travel [extensively?] in connection with the performance of his duties hereunder.

12. Assignment. This Agreement may not be assigned by any party hereto, PROVIDED THAT the Company may assign this Agreement in connection with a merger or consolidation involving the Company or a sale of substantially all its assets to the surviving corporation or purchaser, as the case may be, so long as such assignee assumes the Company's obligations thereunder.

13. Notices. Any notice required or permitted to be given under this Agreement shall be sufficient in writing and sent by registered mail to the [Founder/Key Employee] at the address set out above or to the Company at the address set out above, to the specific attention of [who is the primary contact at the Company?].

14. Waiver of Breach. A waiver by the Company or the [Founder/Key Employee] of a breach of any provision of this Agreement by the other party shall not operate or be construed as a waiver of any subsequent breach by the other party.

15. Entire Agreement. This Agreement contains the entire agreement of the parties. It may be changed only by an agreement in writing signed by a

party against whom enforcement of any waiver, change, modification, extension, or discharge is sought.

IN WITNESS WHEREOF, the parties hereto have executed this Agreement as of the day and year first above written.

[COMPANY]

By

[Sign above, type name here], President

[FOUNDER/KEY EMPLOYEE'S NAME], an Individual

Signature

Independent Contractor Service Agreement

THIS INDEPENDENT CONTRACTOR SERVICE AGREEMENT (the "Agreement") is made as of [month/day/year]

BETWEEN:

[YOUR COMPANY], a [state of incorporation] Corporation with a registered office address at [address—you can also use your business address]

(the "Company")

OF THE FIRST PART

AND:

[INDIVIDUAL NAME], an individual, who resides at [Address]

("[Name]")

[OR, where you are contracting with an individual through their own company]

[NAME of CONTRACTOR'S COMPANY], a [State of incorporation] Corporation with an address for service of [address of Contractor's company],

AND

[NAME OF INDIVIDUAL], an individual who resides at [Address]

("[Corp. Name]" and "[Indiv. Name]," respectively)

OF THE SECOND PART

WHEREAS:

(a) The Company is in the business of [describe briefly the main aspects of your operations] (the "Business");

(b) The Company wishes to engage the services of [Name of Independent Contractor] as its [Job Title], and [Name of Independent Contractor] has agreed to be engaged by the Company in this fashion;

[OR, WHERE YOU ARE CONTRACTING WITH A COMPANY, USE THE FOLLOWING CLAUSE]

(b) The Company wishes to engage the services of [Name of Individual Independent Contractor] in his capacity as the principal of [Name of Corporate Independent Contractor], to act as [Job Title] for the Company, and [Corp. Name] and [Indiv. Name] have agreed to be engaged by the Company in this fashion;

(c) the Company and [Corp. Name or Indiv. Name] have agreed that, as compensation for the services to be provided by [Corp. Name or Indiv. Name], the Company shall pay [Corp. Name or Indiv. Name] the amount of [set out your payment details, including options to purchase stock or stock to be issued as a portion of consideration], on the terms and conditions set forth herein;

NOW, THEREFORE, in consideration of the mutual promises, covenants, terms, and conditions herein, and for other good and valuable consideration, the receipt and sufficiency of which are hereby acknowledged by the parties, the parties agree as follows:

1. *Term*. This Agreement shall be for an initial term of [i.e., one year, six months, etc., or for the length of time it will take to accomplish a specific task] (the "Term"). This Agreement may be renegotiated for such additional Terms, on such terms and conditions as may be agreed between the parties. This Agreement, or any successive agreement(s), shall remain in full force and effect unless terminated by either party in writing, in accordance with the provisions of Section 9 of this Agreement.

2. ***Duties to Be Performed***. The specific duties to be performed by [Corp. Name or Indiv. Name] on behalf of the Company are as follows:

   • [set out in point form or in narrative form what duties and responsibilities you are contracting with this individual to perform]

   (collectively, the "Duties").

   The [Corp. Name or Indiv. Name] may work such hours and days as are required to complete the Duties and which are agreed to by the parties, and may perform the Duties at either the Company's premises or such other premises as may be possible, given the nature of the Duties.

   • [Where applicable to your company, consider adding this clause]

   [Corp. Name or Indiv. Name] shall be wholly responsible for supplying such tools and equipment as may be required to carry out the Duties, and shall be permitted to engage such assistants or subcontractors as may be required to perform the Duties. Where the [Corp. Name or Indiv. Name] engages assistants or subcontractors to assist in carrying out the Duties, the [Corp. Name or Indiv. Name] shall be solely responsible for the payment and supervision of such assistants or subcontractors, including the responsibility to remit any payroll taxes or statutory deductions on behalf of such assistants or subcontractors as may be required.

3. ***Additional Duties***. [Corp. Name or Indiv. Name] may perform such additional duties for the Company as may be requested by the Company and agreed to by [Corp. Name or Indiv. Name].

4. ***Remuneration***. The Company shall pay to [Corp. Name or Indiv. Name] total remuneration of [set out total amount to be paid under this Contract, including any stock to be issued or stock options to be granted], (the "Re-

muneration"), during the Term of this Agreement. The Remuneration shall be paid in equal [monthly? biweekly? weekly?] installments, on the [when? 15th and 30th?, 1st and 15th, etc.] day of each month [or, where payment is to be made in a lump sum amount, "The Remuneration shall be paid by way of a lump-sum payment, on or before the final day of the Term, or earlier, as the parties may agree".]. [For either installment or lump-sum payments, add the following:] [Corp. Name or Indiv. Name] shall be responsible for submitting interim [monthly? weekly? biweekly?] invoices to the Company during the Term [or, . . . shall provide the Company with an invoice covering the Remuneration for the Duties to be performed on or before [date].]

5. Should this Agreement be terminated prior to the completion of the Term, as provided for in Section 9 below, the Remuneration to be paid to [Corp. Name or Indiv. Name] shall be paid on a pro rata basis, as provided for in Section 10 below.

6. *No Employment Relationship.* The parties expressly agree that [Corp. Name or Indiv. Name] or any subcontractors or assistants engaged by [Corp. Name or Indiv. Name] shall be considered an Independent Contractor to the Company, and that no employment relationship shall be formed by the provision of the Duties by [Corp. Name or Indiv. Name] or such subcontractors or assistants as may be engaged by [Corp. Name or Indiv. Name]. Neither [Corp. Name or Indiv. Name] nor any subcontractors or assistants engaged by [Corp. Name or Indiv. Name] shall have any claim whatsoever under this Agreement or otherwise against the Company for vacation pay, sick leave, retirement benefits, Social Security, workers compensation, disability, unemployment insurance benefits, or any other employee benefits, all of which shall be the sole responsibility of [Corp. Name or Indiv. Name]. The Company shall not withhold on behalf of [Corp. Name or Indiv. Name] or any subcontractors or assistants engaged by [Corp. Name or Indiv. Name] to carry out the Duties, any sums for income tax, unemployment insurance, Social Security, or any other withholding pursuant to any law or requirement of any government agency, and all such withholdings and remittances shall be the sole responsibility of [Corp. Name or Indiv. Name]. [Corp. Name or Indiv. Name] shall indemnify and hold the Company harmless from any and all loss or liability arising with respect to any of the foregoing benefits or withholding, including the failure of [Corp. Name or Indiv. Name] to remit any benefits or withholdings on behalf of itself or any subcontractors or assistants engaged by [Corp. Name or Indiv. Name] to carry out the Duties. Furthermore, [Corp. Name or Indiv. Name] agrees to reimburse the Company for any withholdings or benefits which the Company is required to pay to any regulatory authorities arising as a result of the failure of [Corp. Name or Indiv. Name] to remit such payments on their behalf.

7. *Confidentiality.* The parties agree that during the course of performing the Duties, [Corp. Name or Indiv. Name] may receive confidential information with respect to the Business of the Company. [Corp. Name or Indiv. Name] expressly agrees at all times to maintain the confidentiality of all such confidential information provided and follow such appropriate procedures as may be put into place by the Company to ensure that no confidentiality rights of the Company are abridged during the Term of this Agreement or at any time following the expiration or termination of this Agreement.

8. *Costs of Legal Proceedings.* Should the Company be required to commence legal proceedings against [Corp. Name or Indiv. Name] with respect to enforcement of the confidentiality provision of this Agreement or with respect to a breach of the confidentiality provision of this Agreement resulting in damages to the Company being incurred, then the Company shall be entitled to recover from [Corp. Name or Indiv. Name] its reasonable costs of such action, including attorneys' fees and expenses.

9. *Termination.* This Agreement may be terminated as follows:

    (a) by either party, for any reason, upon the provision of thirty (30) days' notice in writing; or

    (b) by the Company, upon [Corp. Name or Indiv. Name] breaching the confidentiality provision set out in Section 7 above, upon twenty-four (24) hours' notice in writing.

    Any written notice to be provided from one party to the other shall be delivered by either registered mail or courier delivery, to the addresses of the parties as set out below, or to such other address as the parties may from time to time advise the other, in writing:

    To the Company: To [Corp. Name or Indiv. Name]:

    _____

    _____

    _____

With a copy to its legal counsel: [optional]

10. *Pro-Rated Remuneration upon Termination.* Upon termination of this Agreement pursuant to the provisions of Section 9 above, the Remuneration will be pro-rated to the date of termination of the Agreement.

11. *Waiver.* No waiver of all or any portion of this Agreement is enforceable unless in writing and signed by such waiving party, and any waiver shall not be construed as a waiver by any other party or of any other or subsequent breach.

12. *Indemnification*. [Corp. Name or Indiv. Name] agrees to indemnify and defend the Company against, and hold the Company harmless from, any and all claims, actions, suits, proceedings, costs, expenses, damages and liabilities, including attorneys fees and costs, resulting from, or arising out of, or connected in any way with any act or omission of [Corp. Name or Indiv. Name] under this Agreement or [Corp. Name or Indiv. Name]'s failure to comply with the provisions of this Agreement.

13. *Entire Agreement*. This Agreement supersedes any and all other agreements, either oral or in writing, between the parties hereto with respect to the subjects discussed herein, and contains the entire agreement between the parties relating to the subject matter.

14. *Amendments*. This Agreement may not be amended except by the mutual consent of the parties hereto, such consent to be provided in writing.

15. *Governing Law*. The parties expressly agree that this Agreement shall be governed by the laws of the United States of America and the State of [State where Company is located]. Each party to this Agreement consents to the exclusive jurisdiction of the state and federal courts sitting in [County where Company is located] County, [State where Company is located], in any action on a claim arising out of, under, or in connection with this Agreement.

16. *Assignment and Binding Effect*. Neither this Agreement nor any of the rights, interests or obligations hereunder shall be assigned by either party hereto without the prior written consent of the other party hereto, except as otherwise provided herein. This Agreement shall be binding upon and shall inure to the benefit of the parties hereto and their respective officers, directors, administrators, permitted successors, assigns, and/or delegates.

17. *Integration and Captions*. This Agreement includes the entire understanding of the parties hereto with respect to the subject matter hereof. The headings herein are solely for convenience and shall not control the interpretation of this Agreement.

18. *Legal Representation*. Each party has been represented by independent legal counsel in connection with this Agreement, or each has had the opportunity to obtain independent legal counsel and has waived such right, and each party shall be responsible for obtaining its own tax counsel at its own expense.

19. *Construction*. Each party acknowledges and agrees that it has had the opportunity to review, negotiate, and approve all of the provisions of this Agreement.

20. *Cooperation*. The parties agree to execute such reasonable necessary documents upon advice of legal counsel in order to carry out the intent and purpose of this Agreement as set forth herein.

21. **Fees, Costs, and Expenses.** Each of the parties hereto acknowledges and agrees to pay, without reimbursement from the other party, the fees, costs, and expenses incurred by it with respect to this Agreement, including the cost of obtaining independent legal advice with respect to entry into this Agreement.

22. **Consents and Authorizations.** Upon the execution of this Agreement, the parties acknowledge and agree that they each have the full right, power, legal capacity, and authority to enter into this Agreement, and the same constitutes a valid and legally binding agreement and obligation of each party in accordance with the terms, conditions, and other provisions contained herein.

23. **Gender and Number.** Unless the context otherwise requires, references in this Agreement in any gender shall be construed to include the other gender, references in the singular shall be construed to include the plural, and references in the plural shall be construed to include the singular.

24. **Severability.** In the event that any one or more of the provisions of this Agreement shall be deemed unenforceable by any court of competent jurisdiction for any reason whatsoever, this Agreement shall be construed as if such unenforceable provision had never been contained herein and the remaining provisions of this Agreement shall remain enforceable and in full effect.

25. **Counterparts and Execution by Facsimile.** This Agreement may be executed in counterpart and/or by facsimile, each of which shall constitute a duplicate original and all of which shall constitute the entire agreement.

IN WITNESS WHEREOF, the parties hereto have executed this Agreement as of the day and year first above written.

[YOUR COMPANY]

By:

[Type Name], President

[Where Independent Contractor is an Individual:]

[Name of Independent Contractor], an Individual

Signature

[Where Independent Contractor is a corporation:]

[NAME OF CORPORATE INDEPENDENT CONTRACTOR]

By:

[Type Name and Title below signature line]

And By:

[Type Individual's name here], as an Individual

Employment Agreement

THIS EMPLOYMENT AGREEMENT (the "Agreement") is made as of _____, 200__

BETWEEN:

[YOUR COMPANY], a [state of incorporation] Corporation with a registered office address at [address—you can also use your business address]

(the "Company")

OF THE FIRST PART

AND:

[INDIVIDUAL NAME], an individual, who resides at [Address]

(the "Employee")

OF THE SECOND PART

WHEREAS:

(a) The Company is in the business of _____ (the "Business");

(b) The Company wishes to engage the services of the Employee as its General Manager of Operations, and the Employee has agreed to be engaged by the Company in this fashion;

(c) The Company and the Employee have agreed that, as compensation for the services to be provided by the Employee, the Company shall pay the Employee an amount equivalent to twenty-five percent (25%) of the Company's net profits, on the terms and conditions set forth herein;

NOW, THEREFORE, in consideration of the mutual promises, covenants, terms, and conditions herein, and for other good and valuable consideration, the receipt and sufficiency of which are hereby acknowledged by the parties, the parties agree as follows:

1. *Agreement to Employ.* The Company agrees to employ the Employee as its [Job Title?] and the Employee agrees to be employed in this capacity.

2. *Employment Term.* The term of this Agreement shall be for a [?? monthly, yearly ??] period, commencing on the date of this Agreement and terminating on [date?].

    [Alternatively, if it is to continue for successive periods, consider the following clause:

    This Agreement shall be for an initial term of [??? months/years] and shall automatically renew for additional [how long? month/year terms] unless terminated by either party in writing, in accordance with the provisions of Section 11 of this Agreement.]

3. ***Duties to be Performed.*** The specific duties to be performed by the Employee on behalf of the Company are as follows:

[List the duties you are hiring this individual to perform for you]

(collectively, the "Duties").

4. ***Additional Employment Duties.*** The Employee may perform such additional duties for the Company as may be requested by the Company and agreed to by the Employee.

5. ***Remuneration.*** The Company shall pay to the Employee [monthly/yearly/hourly?] gross remuneration of [amount, as well as stock or options to purchase stock], (the "Remuneration"). The Employee shall receive the Remuneration on a [monthly?weekly?biweekly?] basis, on the [1st and 15th?/every other Friday?] of each month.

6. Should this Agreement be terminated prior to the completion of the Term, as provided for in Section 11 below, the Remuneration to be paid to the Employee shall be paid on a pro-rata basis, as provided for in Section 12 below.

[Clause 7 may be customized to apply to your specific situation].

7. ***Vacation Time and Medical Leave.*** Following completion of the first year's continuous employment, the Employee will be entitled to received paid vacation time of two (2) calendar weeks. Paid vacation time entitlement will increase as follows:

   (a) following completion of the second year of continuous employment—two (2) calendar weeks per year;

   (b) following completion of the third and fourth years of continuous employment—three (3) calendar weeks per year;

   (c) following completion of the fifth and subsequent years of continuous employment—four (4) calendar weeks per year.

   The Employee shall also be entitled to [how many?] days of paid medical leave per calendar year. Unused medical leave [may?may not?] be banked for use in subsequent years.

8. ***Employment Relationship.*** The parties expressly agree that the Employee shall be considered an employee of the Company, and that an employment relationship has been entered into. As such, the Company will be responsible for deducting and remitting, from the gross Remuneration due to the Employee, all required statutory deductions, including but not limited to: federal and/or state income tax, unemployment insurance, Social Security, and health benefit premiums as may be offered by the Company.

9. ***Confidentiality.*** The parties agree that during the course of performing the Duties, the Employee may receive confidential information with respect to the Business of the Company. The Employee expressly agrees at all times to

maintain the confidentiality of all such confidential information provided and follow such appropriate procedures as may be put into place by the Company to ensure that no confidentiality rights of the Company are abridged during the Term of this Agreement or at any time following the expiration or termination of this Agreement.

10. ***Costs of Legal Proceedings.*** Should the Company be required to commence legal proceedings against the Employee with respect to enforcement of the confidentiality provision of this Agreement or with respect to a breach of the confidentiality provision of this Agreement resulting in damages to the Company being incurred, then the Company shall be entitled to recover from the Employee its reasonable costs of such action, including attorneys' fees and expenses.

11. ***Termination.*** This Agreement may be terminated as follows:

   (a) by either party, for any reason, upon the provision of [how many days'/months'?] notice in writing; or

   (b) by the Company, upon the Employee breaching the confidentiality provision set out in Section 9 above, upon [how many days'?weeks'?hours'?] notice in writing.

Any written notice to be provided from one party to the other shall be delivered by either registered mail or courier delivery, to the addresses of the parties as set out below, or to such other address as the parties may from time to time advise the other, in writing:

To the Company:　　　　　　　　　　To the Employee:

　　　　　　　　　　　　　　　　　_____

　　　　　　　　　　　　　　　　　_____

　　　　　　　　　　　　　　　　　_____

With a copy to its legal counsel: [optional]

12. ***Pro-Rated Remuneration upon Termination.*** Upon termination of this Agreement pursuant to the provisions of Section 11 above, the Remuneration will be pro-rated to the date of termination of the Agreement.

13. ***Waiver.*** No waiver of all or any portion of this Agreement is enforceable unless in writing and signed by such waiving party, and any waiver shall not be construed as a waiver by any other party or of any other or subsequent breach.

14. ***Entire Agreement.*** This Agreement supersedes any and all other agreements, either oral or in writing, between the parties hereto with respect to the subjects discussed herein, and contains the entire agreement between the parties relating to the subject matter.

15. *Amendments*. This Agreement may not be amended except by the mutual consent of the parties hereto, such consent to be provided in writing.

16. *Governing Law*. The parties expressly agree that this Agreement shall be governed by the laws of the United States of America and the State of [State where your business operates]. Each party to this Agreement consents to the exclusive jurisdiction of the state and federal courts sitting in [County and State where your business operates], in any action on a claim arising out of, under, or in connection with this Agreement.

17. *Assignment and Binding Effect*. Neither this Agreement nor any of the rights, interests or obligations hereunder shall be assigned by either party hereto without the prior written consent of the other party hereto, except as otherwise provided herein. This Agreement shall be binding upon and shall inure to the benefit of the parties hereto and their respective officers, directors, administrators, permitted successors, assigns, and/or delegates.

18. *Integration and Captions*. This Agreement includes the entire understanding of the parties hereto with respect to the subject matter hereof. The headings herein are solely for convenience and shall not control the interpretation of this Agreement.

19. *Legal Representation*. Each party has been represented by independent legal counsel in connection with this Agreement, or each has had the opportunity to obtain independent legal counsel and has waived such right, and each party shall be responsible for obtaining its own tax counsel at its own expense.

20. *Construction*. Each party acknowledges and agrees that it has had the opportunity to review, negotiate, and approve all of the provisions of this Agreement.

21. *Cooperation*. The parties agree to execute such reasonable necessary documents upon advice of legal counsel in order to carry out the intent and purpose of this Agreement as set forth herein.

22. *Fees, Costs, and Expenses*. Each of the parties hereto acknowledges and agrees to pay, without reimbursement from the other party, the fees, costs, and expenses incurred by it with respect to this Agreement, including the cost to obtain independent legal advice with respect to entry into this Agreement.

23. *Consents and Authorizations*. Upon the execution of this Agreement, the parties acknowledge and agree that they each have the full right, power, legal capacity, and authority to enter into this Agreement, and the same constitutes a valid and legally binding agreement and obligation of each party in accordance with the terms, conditions, and other provisions contained herein.

24. ***Gender and Number.*** Unless the context otherwise requires, references in this Agreement in any gender shall be construed to include the other gender, references in the singular shall be construed to include the plural, and references in the plural shall be construed to include the singular.

25. ***Severability.*** In the event that any one or more of the provisions of this Agreement shall be deemed unenforceable by any court of competent jurisdiction for any reason whatsoever, this Agreement shall be construed as if such unenforceable provision had never been contained herein and the remaining provisions of this Agreement shall remain enforceable and in full effect.

26. ***Counterparts and Execution by Facsimile.*** This Agreement may be executed in counterpart and/or by facsimile, each of which shall constitute a duplicate original and all of which shall constitute the entire agreement.

IN WITNESS WHEREOF, the parties hereto have executed this Agreement as of the day and year first above written.

[YOUR COMPANY]

By:

[Sign above, Type Name here], President

[EMPLOYEE'S NAME], an Individual

Signature

Chapter 12

How to Use a Buy-Sell Agreement

A buy-sell agreement is used by the owners of a small closely held business entity to cover the buyout of shares upon death, divorce, disability, or withdrawal of an owner. You generally would not see such an agreement with a publicly traded company because, subject to any restrictions, the shares are freely tradeable.

But in a smaller company, where people are working closely together and have to get along, many will want to control who gets to own shares in the company.

Consider the following:

Case No. 14—Herman, Chloe, and Matty

Herman, Chloe, and Matty formed a corporation and contributed into it an awesome technology that was going to change the way e-commerce was done. They incorporated AweTech, Inc. in Nevada and issued Herman 250,000 shares, Chloe 100,000 shares, and Matty 50,000 shares based upon their relative contributions. Herman wanted AweTech, Inc. to institute a buy-sell agreement for very personal reasons. He was the lead developer of this once-in-a-lifetime technology, and was having problems with his new wife, Bambie. He was sensing after all of six weeks of married life that she was a golddigger out for his future prospects. They lived in a community property state whereby half of what the business grew to become would be hers. And in the event of a divorce settlement where she received shares, having her as a shareholder of the company, with her loud and flashy know-nothingness, would be a major embarrassment. A buy-sell agreement, he knew, could address his concerns.

Chloe also wanted a buy-sell agreement. She was a very serious technician and had married her opposite. Dieter was a surfer, a rocker, and a slacker. She loved him for these qualities but knew that he had no business being anywhere near a technical enterprise.

Matty was willing to go along with the group on a buy-sell agreement. He was with them for the experience, which he saw as more of a single, not a home run. He was not married and had no real emotional or business allegiance to the company, so signing another document did not bother him.

AweTech, Inc.'s attorney prepared a fifty-page buy-sell agreement covering every possible contingency with a multitude of terms, conditions, and boilerplate (standard) provisions too lengthy to be reprinted here. Nevertheless, several key sections along with the spousal consent are given below in order to understand what later happened at AweTech, Inc.

At Herman's insistence they established a book value for the purchase price of the shares. And they bought insurance so the corporation would have money to buy the shares.

AweTech, Inc. Buy-Sell Agreement

Section Five—Events Triggering a Buyout Right

A. *Death*. Upon the death of an individual Shareholder, the Corporation and/or remaining Shareholders shall have an option to purchase in accordance with the procedures set forth herein, all (but not less than all) of the decedent's shares at the book value of the corporation.

B. *Disability*. In the event an individual Shareholder is employed by the Corporation in a capacity as an officer, employee, consultant, or director and becomes disabled, as defined below, the Corporation and/or remaining Shareholders shall have an option to purchase, in accordance with the procedures set forth herein, all (but not less than all) of the disabled Shareholder's shares, and all other shares in the Corporation owned by such individual Shareholder, whether such Shareholder is the owner of record or merely the beneficial owner of such shares, at the book value of the corporation.

Definition of Disability. A Shareholder is disabled for purposes of this Agreement if he: (1) has been declared legally incompetent by a final court decree (the date of such decree being deemed to be the date on which the disability occurred); (2) receives disability insurance benefits from his/her State Industrial Insurance System or any disability income insurance policy maintained by the Corporation for a period of twelve (12) consecutive months; or (3) has been found to be disabled pursuant to a Disability Determination. A "Disability Determination" means a finding that the Shareholder, because of a medically determinable disease, injury, or other mental or physical disability, is unable to perform substantially all of his regular duties to the Corporation and that such disability is determined or reasonably expected to last at least twelve (12) months. The Disability Determination shall be based on the written opinion of the physician regularly attending the Shareholder whose disability is in question. If a majority of the members of the Board of Directors of the Corporation disagree with the opinion of this physician (the "First Physician"), the Corporation may engage, at its own expense, another physician (the "Second Physician") to examine the Shareholder. If the First and Second Physicians disagree on the disability of the Shareholder, they shall choose a third consulting physician (whose expense shall also be borne by the Corporation), and the written opinion of a majority of these three (3) physicians shall, except as otherwise provided in this Subsection, be conclusive as to the Shareholder's disability. The date of any written opinion conclusively finding the Shareholder to be disabled is the date on which the disability will be deemed to have occurred. If there is a conclusive finding that the Shareholder is not disabled, the remaining Shareholders shall have the right to request additional Disability Determinations, provided they agree to pay all the expenses of the Disability Determinations and do not request an additional Disability Determination more frequently than once every six (6) months. In conjunction with a Disability Determination, each Shareholder hereby consents to any required medical examination, and agrees to furnish any medical information requested by any examining physician and to waive any applicable physician-patient privilege that may arise because of such examination. All physicians except the First Physician must be board-certified in the speciality most closely related to the nature of the disability alleged to exist.

C. *Termination of Employment.* If any individual Shareholder is employed by the Corporation on a part-time or full-time basis as an officer, employee, director, or consultant, and ceases to be employed by the Corporation for any reason other than death or disability, whether the termination results from retirement because of age under a retirement policy adopted by the Corporation that applies to the Shareholder, voluntary termination of employment, termination of employment by the mutual consent of the Shareholder and the Corporation, or termination by the unilateral act of the Corporation for cause, with cause being defined as (i) a final nonappealable conviction of or a plea of guilty or nolo contendere by the Shareholder to a felony or a misdemeanor involving dishonesty or other criminal conduct against the Corporation or any affiliate of the Corporation, (ii) the Shareholder's continual breach of his duties and obligations arising under an employment contract with the Corporation or continued breach of any written policy, rule, or regulation of the Corporation or any affiliate of the Corporation for a period of at least five (5) days following receipt of written notice from an officer of the Corporation of any affiliate of the Corporation specifying such breach, or the receipt by the Shareholder of three (3) or more such notices in any twelve (12) month period. The Corporation and/or remaining Shareholders shall have an option to purchase, in accordance with the procedures set forth herein, all, (but not less than all), of the terminated Shareholder's shares, and all other shares in the Corporation owned by such individual Shareholder and his spouse, if any, whether such Shareholder and his spouse are the owner of record or merely the beneficial owners of such shares, at the book value of the corporation.

D. *Transfers by Operation of Law.* In the event any Shareholder: (a) files a voluntary petition under any bankruptcy or insolvency law or a petition for the appointment of a receiver, or makes an assignment for the benefit of creditors; (b) is subjected involuntarily to such a petition or assignment or to an attachment or other legal or equitable interest with respect to his or her shares in the Corporation and such involuntary petition, assignment, or attachment is not discharged within thirty (30) days after its effective date; or (c) is subjected to any other possible involuntary transfer of his shares in the Corporation by legal process, the Corporation and/or other Shareholders shall have the option to purchase, in accordance with the procedures set forth herein, all (but not less than all) of the shares that are subject to the involuntary transfer, for the book value of the corporation.

E. *Divorce.* If, at the time of their divorce, both spouses are Shareholders in the Corporation and the court awarding the divorce does not order all the shares owned by one spouse to be transferred to the other spouse as part of the divorce decree or any property settlement incorporated into the divorce decree, then: if only one of the spouses is, at the time of the divorce decree, employed by the Corporation as an officer, employee, director, or paid consultant, the shares owned by the other spouse shall be offered for sale at the book value of the corporation as follows:

(a) The spouse who is an employee of the Corporation shall have a first option to purchase some or all of the shares in question. This option must be exercised within twenty (20) days after the entry of the divorce decree.

(b) The Corporation shall have a second opinion to purchase the shares in question not purchased pursuant to Paragraph (a). Within twenty (20) days after the date the Corporation's Secretary receives written notification of the divorce and the purchase right granted by this Subsection, the Corporation will call a special Board of Directors meeting, to be held not more than forty (40) days after the call, to decide whether the Corporation should purchase any of the shares not purchased by the employee-spouse. The option to purchase must be approved by the affirmative vote of the holder of a majority of votes entitled to be cast at the meeting, excluding the vote of the selling spouse. The Corporation shall, within twenty (20) days of this Shareholder meeting, notify the spouse required to offer shares for sale, in writing, whether it has or has not exercised its option to purchase. If the Corporation exercises the option to purchase, it may allocate some or all of the shares it agrees to purchase to one or more of the remaining Shareholders or other persons if all the Directors who voted in favor of the purchase approve the allocation.

The shares of the spouse required to offer shares for sale pursuant to this sub-section that are not purchased pursuant to paragraphs (a) and (b) shall continue to be subject to the terms and conditions of this Agreement.

* * *

SPOUSAL CONSENT

Each of the undersigned, being the spouse of a Shareholder who has signed this Agreement, hereby acknowledges that he or she has read and is familiar with its provisions of the AweTech, Inc. Stock Transfer Restrictions and Buy-Sell Agreement dated _____, 200__, and agrees to be bound thereby and to join therein to the extent, if any, that his or her joinder may be necessary. The undersigned hereby agrees that his or her spouse may join in any future amendment or modification of this Agreement without any further signature, acknowledgment, agreement, or consent on his or her part; and further agrees that any interest which he or she may have in the shares of stock in the Corporation owned directly or beneficially by his or her spouse shall be subject to the provisions of this Agreement.

Six months after signing the buy-sell agreement a terrible thing happened. Chloe became disabled in a car accident. While she was going to be able to live a somewhat comfortable life, she would never be able to work again. She fit the definition of disability in the buy-sell agreement. The corporation decided to use the insurance money to buy Chloe's 100,000 shares for their book value of $1.00 per share.

Surprising everyone, Dieter emerged from his slackerdom and challenged the valuation of the shares. It was way too low, he argued. He knew the company was worth far more than $1.00 per share. He argued that the $100,000 AweTech, Inc. was going to pay for Chloe's shares was less than a tenth of their true value. Book value was the lowest measure of shares a company could use. It did not take into account the fair market value of their patent, which was worth many times more on the open market. He argued that an independent appraisal by a CPA could be prepared to gauge the true value of the company.

But Dieter had been a slacker when he signed the spousal consent. His signature was on the document agreeing to a buyout based on book value. He and Chloe were obligated to accept $100,000 for their shares.

With Chloe no longer with the company, Matty grew less interested and more and more easily frustrated by Herman's demanding management style. One day Matty blew a fuse and lashed out at Herman. He quit his job in a very loud and obnoxious way, a story he regaled his friends with over beers that night. He did not care. The company was going public soon and he would get his millions when he cashed in his shares.

Matty had forgotten all about signing the buy-sell agreement. He only recalled it the next day when Herman demanded his stock certificate for 50,000 shares back in exchange for a check of $50,000. Matty hired a lawyer to argue that the share value was worth at least $500,000. But Matty had signed the agreement consenting to a book value valuation. Quitting his job three months before the public offering cost Matty a lot of money.

Herman was now the only founder left. But he still had a problem. Bambie. He knew it would never work out. He was constantly embarrassed by her and now more convinced than ever that all she wanted was his money.

He filed for divorce. She hired the biggest divorce-shark attorney she could find. The attorney threatened to prove that she had signed the buy-sell agreement under duress and was not properly counseled as to its meaning or contents. He argued that book value was a standard that no court would uphold in caring for the future of a material community component to the success of the business. He threatened to show pictures of Herman involved in unnatural acts.

Herman's attorney withstood the assault but realized they had to settle. A compromise was reached where Bambie received a property settlement based on the difference between the shares' book value and their soon to be public value. Herman was satisfied with the settlement. Without the buy-sell in place he (or the corporation) would have had to pay top dollar for all the shares.

The others were not so happy. By setting the shares at less than their fair market value they had been negatively affected by the buy-sell. A lesson learned.

Rich Dad Tips

- Always have the terms of a buy-sell agreement reviewed by your own independent attorney.
- Remember, the corporation's attorney represents the company—not you as an individual.

Chapter 13

What Happens at the End

Because hopes are high upon creating a business, people often avoid think-ing about what will happen if the business comes to an end. But the subject of dissolution is one that should not be ignored. Planning ahead by under-standing some basic principles of dissolution is important. Whether you go out of business or enter into a relationship with another business where your existing business dissolves, there are procedures that must be prepared for from the start. What follows are considerations concerning conse-quences related to the dissolution of various business entities. And, as dis-cussed in this chapter's final section, dissolution may not be appropriate.

Limited Partnership

In a limited partnership, the partnership agreement should include express provisions for dissolution, liquidation, termination, and winding up of the partnership. Dissolution of the partnership means the triggering moment when provisions for winding up and liquidation shall begin; termination oc-curs only upon the conclusion of all such activities.

When designing the partnership agreement, a variety of possible trigger-ing events should be considered that could allow for or require dissolution. Dissolution provisions for short-term activities may specify an exact date when the partnership will dissolve. More frequently, provisions invoke dissolution:

- When a final general partner leaves the partnership, unless a majority—or greater percentage—of the remaining limited partners are allowed a brief time to keep the business and find a new general partner;
- If the business does not achieve expected financing goals within a given period of time;
- Upon a judicial decree;
- If it is found that the partnership's status is unlawful; or
- Upon the sale of substantially (over 90 percent) all assets and other property of the business.

Commonly, an express provision requires the prior written consent of the limited partners before a general partner can initiate the dissolution of the partnership. Alternatively, provisions may require unanimous written consent of all general partners in addition to a majority of limited partners. Additionally, if a general partner is in default without meeting the deadline and conditions to cure the default, a provision in the partnership agreement can allow a nondefaulting general partner and, typically, a minimum of a majority of the limited partners to elect to dissolve the partnership at once.

An express provision should state the order of operations for the winding-up phase of the business upon dissolution, during which a brief but sufficient amount of time is allowed for liquidation of assets, a final accounting, and the closing of the business's books. Unless dissolution is invoked by a judicial decree, which will state who will be in charge of the winding-up process, the general partner(s) ordinarily take on the task unless, where no general partner is left, the limited partners may jointly conduct the winding-up process. Your state will very likely require a form to be filed with the appropriate authority.

Sometimes state law specifies the order in which liquidation proceeds are distributed, but many states also allow the partnership agreement to control such distribution if the agreement specifies reasonable provisions. A common pattern is first to pay all creditors, other than partners who may have made loans to the business whose debts are to be paid. Those partner debts get paid second. Finally, if money is left, profit and loss is computed for the taxable year during which liquidation is taking place. Distributions are then made according to each partner's capital account balance (providing the balance is positive). Usually all distributions must be made by the end of the taxable year in question or within a period specified by law (often, ninety days after the date set for liquidation).

But what if there's a deficit? Generally, if, after the calculations described above, there is a deficit in a general partner's capital account, that general partner will have until the end of the applicable distribution period to furnish sufficient funds to eliminate that deficit from the books before they are closed. Limited partners may be protected from restoring funds to eliminate any deficit in their account because the idea itself is counter to the fundamental principle that limited partners are protected from the business's liabilities. This needs to be provided for specifically in the partnership agreement with provisions for loss limitations and offsets for qualified income with respect to limited partners.

Limited Liability Company

Limited liability companies are also subject to rules covering dissolution specific to this type of entity. As discussed earlier in this book, the statutory provisions for LLCs vary widely from one state to another and, because the LLC remains a fairly new phenomenon, not a great deal of guidance can be found in case law supporting the fine points involved. Thus, you'll need to be very careful about determining what rules apply in the state where you form the LLC. Here are some frequently specified provisions (but, again, you'll need to check your own state's requirements and guidelines for LLCs):

• Dissolution requires advance approval by a vote for dissolution passed by at least a majority percentage of membership interests (sometimes a larger percentage is specified in the articles of organization or operating agreement).

• There are limitations on a member's ability to have his capital contribution returned upon termination or withdrawal (often a unanimous vote of members is required to allow lower values to be set for a membership interest differing from capital contributions of other members), and even where allowed under an operating agreement, liability for capital contributions existing at the time when a debt is undertaken may allow for continued rights of a creditor even after membership ceases with respect to that part of the capital contribution. Also, unless allowable with a specific provision in the operating agreement, members usually cannot withdraw capital contributions before the process of dissolution and winding up has been completed.

- Note that corporate members may endure dissolution and winding up of their own entities, in which case such an event in some states may cause the LLC to dissolve as well, unless the remaining members purchase the interest and have an agreement to continue the LLC (again, at least a majority of membership interests are required to do so).

- Much like limited partnerships, LLCs often have similar triggering events for dissolution: a specific date upon which the LLC is to end; sale of the LLC's assets; judicial decrees; or a vote for dissolution by at least a majority percentage of membership interests (sometimes a majority of members or a unanimous vote by all eligible voting members). Also, the death, dissolution, withdrawal, or any other event that renders a member's position untenable may require dissolution (with similar requirements of votes to continue operating, and with similar requirements to provide for the company's future as discussed above with respect to limited partnerships).

- The winding-up process is conducted by the managing member or, if the managing member is in default or has left the LLC, then by the remaining members. The LLC can't do any other business at that point other than address itself to matters directly related to winding up. Almost always, notice of the dissolution must be given to all of the LLC's creditors and others with a legal interest at stake (such as a plaintiff with a judgment against the LLC) as well.

- The order of payment, included—and sometimes modifiable—in the articles of organization or operating agreement, begins with payment to all creditors of the LLC; next, the costs involved in the liquidation process (including reasonable compensation fees for those undertaking the job of winding up); then a reserve account if there are any other expected needs (a potential debt that may become due or a lawsuit that has yet to reach a judgment); repayment of any loans to the LLC made by its own members; and finally, distribution of remaining funds to members (as with limited partnerships, similarly calculated according to positive account balances). Again, a judicially decreed dissolution will usually set forth the details of the process within the declaratory documents.

- Deficits are not normally subject to further contributions by members, although, if provided for in the articles or operating agreement, a member whose capital contribution was not received or was insufficient may be reachable to the amount still owing by the other members. Usually this is provided for prior to dissolution, but if properly documented as ongoing, it may be possible to reach the member after the dissolution. Nearly all LLCs give no remedy by members versus other members if insufficient funds are available at the point where member distributions would occur. Only the company's own assets are at stake unless, where applicable, an agreement to the contrary allows members to look to others for reimbursement or even indemnification or contribution of that member's liabilities.

Corporation

For a corporation, dissolution requires the approval of the board of directors and the shareholders. In most jurisdictions, when the approvals are obtained, the corporation (and in some states, LLCs and LPs too) must file with the state certifying the dissolution has been approved along with a list of the directors who will wind up the affairs.

The directors then collect monies owed, sell real and personal property, and generally settle the corporate accounts. After paying expenses, costs, and all general and special liens, the directors pay any other debts due. If not enough money is available, the debtors receive a pro rata distribution. If any funds remain after the payment of debts and expenses, the shareholders are then paid according to their priority. Recall that preferred shareholders may have a liquidation preference over common shareholders.

It is important to be cautious in this process. If the directors distribute money to a shareholder without properly paying a creditor they may be held personally liable.

In some states a holder of a specified percentage of the issued stock (in Nevada, for example, it is 10 percent) may apply to the local court for an order dissolving the corporation and appointing a receiver to wind up its affairs. This is known as involuntary dissolution, and if you are hit with it you are going to need an attorney. Note that you, as an officer, director, or shareholder, cannot legally represent the corporation in pro per (without a lawyer) as an individual. A corporation, as a separate legal entity, can only be represented in court by an attorney.

The circumstances by which a court will appoint a receiver include:

- Willful violation of the corporate charter;
- Corporate insolvency or inability to pay debts;
- Abandonment of the business;
- Fraud or mismanagement by the directors; or
- Corporate assets in danger of loss or waste.

A receiver is an independent third party, like a bankruptcy trustee, who will take over the affairs of the company, investigate any claims, and report back to the court. A receivership should be avoided at all costs because (1) you lose control of your company; (2) receivers (and the lawyers they get to hire) can be very expensive; and (3) receivers are not always 100 percent objective. There is a good chance that all parties involved will be upset with how things turn out in a receivership. You are better advised to try and work things out.

But Why Dissolve?

A final point on dissolution. As mentioned, the directors (or trustees in some states) charged with winding up the affairs of a dissolved corporation can be held personally liable for a failure to pay creditors. In some cases, the directors were unaware of the creditor claims, paid the remaining corporate monies to the shareholders, and several years later were held personally liable to the unknown creditors. Likewise, once dissolved, a lawsuit against the corporation may instead by brought personally against the directors.

You need to carefully review whether you want to be in that position.

An option to consider: Do not dissolve the company. If there are claims lurking out there, and no great monies to distribute to the shareholders anyway, keep the corporation intact. In Nevada for example, to keep the corporation alive is only $85 a year to the state and a little more for a resident agent and annual tax return. Keep your shield up for several years until the statute of limitations for bringing claims has run out. And even then, do not file dissolution papers with your secretary of state but rather just stop paying the annual renewal fees. In most states your charter will be revoked, but you can pay extra fees and reinstate it for two or three years after revocation, buying you even more time and protection.

It is hard to understand why some people are in such a rush to dissolve their entities. They were formed to limit liability and provide asset protection. If they have done any kind of business at all, they need to be left on the corporate rolls for as long as possible to carry out the objectives of their formation.

Chapter 14

Some Miscellaneous Traps and Thoughts

You have learned quite a bit reading this book. You now know how informed businesspeople and investors use good entities to shield their assets and protect their business.

Before we close there are three additional tax traps to review. They serve as a closing reminder that what the IRS sees as too beneficial to the taxpayer it will attempt to rule out.

Personal Service Company

A personal service company is defined as any company where substantially all of the activities involve the performance of services in the fields of health, law, engineering, architecture, accounting, actuarial science, performing arts, or consulting. Further, a personal service company is a corporation whereby personal services are substantially performed by employee-owners. An employee-owner is any employee who owns more than 10 percent of the outstanding stock of the corporation.

The corporate tax rate for a personal service company is a flat 35 percent, without a graduation of tax rates as in a regular corporation. The purpose is to prevent people who perform personal services from claiming lower corporate tax rates than they would ordinarily have to pay as an individual.

Personal Holding Company

A corporation is a personal holding company when (1) at any time during the last half of the tax year more than 50 percent in value of its outstanding stock is owned, directly or indirectly, by or for not more than five individuals, and (2) at least 60 percent of adjusted ordinary gross income for the tax year is personal holding company income. Personal holding company income consists of passive types of income: interest, dividends, royalties, and rents. The kind of income we all like to have because you do not have to work every day to earn it.

There are extremely complicated rules associated with personal holding company income. So see your accountant. What you need to know here is that if you do not distribute the income from a personal holding company to yourself, the corporation can be assessed with a 39.6 percent tax on top of its normal tax rate. Again, the purpose is to ensure that taxes are paid on this income as if the individual had to pay it at individual rates.

Accumulated Earnings

Accumulated earnings are past profits, the previously taxed income reduced by any capital gain, within a C corporation. They are the retained earnings held by the corporation without any capital gains reflected and the monies that the company needs for the future to operate and expand its business.

The problem is that the IRS likes to see those profits distributed to shareholders, where they can tax it again. They do not want you using it for such mundane and prudent needs as working capital or retaining it as a reserve in case of an economic downturn. As so every C corporation with accumulated earnings greater than $250,000 (or $150,000 for personal service companies) is at risk of being taxed an additional 39.6 percent on top of regular corporate tax rates.

As one would suspect, this is a greatly litigated issue. Courts have generally supported business owners who claim that retained earnings are needed for future expansion, additional inventory, and other legitimate business needs. But beware of this provision. If it becomes an issue for you, consult your tax professional. As with all the advice you have received in this book, be sure to review it with professionals competent to give you the advice you need to succeed.

While there are a number of traps out there for the unsuspecting, like the ones above, they should not deter you from your business and asset protection objectives. As we have discussed throughout the book, with a team of professional advisors assisting you, all of the various traps (and there aren't that many) are easily avoided.

In selecting and building a group of advisors be sure to work with people you like and trust. You are going to want your attorney, accountant, graphic designer, engineers, consultants, and other professionals you bring in to be team players. There should be no room for individuals who are egocentric, abrasive, negative, or nonresponsive. Your team members should be able to work with you and the other team members to achieve a common goal— protecting and advancing your business interests. This is not that much to ask, especially since you are paying these people.

To that end, consider interviewing for your professional team. Meet with several accountants, attorneys, and other service providers to get a feel for them and their practice. Ask specific questions such as how much their fees are and what their level of experience is in certain areas. Be a comparison shopper. For example, our firm charges $695 plus state filing fees for a complete corporate (or LLC and LP) package, including articles of incorporation, bylaws, minutes of shareholder and directors meetings, and issuance of stock. Any attorney who charges $1,000 or more (and some charge $2,000 to $5,000) for this service may not be the right person for you.

And, like any coach or manager, feel free to replace members of your team if they are not performing for you. If, for example, your accountant won't return your phone calls for weeks at a time you may want to start looking for someone who's more responsive.

By building and cultivating a team of professionals that care about you and your business, you will be able both to concentrate on your core goals and succeed in the future.

Of course, your advisory team can only take you so far. The true source of your success is going to come from within you. The choices and decisions you make, the means by which you approach your business, and the ways in which you deal with people and situations will all be determinative factors in your achievement. The balance you strike between the obligations of work, family, and community will also be important.

Please also remember to focus on working smarter, not harder. As Richard

Kiyosaki's rich dad taught him, by using the same strategies the rich use to your advantage you too can become wealthy.

All the strategies discussed herein—the use of corporations, LLCs, and LPs, the strategic utilization of Nevada entities, and maximizing the use of the tax code to your advantage—can be implemented easily and without great expense. They are all present to help you achieve your greatest dreams and goals.

Good luck.

Appendix
Summary of State Corporation
Formation Requirements

Following, you will find a brief synopsis of the formation requirements for corporations in each of the fifty states. While we have provided the requirements as they appear on the statutes of each state, it is your responsibility to review the statutes, consult with legal and tax counsel, and comply with the laws of whichever state you decide to enter into business in.

Alabama

State Corporation Statute: Al. Code §§ 10-2B-1.01 through 10-2B-17.03.

Formation: Before filing its articles of incorporation, a domestic for-profit corporation may reserve a name with the secretary of state's office. Articles of incorporation must include the following:

• The name of the corporation, which must include the word "corporation" or "incorporated" or an abbreviation of one of those words ("Inc." or "Corp.") The name may not contain language stating or implying that the corporation is organized for a purpose other than that permitted by its articles of incorporation. Except as provided below, a corporate name shall not be the same as, or deceptively similar to: (1) the corporate name of a corporation incorporated or authorized to transact business in Alabama; (2) a reserved or registered corporate name; or (3) the fictitious name adopted by a foreign corporation authorized to transact business in Alabama because its real name is unavailable. A corporation may apply to the secretary of state for authorization to use a name that is the same as, or deceptively similar to a name described above. The secretary of state shall authorize use of the name applied for if: (1) the other corporation consents to the use in writing and submits an undertaking in form satisfactory to the secretary of state to change its name to a name that is not the same as or deceptively similar to the name of the applying corporation; or (2) the applicant delivers to the secretary of state a certified copy of the final judgment of a court of competent jurisdiction establishing the applicant's right to use the name applied for in Alabama. A corporation may use the name (including the fictitious name) of another domestic or foreign corporation that is used in Alabama if the other corporation is incorporated or authorized to transact business in Alabama and the proposed user corporation: (1) has merged with the other corporation; (2) has been formed by reorganization of the other corporation; or (3) has acquired all or substantially all of the assets, including the corporate name, of the other corporation.

- The duration or life of the corporation, if not perpetual;
- The purpose of organizing the corporation;
- The number of authorized shares the corporation may issue;
- The name of registered agent and address of resident office;
- The names and addresses of directors of the corporation; and
- The names and addresses of incorporators of the corporation.

You must file the original and two copies of the articles of incorporation and the certificate of name reservation in the county where the corporation's registered office is located.

A probate judge will collect and assess the secretary of state filing fee. As of January 2001, the secretary of state's filing fee was $50.00 and the minimum probate judge fee was $35.00. The filing of the articles of incorporation by the probate judge signifies the acceptance of the articles and the existence of the corporation begins immediately upon the filing thereof.

Upon creation, the corporation may have a meeting of its board of directors to elect officers, adopt bylaws (which may contain any provision consistent with law and the articles of incorporation), and carry on any other business of the corporation. This meeting may be held inside or outside of Alabama.

Minimum Number of Incorporators: One.

Management Requirements: Directors must approve bylaws for the corporation, directors must be natural persons of at least 19 years of age, and there must be at least one director of the corporation.

State Tax Classification: Corporations are charged a state franchise tax and tax on corporate shares of stock. Business privilege tax assessed at $.25 per $1,000. Corporate income tax is assessed at the rate of 6.5%.

Contact Information: Corporations Division
Office of the Secretary of State
P.O. Box 5616
Montgomery, Alabama 36103-5616
Phone: (334) 242-5324
Facsimile: (334) 240-3138
http://www.sos.state.al.us/business/
corporations.cfm

Alaska

State Corporation Statute: Ak. Code §§ 10.06.005 through 10.06.990.

Formation: Before filing its articles of incorporation, a domestic for-profit corporation must reserve a name with the secretary of state's office. Articles of incorporation must include the following:

• The name of the corporation, which must contain the words "Corporation," "Company," "Incorporated," "Limited," or an abbreviation of these words, but which cannot contain the words "city," "borough," or "village," or otherwise imply that the corporation is a municipality. The name of a city, borough, or village may be used in the corporate name;

• The purpose for which the corporation is being organized, which may be stated as any lawful business allowed by the Alaska Corporation Code and/or a more specific purpose. In addition, the Standard Industrial Classification Code(s) (SIC) which most closely describe the business activities of the corporation must be stated (see SIC code list);

• If the corporation is authorized to issue only one class of shares, the total number of shares that the corporation is authorized to issue must be stated;

• If the corporation is authorized to issue more than one class of shares or if a class of shares is to have two or more series, a statement reflecting one or more of the following conditions must be included: (1) the total number of shares of each class the corporation is authorized to issue, and the total number of shares of each series that the corporation is authorized to issue, or a statement that the board is authorized to fix the number of shares; (2) the designation of each class, and the designation of each series or a statement that the board may determine the designation of any series; (3) the rights, preferences, privileges, and restrictions granted to or imposed on the respective classes or series of shares or the holders of the shares, or that the board, within any limits and restrictions stated, may determine or alter the rights, prefer-ences, privileges, and restrictions granted to or imposed on a wholly unissued class of shares or a wholly unissued series of any class of shares; and (4) if the number of shares of a series is authorized to be fixed by the board, the articles of incorporation may also authorize the board to increase or decrease, but not below the number of shares of the series then outstanding, the number of shares of a series after the issue of shares of that series;

• The physical address of its initial registered office and the name of its initial registered agent (a mailing address must also be given if different from the physical address);

• The name and address of each alien affiliate or a statement that there are no alien affiliates (alien means any person who is not a U.S. citizen or na-tional of the U.S., or who is not lawfully admitted to the U.S. for permanent residence).

You must sign, verify (by notary public) and deliver to the division an original and an exact copy of the articles of incorporation together with a check or money order payable to the State of Alaska in the amount of $250.00. The articles should contain a statement that they are being filed un-der the provisions of the Alaska Corporations Code.

The existence of the corporation begins upon the issuance of a certifi-cate of incorporation. Upon creation, the corporation must have a meeting of its board of directors to elect officers, adopt bylaws (which may contain any provision consistent with law and the articles of incorporation), and car-rying on any other business of the corporation. This meeting may be held in-side or outside of Alaska.

Minimum Number of Incorporators: One natural person, at least 18 years of age.

Management Requirements: Directors must approve bylaws for the cor-poration, directors must be at least 18 years of age, and there must be at least one director of the corporation. If, at the initial organizational meeting of the corporation, more than 16⅔% of the then-current directors or incorpora-tors refuse to adopt a motion to set the number of directors at less than five directors, there may not be fewer than five directors of the corporation.

State Tax Classification: Alaska corporations are charged a state income tax, at a variable rate, and a biennial corporation fee of $100.00.

Contact Information: The Division of Banking, Securities and
Corporations
Department of Community and Economic
Development
P.O. Box 110808
Juneau, AK 99801-0808
Phone: (907) 465-2521
Facsimile: (907) 465-2549
http://www.dced.state.ak.us/bsc/
corpdoc.htm

Arizona

State Corporation Statute: Az. Code §§ 10.120 through 10.2742.

Formation: Before filing its articles of incorporation, a domestic for-profit corporation may reserve a name with the secretary of state's office. Application and filing fees are associated with the reservation of a name. When filing its articles, you must include a cover sheet, a trade name certificate, or declaration of trade name assignee, or declaration of holder of trade name, and a certificate of disclosure. The articles of incorporation must include the following:

• The proposed name of the corporation, which must include the word "association," "bank," "company," "corporation," "limited," or "incorporated," but which shall not include the word "bank," "trust," "deposit," or "trust company" unless the corporation is or intends to become substantially involved in the banking or trust business;

• The initial business or affairs of the corporation;

• The fiscal year end date of the corporation;

• The number of shares of stock the corporation will be authorized to issue, series, class and preference, if any;

• The street address of the known place of business in Arizona. May be in care of the address of the statutory agent (if agent, cannot be a P.O. Box.);

• The name and address of the statutory agent (cannot be a P.O. Box.);

• The name(s) and address(es) of the initial board of directors (minimum of one);

• The name(s) and address(es) of the incorporators (minimum of one);

• The signatures of all incorporators; and

• The signature of statutory agent (acknowledge acceptance).

You must file a cover sheet, one or more exact copy of the articles of incorporation, a trade name certificate, or declaration of trade name assignee, or declaration of holder of trade name, and a certificate of disclosure with the Arizona corporations commission. Such filings must be accompanied by a filing fee of $60.00

Within sixty (60) days after filing with the commission, there must be published in a newspaper of general circulation in the county of the known place of business in Arizona, three (3) consecutive publications of a copy of the approved articles of incorporation or application for authority. Within 90 days after filing, an affidavit evidencing the publication must be filed with the commission.

The existence of the corporation begins upon the filing of the articles and related documents. Upon creation, the corporation must have a meeting of its board of directors to elect officers, adopt bylaws (which may contain any provision consistent with law and the articles of incorporation), and carry on any other business of the corporation. This meeting may be held inside or outside of Arizona.

Minimum Number of Incorporators: One.

Management Requirements: Directors must approve bylaws for the corporation, directors must be at least 18 years of age, and there must be at least one director of the corporation.

State Tax Classification: Corporations are charged state income tax at the rate of 6.968%, and a transaction privilege tax at 5%.

Contact Information: Arizona Corporation Commission
Corporations Division
1300 West Washington
Phoenix, AZ 85007-2996
Phone: (602) 542-3026
http://www.cc.state.az.us/

Arkansas

State Corporation Statute: Ar. Code §§ 10-2B-1.01 through 10-2B-17.03.

Formation: Before filing its articles of incorporation, a domestic for-profit corporation may reserve a name with the secretary of state's office. Articles of incorporation must include the following:

- Name of the corporation, which must include the word "Corporation" or "Incorporated" or an abbreviation of one of these words ("Inc." or "Corp."). The name must not be the same as or confusingly similar to the name of any domestic corporation or foreign corporation authorized to transact business in Arkansas;
- Duration or life of the corporation, if not perpetual;
- Purpose of organizing the corporation;
- Number of authorized shares the corporation may issue, classes and par value;
- Name of registered agent and address of resident office;
- Names, addresses, and number of directors of the corporation;
- Names and addresses of incorporators of the corporation;

You must file the original and two copies of the articles of incorporation with the secretary of state. As of January 2001, the secretary of state's filing fee was $50.00.

The existence of the corporation begins immediately upon the filing of the articles of incorporation. Upon creation, the corporation may have a meeting of its board of directors to elect officers, adopt bylaws (which may contain any provision consistent with law and the articles of incorporation), and carry on any other business of the corporation. This meeting may be held inside or outside of Arkansas.

Minimum Number of Incorporators: One.

Management Requirements: Directors must approve bylaws for the corporation. Any two or more offices may be held by the same person, except the offices of president and secretary. When only one stockholder, all offices may be held by the same person.

State Tax Classification: Corporations are charged state franchise tax, assessed at the rate of .27% against the corporation's outstanding stock, and a variable corporate income tax.

Contact Information: Secretary of State
256 State Capital Building
Little Rock, AR 72201
Phone: (501) 682-1010
Facsimile: (501) 682-3510
http://www.sosweb.state.ar.us/

California

State Corporation Statute: Ca. Corporations Code §§ 100 through 2319.

Formation: Before filing its articles of incorporation, a domestic for-profit corporation may reserve a name with the secretary of state's office. Articles of incorporation must include the following:

• The name of the corporation; provided, however, that in order for the corporation to be subject to the provisions of this division applicable to a close corporation, the name of the corporation must contain the word "corporation," "incorporated," or "limited," or an abbreviation of one of such words. The name shall not include the word "bank," " trust," "trustee," or related words, unless a certificate of approval of the Commissioner of Financial Institutions is attached to the articles of incorporation. The name shall also not be likely to mislead the public or be the same as, or resemble so closely as to tend to deceive, the name of a domestic corporation, the name of a foreign corporation which is authorized to transact intrastate business or has registered its name, a name which a foreign corporation, a name which will become the record name of a domestic or foreign corporation upon the effective date of a filed corporate instrument where there is a delayed effective date, or a name which is under reservation for another corporation, except that a corporation may adopt a name that is substantially the same as an existing domestic corporation or foreign corporation which is authorized to transact intrastate business or has registered its name, upon proof of consent by such domestic or foreign corporation and a finding by the secretary of state that under the circumstances the public is not likely to be misled.

• The applicable one of the following statements: (1) the purpose of the corporation is to engage in any lawful act or activity for which a corporation may be organized under the General Corporation Law of California other than the banking business, the trust company business or the practice of a profession permitted to be incorporated by the California Corporations Code; or (2) the purpose of the corporation is to engage in the profession of (with the insertion of a profession permitted to be incorporated by the California Corporations Code) and any other lawful activities (other than the banking or trust company business) not prohibited to a corporation engaging in such profession by applicable laws and regulations.

- In case the corporation is a corporation subject to the Banking Law, the articles shall set forth a statement of purpose which is prescribed in the applicable provision of the Banking Law;
- In case the corporation is a corporation subject to the Insurance Code as an insurer, the articles shall additionally state that the business of the corporation is to be an insurer;
- If the corporation is intended to be a "professional corporation," the articles shall additionally contain the statement required by Section 13404 of the California Corporations Code;
- The articles shall not set forth any further or additional statement with respect to the purposes or powers of the corporation, except by way of limitation or except as expressly required by any law of California or any federal or other statute or regulation (including the Internal Revenue Code and regulations thereunder as a condition of acquiring or maintaining a particular status for tax purposes);
- The name and address in California of the corporation's initial agent for service of process;
- If the corporation is authorized to issue only one class of shares, the total number of shares which the corporation is authorized to issue;
- If the corporation is authorized to issue more than one class of shares, or if any class of shares is to have two or more series: (1) the total number of shares of each class the corporation is authorized to issue, and the total number of shares of each series which the corporation is authorized to issue or that the board is authorized to fix the number of shares of any such series; (2) the designation of each class, and the designation of each series or that the board may determine the designation of any such series; and (3) the rights, preferences, privileges and restrictions granted to or imposed upon the respective classes or series of shares or the holders thereof, or that the board, within any limits and restrictions stated, may determine or alter the rights, preferences, privileges and restrictions granted to or imposed upon any wholly unissued class of shares or any wholly unissued series of any class of shares. As to any series the number of shares of which is authorized to be fixed by the board, the articles may also authorize the board, within the limits and restrictions stated therein or stated in any resolution or resolutions of the board originally fixing the number of shares constituting any series, to increase or decrease (but not

below the number of shares of such series then outstanding) the number
of shares of any such series subsequent to the issue of shares of that series.
In case the number of shares of any series shall be so decreased, the shares
constituting such decrease shall resume the status which they had prior to
the adoption of the resolution originally fixing the number of shares of
such series.

You must file the original and two copies of the articles of incorporation
with the secretary of state. As of January 2001, the secretary of state's filing
fee was $100.00.

The corporate existence begins upon the filing of the articles of incorporation in the office of the secretary of state. Upon creation, the corporation
may have a meeting of its board of directors to elect officers, adopt bylaws
(which may contain any provision consistent with law and the articles of incorporation), and carry on any other business of the corporation. This meeting may be held inside or outside of California.

Minimum Number of Incorporators: One or more natural persons,
partnerships, associations or corporations, domestic or foreign.

Management Requirements: Except for close corporations, the number
or minimum number of directors shall not be less than three; provided,
however, that (1) before shares are issued, the number may be one, (2) before shares are issued, the number may be two, (3) so long as the corporation has only one shareholder, the number may be one, (4) so long as the
corporation has only one shareholder, the number may be two, and (5) so
long as the corporation has only two shareholders, the number may be two.
Directors may approve bylaws for the corporation, establishing the number
of directors and other rules governing the corporation.

State Tax Classification: The state charges a minimum annual franchise
tax of $800.00, assessed at the rate of 8.84% of net income. The State also as-
sesses sales and use taxes, each at the rate of 5.75%.

Contact Information: Business Programs Division
                                  1500 11th Street
                                  Sacramento, CA 95814
                                  Phone: (916) 653-2318
                                  http://www.ss.ca.gov/business/corp/
                                  corporate.htm

Colorado

State Corporation Statute: CRS §§ 7-101-100 through 7-117.105.

Formation: Before filing its articles of incorporation, a domestic for-profit corporation may reserve a name with the secretary of state's office. Articles of incorporation must include the following:

- Name of the corporation, which contain the term "corporation," "incorporated," "company," or "limited," or an abbreviation of such words. The name must not contain any term the inclusion of which would violate any statute of Colorado. The name must be distinguishable on the records of the secretary of state from every: (1) other entity name; (2) name that is reserved with the secretary of state under the laws of Colorado for another entity; (3) trade name that is registered with the secretary of state by another entity; and (4) trademark registered with the secretary of state by another entity. An entity name need not be in English if written in English letters or Arabic or Roman numerals.

- The classes of shares and the number of shares of each class that the corporation is authorized to issue. If more than one class of shares is authorized, the articles of incorporation shall prescribe a distinguishing designation for each class, and, before the issuance of shares of any class, the preferences, limitations, and relative rights of that class shall be described in the articles of incorporation. All shares of a class shall have preferences, limitations, and relative rights identical with those of other shares of the same class except to the extent otherwise permitted by section 7-106-102 of the Revised Colorado Statutes.

- The articles of incorporation shall authorize: (1) one or more classes of shares that together have unlimited voting rights; and (2) one or more classes of shares, which may be the same class or classes as those with voting rights, that together are entitled to receive the net assets of the corporation upon dissolution;

- The street address of the corporation's initial registered office and the name of its initial registered agent at that office;

- The address of the corporation's initial principal office;

- The name and address of each incorporator; and

- The written consent of the initial registered agent to the appointment unless such consent is provided in an accompanying document.

You must file the articles of incorporation with the secretary of state. As of January 2000, the secretary of state's filing fee was $50.00. The existence of the corporation begins immediately upon the filing of the articles of incorporation by the secretary of state.

Upon creation, the corporation may have a meeting of its board of directors (or incorporators if board members have not yet been selected) to elect officers, adopt bylaws (which may contain any provision consistent with law and the articles of incorporation), and carry on any other business of the corporation. This meeting may be held inside or outside of Colorado.

Minimum Number of Incorporators: One or more natural persons of at least 18 years of age.

Management Requirements: Directors must approve bylaws for the corporation at the corporation's initial meeting. Any officers of the corporation must be at least one director. Any officers of the corporation must be at least 18 years of age.

State Tax Classification: The State assesses corporate income tax at the rate of 4.63%, charges a fee of $25.00 for a domestic biennial report, and a 2.9% sales and use tax.

Contact Information: Department of State
Business Services
1560 Broadway, Suite 200
Denver, CO 80202
Phone: (303) 894-2251
E-mail: sos.business@state.co.us
http://www.sos.state.co.us/pubs/
business/main.htm

Connecticut

State Corporation Statute: Conn. General Statutes §§ 33-600 through 33-999.

Formation: Before filing its certificate of incorporation, a domestic for-profit corporation may reserve a name with the secretary of state's office. A certificate of incorporation must include the following:

• The name of the corporation, which must contain one of the following designations: "corporation," "incorporated," "company," "Societa per Azioni," or "limited," or the abbreviation "corp.," "inc.," "co.," "S.p.A.," or "ltd.," or words or abbreviations of like import in another language. The name must not contain language stating or implying that the corporation is organized for a purpose other than that permitted by law and its certificate of incorporation. Except as provided below, a corporate name must be distinguishable upon the records of the secretary of the state from: (1) the corporate name of a corporation incorporated or authorized to transact business in Connecticut; (2) a reserved or registered corporate name; (3) the fictitious name adopted by a foreign corporation authorized to transact business in Connecticut; (4) the corporate name of a nonprofit corporation incorporated or authorized to transact business in Connecticut because its real name is unavailable; (5) the corporate name of any domestic or foreign nonstock corporation incorporated or authorized to transact business in Connecticut; (6) the name of any domestic or foreign limited partnership organized or authorized to transact business in Connecticut; (7) the name of any domestic or foreign limited liability company organized or authorized to transact business in Connecticut; and (8) the name of any domestic or foreign limited liability partnership organized or authorized to transact business in Connecticut. A corporation may apply to the secretary of state for authorization to use a name that is not distinguishable upon his records from one or more of the names described above. The secretary of state may authorize the use of the name applied for if: (1) the other corporation, limited partnership, limited liability company, or limited liability partnership, as the case may be, consents to the use in writing and submits an undertaking in a form satisfactory to the secretary of state to change its name to a name that is distinguishable upon the records of the secretary of state from the name of the applying corporation; or (2) the applicant delivers to the secretary of state a certified copy of the final judgment of a court of competent jurisdiction establishing the applicant's right to use the name applied for in Connecticut. A corporation may use the name, including the fictitious name, of another domestic or foreign corporation that is used in Connecticut if the other corporation is incorporated or authorized to transact business in Connecticut and the corporation seeking to use the name: (1) has merged with the other corporation; (2) has been formed by reorganization of the other corporation; or (3) has acquired all or substantially all of the assets, including the corporate name, of the other corporation.

- The number of shares the corporation is authorized to issue;

- The classes of shares and the number of shares of each class that the corporation is authorized to issue. If more than one class of shares is authorized, the certificate of incorporation must prescribe a distinguishing designation for each class, and, prior to the issuance of shares of a class, the preferences, limitations and relative rights of that class must be described in the certificate of incorporation. All shares of a class shall have preferences, limitations and relative rights identical with those other shares of the same class.

- The certificate of incorporation shall authorized (1) one or more classes of shares that together have unlimited voting rights, and (2) one or more classes of shares, which may be the same class or classes as those with voting rights, that together are entitled to receive the net assets of the corporation upon dissolution;

- The street address of the corporation's initial registered office and the name of its initial registered agent at that office; and

- The name and address of each incorporator.

You must file the certificate of incorporation with the secretary of state. As of January 2001, the secretary of state's filing fee was $50.00.

Upon creation, the corporation must have a meeting of its board of directors to elect officers, adopt bylaws (which may contain any provision consistent with law and the certificate of incorporation), and carry on any other business of the corporation. This meeting may be held inside or outside of Connecticut.

Minimum Number of Incorporators: One individual or entity.

Management Requirements: Directors must approve bylaws for the corporation. Directors must be at least 18 years of age, and there must be at least one director of the corporation.

State Tax Classification: The State assesses a 7.5% corporate business tax, charges a fee of $75.00 for biennial reports, and assesses both sales and use taxes at 6%.

Contact Information: Secretary of the State's Office
210 Capitol Ave., Suite 104
Hartford, CT 06106
Phone: (860) 509-6001
E-mail: crd@po.state.ct.us
http://www.sots.state.ct.us/

Delaware

State Corporation Statute: De. Gen. Code §§ 8-1-101 through 8-1-398.

Formation: Before filing its certificate of incorporation, a domestic for-profit corporation must reserve a name with the department of state's office. The certificate of incorporation must include the following:

- The name of the corporation, which: (1) shall contain 1 of the words "association," "company," "corporation," "club," "foundation," "fund," "incorporated," "institute," "society," "union," "syndicate," or "limited," (or abbreviations thereof, with or without punctuation), or words (or abbreviations thereof, with or without puncuation) if like import of foreign countries or jurisdictions; provided, however that the division of corporations in the department of state may waive such requirement if such corporation executes, acknowledges and files with the department of state a certificate stating that its total assets are not less than $10,000,000; (2) shall be such as to distinguish it upon the records in the office of the division of corporations in the department of state from the names of other corporations or limited partnerships organized, reserved or registered as a foreign corporation or foreign limited partnership under the laws of Delaware, except with the written consent of such other foreign corporation or domestic or foreign limited partnership, executed, acknowledged and filed with the department of state; and, (3) shall not contain the word "bank," or any variation thereof, except for the name of a bank reporting to and under the supervision of the State Bank Commissioner or a subsidiary of a bank or savings association, or a corporation regulated under the Bank Holding Company Act of 1956, as amended, or the Home Owners' Loan Act, as amended; provided, however, this shall not be construed to prevent the use of the word "bank," or any variation thereof, in a context clearly not purporting to refer to a banking business or otherwise likely to mislead the public about the nature of the business of the corporation or to lead to a pattern and practice of abuse that might cause harm to the interests of the public or Delaware as determined by the division of corporations in the department of state;

- The address (which shall include the street, number, city and county) of the corporation's registered office in Delaware, and the name of its registered agent at such address;

- The nature of the business or purposes to be conducted or promoted. It shall be sufficient to state, either alone or with other businesses or purposes, that the purpose of the corporation is to engage in any lawful act or activity for which corporations may be organized under the General Corporation Law of Delaware, and by such statement all lawful acts and activities shall be within the purposes of the corporation, except for express limitations, if any;

- If the corporation is to be authorized to issue only 1 class of stock, the total number of shares of stock which the corporation shall have authority to issue and the par value of each of such shares, or a statement that all such shares are to be without par value. If the corporation is to be authorized to issue more than 1 class of stock, the certificate of incorporation shall set forth the total number of shares of all classes of stock which the corporation shall have authority to issue and the number of shares of each class and shall specify each class the shares of which are to be without par value and each class the shares of which are to have par value and the par value of the shares of each such class. The certificate of incorporation shall also set forth a statement of the designations and the powers, preferences and rights, and the qualifications, limitations or restrictions thereof, which are permitted in respect of any class or classes of stock or any series of any class of stock of the corporation and the fixing of which by the certificate of incorporation is desired, and an express grant of such authority as it may then be desired to grant to the board of directors to fix by resolution or resolutions any thereof that may be desired but which shall not be fixed by the certificate of incorporation. The foregoing provisions do not apply to corporations which are not to have authority to issue capital stock. In the case of such corporations, the fact that they are not to have authority to issue capital stock shall be stated in the certificate of incorporation. The conditions of membership of such corporations shall likewise be stated in the certificate of incorporation or the certificate may provide that the conditions of membership shall be stated in the bylaws;

- The name and mailing address of the incorporator or incorporators;

- If the powers of the incorporator or incorporators are to terminate upon the filing of the certificate of incorporation, the names and mailing addresses of the persons who are to serve as directors until the first annual meeting of stockholders or until their successors are elected and qualify.

You must file a certificate of incorporation with the division of corporations in the department of state. As of January 2001, the filing fee was $50.00, with additional charges of $20.00 for each requested certified copy of the certificate, $15.00 to record the certificate with a county recorder, and an additional $9.00 for the second and subsequent pages recorded.

The existence of the corporation begins upon the filing of the certificate of incorporation with the division of corporations. Upon creation, the corporation may have a meeting of its board of directors to elect officers, adopt bylaws (which may contain any provision consistent with law and the certificate of incorporation), and carry on any other business of the corporation. This meeting may be held inside or outside of Delaware.

Minimum Number of Incorporators: Any person, partnership, association or corporation, singly or jointly with others, and without regard to such person's or entity's residence, domicile or state of incorporation, may incorporate or organize a corporation.

Management Requirements: Directors or original incorporators, depending upon the terms of the certificate of incorporation, may approve bylaws for the corporation. There must be at least one director on the corporation's board of directors.

State Tax Classification: The State assesses a variable franchise tax and a state corporation income tax at 8.7%.

Contact Information: State of Delaware
Division of Corporations
401 Federal Street, Suite 4
Dover, Delaware 19901
Phone: (302) 739-3073
Facsimile: (302) 739-3812
http://www.state.de.us/corp/index.htm

Florida

State Corporation Statute: Fl. Code §§ 601.0101 through 607.193.

Formation: Before filing its articles of incorporation, a domestic for-profit corporation may reserve a name with the division of corporations of the secretary of state. The articles of incorporation must include the following:

- The name of the corporation, which must contain the word "corporation," "company," or "incorporated," or the abbreviation "corp.," "Inc.," or "Co.," or words or abbreviations of like import in language, as will clearly indicate that it is a corporation instead of a natural person or partnership. The name may not contain language stating or implying that the corporation is organized for a purpose other than that permitted by statute or its articles of incorporation, and it may not contain language stating or implying that the corporation is connected with a state or federal government agency or a corporation chartered under the laws of the United States. The name must also be distinguishable from the names of all other entities or filings, except fictitious name registrations organized, registered, or reserved under the laws of Florida, which names are on file with the division of corporations.
- The street address of the initial principal office and, if different, the mailing address of the corporation;
- The number of shares the corporation is authorized to issue;
- If any preemptive rights are to be granted to shareholders, the provision therefor;
- The street address of the corporation's initial registered office and the name of its initial registered agent at that office together with a written acceptance; and
- The name and address of each incorporator.

You must file the articles of incorporation with the secretary of state. As of January 2001, the filing fee was $35.00, with an additional resident agent fee of $35.00. Certified copies of the articles cost $8.75 per page.

The existence of the corporation begins upon the filing of the articles of incorporation with the secretary of state. Upon creation, the corporation may have a meeting of its board of directors to elect officers, adopt bylaws (which may contain any provision consistent with law and the articles of incorporation), and carry on any other business of the corporation. This meeting may be held inside or outside of Florida.

Minimum Number of Incorporators: One or more entities or natural persons.

Management Requirements: Directors or original incorporators, depending upon the terms of the certificate of incorporation, may approve bylaws for the corporation. There must be at least one director on the corporation's board of directors.

State Tax Classification: The State assesses a corporate franchise (income) tax at the rate of 5.5%, documentary excise tax at $.35 per $100.00 of transfer, and sales and use tax assessed at 6%.

Contact Information:	Division of Corporations
	P.O. Box 6327
	Tallahassee, FL 32314
	Phone: (850) 488-9000
	http://www.dos.state.fl.us/doc/index.html

Georgia

State Corporation Statute: Ga. Code §§ 14-2-101 through 14-2-1703.

Formation: Before filing its articles of incorporation, a domestic for-profit corporation must reserve a name with the secretary of state's office. The articles of incorporation must include the following:

• The name of the corporation, which must contain the word "corporation," "incorporated," "company," or "limited," or the abbreviation "corp.," "inc.," "co.," or "ltd.," or words or abbreviations of like import in another language. The name may not contain language stating or implying that the corporation is organized for a purpose other than that permitted by law and its articles of incorporation. It may not contain anything which, in the reasonable judgment of the secretary of state, is obscene, and may not in any instance exceed 80 characters, including spaces and punctuation. Except as provided below, a corporate name must be distinguishable upon the records of the secretary of state from: (1) the corporate name of a corporation incorporated or authorized to transact business in Georgia; (2) a reserved or registered corporate name; (3) the fictitious name adopted by a foreign corporation authorized to transact business in Georgia because its real name is unavailable; (4) the corporate name of a nonprofit corporation incorporated or authorized to transact business in Georgia; (5) the name of a limited partnership or professional association filed with the secretary of state; and (6) the name of a limited liability company formed or authorized to transact business in Georgia. A corporation may apply to the secretary of state for authorization to use a name that is not distinguishable upon his records from one or more of the names described above. The secretary of state shall authorize use of the name applied for if the other corporation consents to the use in writing and files with the secretary of state articles of amendment to its articles of incorporation changing its name to a name that is distinguishable upon the records of the secretary of state from the name of the applying corporation. A corporation may use the name (including the fictitious name) of another domestic or foreign corporation that is used in Georgia if the other corporation is incorporated or authorized to transact business in Georgia and: (1) the proposed user corporation has merged with the other corporation; (2) the proposed user corporation has been formed by reorganization of the other corporation; or (3) the other domestic or foreign corporation has taken the steps required by law to change its name to a name that is distinguishable upon the records of the secretary of state from the name of the foreign corporation applying to use its former name.

- The number of shares the corporation is authorized to issue;
- The classes of shares and the number of shares of each class that the corporation is authorized to issue. If more than one class of shares is authorized, the articles of incorporation must prescribe a distinguishing designation for each class and, prior to the issuance of shares of a class, the preferences, limitations, and relative rights of that class must be described in the articles of incorporation.
- The articles of incorporation must authorize: (1) one or more classes of shares that together have unlimited voting rights; and (2) one or more classes of shares (which may be the same class or classes as those with voting rights) that together are entitled to receive the net assets of the corporation upon dissolution.
- The street address and county of the corporation's initial registered office and the name of its initial registered agent at that office;
- The name and address of each incorporator; and
- The mailing address of the initial principal office of the corporation, if different from the initial registered office.

You must file an original and a copy of the articles of incorporation with the secretary of state. As of January 2001, the filing fee was $60.00. You also must publish in a newspaper of general circulation of the county of the corporation's registered agent, once a week for two consecutive weeks, a form which states the name of the corporation, the name of the registered agent, and the address of the registered agent.

The existence of the corporation begins upon the filing of the articles of incorporation with the secretary of state. Upon creation, the corporation may have a meeting of its board of directors to elect officers, adopt bylaws (which may contain any provision consistent with law and the articles of incorporation), and carry on any other business of the corporation. This meeting may be held inside or outside of Georgia.

Minimum Number of Incorporators: Any person, partnership, association or corporation, singly or jointly with others, and without regard to such person's or entity's residence, domicile or state of incorporation, may incorporate or organize a corporation.

Management Requirements: Directors or original incorporators, depending upon the terms of the certificate of incorporation, may approve bylaws for the corporation. There must be at least one director on the corporation's board of directors. Such director must be a natural person of at least 18 years of age.

State Tax Classification: The State assesses a graduated corporate franchise tax, charges $15.00 for corporate annual reports, assesses corporate income tax at the rate of 6%, and collects sales and use taxes at the rate of 4%.

Contact Information: Corporations Division
315 West Tower
2 Martin Luther King, Jr. Drive
Atlanta, Georgia 30334
Phone: (404) 656-2817
Facsimile: (404) 657-2248
http://www.sos.state.ga.us/corporations/

Hawaii

State Corporation Statute: Hi. Code §§ 415-1 through 415-172.

Formation: Before filing its articles of incorporation, a domestic for-profit corporation may reserve a name with the director of the department of commerce and consumer affairs. The articles of incorporation must include the following:

- The name of the corporation, which: (1) shall contain the word "corporation," "incorporated," or "limited," or shall contain an abbreviation of one of the words; and (2) shall not be the same as, or substantially identical to, the name of any domestic corporation, partnership, limited liability company, or limited liability partnership existing or registered under the laws of Hawaii, or any foreign corporation, partnership, limited liability company, or limited liability partnership authorized to transact business in Hawaii, or any trade name, trademark, or service mark registered in Hawaii, or a name the exclusive right to which is, at the time, reserved in Hawaii, except that this shall not apply if the applicant files with the director either of the following: (a) the written consent from the entity or holder of a reserved or registered name to use the same or substantially identical name, and one or more words are added to make the name distinguishable from the other name; or (b) a certified copy of a final decree of a court of competent jurisdiction establishing the prior right of the applicant to the use of the name in Hawaii.

• The aggregate number of shares which the corporation shall have authority to issue, and, if the shares are to be divided into classes, the number of shares of each class;

• The mailing address of its initial or principal office and, if the corporation is required at the time of incorporation to have a registered office and registered agent in Hawaii, the street address of the corporation's initial registered office and the name of its initial registered agent at that office; provided that where no specific street address is available for the corporation's initial or principal office or for the corporation's registered office, the rural route post office number or post office box designated or made available by the United States Postal Service;

• The number of directors constituting the initial board of directors and the names and addresses of the individuals who are to serve as directors until the first annual meeting of shareholders or until their successors are elected and qualified; and

• The name, title, and address of each officer.

You must file the articles of incorporation with the director of the department of commerce and consumer affairs. As of January 2001, the filing fee was $100.00, with additional charges of $10.00 for each requested certified copy of the articles, and $.25 for the second and additional pages.

The existence of the corporation begins upon the delivery of the articles to the director of commerce and consumer affairs for filing. Upon creation, the corporation may have a meeting of its board members to elect officers, adopt bylaws (which may contain any provision consistent with law and the articles of incorporation), and carry on any other business of the corporation. This meeting may be held inside or outside of Hawaii.

Minimum Number of Incorporators: One or more individuals.

Management Requirements: Directors may approve bylaws for the corporation. If the corporation has only one shareholder, the corporation shall have one or more directors. If the corporation has two shareholders, the corporation shall have two or more directors. If the corporation has three or more shareholders, the corporation shall have three or more directors. The number of directors shall be fixed by, or in the manner provided in, the articles of incorporation or the bylaws, except as to the number constituting the initial board of directors, which number shall be fixed by the articles of incorporation.

The officers of a corporation shall consist of a president, one or more vice-presidents as may be prescribed by the bylaws, a secretary, and a treasurer, each of whom shall be elected or appointed by the board of directors at such time and in such manner as may be prescribed by the bylaws.

State Tax Classification: The state charges $25.00 for annual corporation reports and assesses a corporate income tax at a variable rate.

Contact Information: Department of Commerce and Consumer Affairs
Business Registration Division
P.O. Box 40
Honolulu, Hawaii 96810
Phone: (808) 586-2744
Facsimile: (808) 586-2733
http://www.businessregistrations.com/index.html

Idaho

State Corporation Statute: Id. Code §§ 30-1-101 through 30-1-1704.

Formation: Before filing its certificate of incorporation, a domestic for-profit corporation may reserve a name with the secretary of state's office. The certificate of incorporation must include the following:

- The name of the corporation, which must contain the word "corporation," "incorporated," "company," or "limited," or the abbreviation "corp.," "inc.," "co.," or "ltd.," or words or abbreviations of like import in another language; provided however, that if the word "company" or its abbreviation is used it shall not be immediately preceded by the word "and" or by an abbreviation of or symbol representing the word "and." The name may not contain language stating or implying that the corporation is organized for any unlawful purpose or any purpose inconsistent with its articles of incorporation. Except as provided below, a corporate name must be distinguishable upon the records of the secretary of state from: (1) the corporate name of a corporation incorporated or authorized to transact business in Idaho; (2) a name reserved or registered under Idaho Code; (3) the fictitious name adopted by a foreign corporation authorized to transact business in Idaho because its real name is unavailable; (4) the corporate name of a nonprofit corporation incorporated or authorized to transact business in Idaho; and (5) the name of any limited partnership, limited liability partnership or limited liability company which is organized under the laws of Idaho or registered to do business in Idaho. A corporation may apply to the secretary of state for authorization to use a name that is not distinguishable on his records from one or more of the names described above. The secretary of state shall authorize use of the name applied for if (1) the other corporation, holder of a reserved or registered name, limited partnership, limited liability partnership or limited liability company consents to the use in writing and submits an undertaking in a form satisfactory to the secretary of state to change its name to a name that is distinguishable upon the records of the secretary of state from the name of the applying corporation; or (2) the applicant delivers to the secretary of state a certified copy of the final judgment of a court of competent jurisdiction establishing the applicant's right to use the name applied for in Idaho. A corporation may use the name, including the fictitious name, of another domestic or foreign corporation or limited liability company that is used in Idaho if the other corporation or limited liability company is organized or authorized to transact business in Idaho and the proposed user corporation: (1) has merged with the other corporation or limited liability company; (2) has been formed by reorganization of the other corporation or limited liability company; or (3) has acquired all or substantially all of the assets, including the name, of the other corporation or limited liability company.

- The number of shares the corporation is authorized to issue;
- The street address of the corporation's initial registered office and the name of its initial registered agent at that office; and
- The name and address of each incorporator.

You must file the articles of incorporation with the secretary of state. As of January 2001, the filing fee was $100.00, if the articles were typed, and $120.00, if the articles were handwritten. There were additional charges of $10.00 for each requested certified copy of the certificate.

The existence of the corporation begins upon the filing of the certificate of incorporation with the secretary of state. Upon creation, the corporation may have a meeting of its incorporators or initial board members to elect directors, officers, adopt bylaws (which may contain any provision consistent with law and the articles of incorporation), and carry on any other business of the corporation. This meeting may be held inside or outside of Idaho.

Minimum Number of Incorporators: Any individual or entity may incorporate or organize a corporation.

Management Requirements: Directors or original incorporators, depending upon the terms of the articles of incorporation, may approve bylaws for the corporation. There must be at least one director on the corporation's board of directors.

State Tax Classification: Idaho assesses a corporate income tax at 8% and a use tax at 5%.

Contact Information: Office of the Secretary of State
700 W Jefferson, Room 203
P.O. Box 83720
Boise, ID 83720-0080
Telephone (208) 334-2300
Facsimile (208) 334-2282
http://www.idsos.state.id.us/

Illinois

State Corporation Statute: Il. Code §§ 805 5/1.01 through 805 5/17.05.

Formation: Before filing its articles of incorporation, a domestic for-profit corporation may reserve a name with the secretary of state's office. The articles of incorporation must include the following:

- The name of the corporation, which must contain, separate and apart from any other word or abbreviation in such name, the word "corporation," "company," "incorporated," or "limited," or an abbreviation of one of such words, and if the name of a foreign corporation does not contain, separate and apart from any other word or abbreviation, one of such words or abbreviations, the corporation shall add at the end of its name, as a separate word or abbreviation, one of such words or an abbreviation of one of such words. The name must not contain any word or phrase which indicates or implies that the corporation: (1) is authorized or empowered to conduct the business of insurance, assurance, indemnity, or the acceptance of savings deposits; (2) is authorized or empowered to conduct the business of banking unless otherwise permitted by the Commissioner of Banks and Real Estate pursuant to Section 46 of the Illinois Banking Act; or (3) is authorized or empowered to be in the business of a corporate fiduciary unless otherwise permitted by the Commissioner of Banks and Real Estate. The word "trust," "trustee," or "fiduciary," may be used by a corporation only if it has first complied the Corporate Fiduciary Act. The word "bank," "banker," or "banking," may only be used by a corporation if it has first complied with the Illinois Banking Act. The name must be distinguishable upon the records in the office of the secretary of state from the corporate name or assumed corporate name of any domestic corporation, whether profit or not for profit, existing under any act of Illinois or of any foreign corporation, whether profit or not for profit, authorized to transact business in Illinois, or a name the exclusive right to which is, at the time, reserved or registered, except that, subject to the discretion of the secretary of state, a foreign corporation that has a name otherwise prohibited may be issued a certificate of authority to transact business in Illinois, if the foreign corporation: (1) elects to adopt an assumed corporate name or names in accordance with Illinois statutes; and (2) agrees in its application for a certificate of authority to transact business in Illinois only under such assumed corporate name or names. Furthermore, the name must contain the word "trust," if it be a domestic corporation organized for the purpose of accepting and executing trusts, shall contain the word "pawners," if it be a domestic corporation organized as a pawners' society, and shall contain the word "cooperative," if it be a domestic corporation organized as a cooperative association for pecuniary profit. The name must not contain a word or phrase, or an abbreviation or derivation thereof, the use of which is prohibited or restricted by any statute of Illinois unless such restriction has been complied with. The name must consist of letters of the English alphabet, Arabic or Roman numerals, or symbols capable of being readily reproduced by the office of the secretary of state. It must be the name under which the corporation shall transact business in Illinois unless the corporation shall also elect to adopt an assumed corporate name or names; provided, however, that the corporation may use any divisional designation or trade name without complying with the requirements listed above, provided the corporation also clearly discloses its corporate name. For the purposes of the foregoing, the secretary of state shall determine whether a name is "distinguishable" from another name. Without excluding other names which may not constitute distinguishable names in Illinois, a name is not considered distinguishable solely because it contains one or more of the following: (1) the word "corporation," "company," "incorporated," or "limited," or an abbreviation of one of such words; (2) articles, conjunctions, contractions, abbreviations, different tenses or number of the same word.

- The purpose or purposes for which the corporation is organized, which may be stated to be, or to include, the transaction of any or all lawful businesses for which corporations may be incorporated under Illinois statutes;
- The address of the corporation's initial registered office and the name of its initial registered agent at that office;
- The name and address of each incorporator;
- The number of shares of each class the corporation is authorized to issue;
- The number and class of shares which the corporation proposes to issue without further report to the secretary of state, and the consideration to be received, less expenses, including commissions, paid or incurred in connection with the issuance of shares, by the corporation.
- If shares of more than one class are to be issued, the consideration for shares of each class shall be separately stated;
- If the shares are divided into classes, the designation of each class and a statement of the designations, preferences, qualifications, limitations, restrictions, and special or relative rights with respect to the shares of each class; and

- If the corporation may issue the shares of any preferred or special class in series, then the designation of each series and a statement of the variations in the relative rights and preferences of the different series, if the same are fixed in the articles of incorporation, or a statement of the authority vested in the board of directors to establish series and determine the variations in the relative rights and preferences of the different series.

You must file one original and one copy of the articles of incorporation with the business services division of the secretary of state. As of January 2001, the filing fee was $75.00.

The existence of the corporation begins upon issuance of a certificate of incorporation by the secretary of state. Upon creation, the corporation may have a meeting of its incorporators or initial board members to elect directors, officers, adopt bylaws (which may contain any provision consistent with law and the articles of incorporation), and carry on any other business of the corporation. This meeting may be held inside or outside of Illinois.

Minimum Number of Incorporators: Any one individual over the age of 18 or any one foreign or domestic corporation.

Management Requirements: Directors or original incorporators, depending upon the terms of the articles of incorporation, may approve bylaws for the corporation. There must be at least one director on the corporation's board of directors.

State Tax Classification: Illinois assesses a corporate income tax at 4.8%, sales and use taxes at 1.25% and a franchise tax. The franchise tax is initially assessed at the rate of 0.15% of paid-in capital, but decreases to 0.1% after the first year of corporate existence.

Contact Information: Secretary of State
Department of Business Services
Springfield, IL 62756
Phone: (217) 782-6961
http://www.sos.state.il.us

Indiana

State Corporation Statute: In. Code §§ 23-1-1 through 23-1-54-3.
Formation: Before filing its articles of incorporation, a domestic for-

profit corporation may reserve a name with the secretary of state's office. The articles of incorporation must include the following:

- The name of the corporation, which must contain the word "corporation," "incorporated," "company," or "limited," or the abbreviation "corp.," "inc.," "co.," or "ltd.," or words or abbreviations of like import in another language. The name may not contain language stating or implying that the corporation is organized for a purpose other than that permitted by statute and its articles of incorporation. Except as discussed below, a corporate name must be distinguishable upon the records of the secretary of state from: (1) the corporate name of a corporation incorporated or authorized to transact business in Indiana; (2) a reserved or registered corporate name; and (3) the corporate name of a not-for-profit corporation incorporated or authorized to transact business in Indiana. A corporation may apply to the secretary of state for authorization to use a name that is not distinguishable upon the secretary of state's records from one or more of the names described above The secretary of state shall authorize use of the name applied for if: (1) the other corporation files its written consent to the use, signed by any current officer of the corporation; or (2) the applicant delivers to the secretary of state a certified copy of the final judgment of a court of competent jurisdiction establishing the applicant's right to use the name applied for in Indiana. A corporation may use the name, including the fictitious name, of another domestic or foreign corporation that is used in Indiana if the other corporation is incorporated or authorized to transact business in Indiana and the proposed user corporation: (1) has merged with the other corporation; (2) has been formed by reorganization of the other corporation; or (3) has acquired all or substantially all of the assets, including the corporate name, of the other corporation.
- The number of shares the corporation is authorized to issue;
- The street address of the corporation's initial registered office in Indiana and the name of its initial registered agent at that office; and
- The name and address of each incorporator.

You must file the articles of incorporation with the secretary of state. As of January 2001, the filing fee was $90.00.

The existence of the corporation begins upon the filing of the articles of incorporation with the secretary of state. Upon creation, the corporation may have a meeting of its incorporators or initial board members to elect directors, officers, adopt bylaws (which may contain any provision consistent with law and the articles of incorporation), and carry on any other business of the corporation. This meeting may be held inside or outside of Indiana.

Minimum Number of Incorporators: Any individual or entity may incorporate or organize a corporation.

Management Requirements: Directors or original incorporators, depending upon the terms of the articles of incorporation, may approve bylaws for the corporation. If there are fewer than 50 stockholders in the corporation, the corporation may operate without a board of directors, provided it set forth in its articles of incorporation who will perform management functions for the corporations. A corporation must, however, have at least one officer.

State Tax Classification: The State charges $30.00 for corporate biennial reports, assesses a corporate income tax against gross income at the rate of 3.4%, and a supplemental net income tax at the rate of 4.5%. The State also assesses sales and use taxes at the rate of 5%.

Contact Information: Indiana Secretary of State
                                Business Services
                                302 W. Washington
                                Room E-018
                                Indianapolis, IN 46204
                                Phone: (317) 232-6576
                                Facsimile: (317) 233-3387
                                http://www.ai.org/sos/bus_service/

Iowa

State Corporation Statute: Ia. Code §§ 490.101 through 490.1705.

Formation: Before filing its certificate of incorporation, a domestic for-profit corporation may reserve a name with the secretary of state's office. The certificate of incorporation must include the following:

• The name of the corporation, which must contain the word "corporation," "incorporated," "company," or "limited," or the abbreviation "corp.," "inc.," "co.," or "ltd.," or words or abbreviations of like import in another language. The name must not contain language stating or implying that the corporation is organized for a purpose other than that permitted by law and its articles of incorporation. Except as provided below, a corporate name must be distinguishable upon the records of the secretary of state from all of the following: (1) the corporate name of a corporation incorporated or authorized to transact business in Iowa; (2) a reserved or registered corporate name; (3) the fictitious name adopted by a foreign corporation or a not-for-profit foreign corporation authorized to transact business in Iowa because its real name is unavailable; and (4) the corporate name of a not-for-profit corporation incorporated or authorized to transact business in Iowa. A corporation may apply to the secretary of state for authorization to use a name that is not distinguishable upon the secretary's records from one or more of the names described above. The secretary of state shall authorize use of the name applied for if one of the following conditions applies: (1) the other corporation consents to the use in writing and submits an undertaking in form satisfactory to the secretary of state to change its name to a name that is distinguishable upon the records of the secretary of state from the name of the applying corporation; (2) the applicant delivers to the secretary of state a certified copy of the final judgment of a court of competent jurisdiction establishing the applicant's right to use the name applied for in Iowa. A corporation may use the name, including the fictitious name, of another domestic or foreign corporation that is used in Iowa if the other corporation is incorporated or authorized to transact business in Iowa and the proposed user corporation submits documentation to the satisfaction of the secretary of state establishing one of the following conditions: (1) it has merged with the other corporation; (2) it has been formed by reorganization of the other corporation; or (3) it has acquired all or substantially all of the assets, including the corporate name, of the other corporation.

- The number of shares the corporation is authorized to issue;
- The street address of the corporation's initial registered office and the name of its initial registered agent at that office; and
- The name and address of each incorporator.

You must file the articles of incorporation with the secretary of state. As of January 2001, the filing fee was $50.00.

The existence of the corporation begins upon the filing of the certificate of incorporation with the secretary of state. Upon creation, the corporation may have a meeting of its incorporators or initial board members to elect directors, officers, adopt bylaws (which may contain any provision consistent with law and the articles of incorporation), and carry on any other business of the corporation. This meeting may be held inside or outside of Iowa.

Minimum Number of Incorporators: Any individual or entity may incorporate or organize a corporation.

Management Requirements: Directors or original incorporators, depending upon the terms of the articles of incorporation, may approve bylaws for the corporation. There must be at least one director on the corporation's board of directors.

State Tax Classification: The State charges $30.00 for corporate annual reports, assesses a variable rate corporate income tax, and assesses sales and use taxes at the rate of 5%.

Contact Information:
Business Services Division
Office of the Secretary of State
1305 E. Walnut
2nd Floor Hoover Bldg.
Des Moines, Iowa 50319
Phone: (515) 281-5204
http.//www.sos.state.ia.us/business/
    services.html

Kansas

State Corporation Statute: Ks. Statutes §§ 17-6001 through 17-7515.

Formation: Before filling its articles of incorporation, a domestic for-profit corporation may reserve a name with the secretary of state's office. The articles of incorporation must include the following:

• The name of the corporation, which, except for banks, must contain one of the words "association," "church," "college," "company," "corporation," "club," "foundation," "fund," "incorporated," "institute," "society," "union," "syndicate," or "limited," or one of the abbreviations "co.," "corp.," "inc.," "ltd.," or words or abbreviations of like import in other languages if they are written in Roman characters or letters. The name must be such as to distinguish it upon the records of the office of the secretary of state from the names of other corporations, limited liability companies and limited partnerships organized, reserved or registered under the laws of Kansas, unless there shall be obtained the written consent of such other corporations, limited liability company or limited partnership executed, acknowledged and filed with the secretary of state.

- The address, which shall include the street, number, city and county of the corporation's registered office in Kansas, and the name of its resident agent at such address;
- The nature of the business or purposes to be conducted or promoted. It is sufficient to state, either alone or with other businesses or purposes, that the purpose of the corporation is to engage in any lawful act or activity for which corporations may be organized under the Kansas general corporations code, and by such statement all lawful acts and activities shall be within the purposes of the corporation, except for express limitations, if any;
- If the corporation is to be authorized to issue only one class of stock, the total number of shares of stock which the corporation shall have authority to issue and the par value of such shares, or a statement that all such shares are to be without par value. If the corporation is to be authorized to issue more than one class of stock, the articles of incorporation must set forth the total number of shares of all classes of stock which the corporation will have authority to issue and the numbers of shares of each class, and shall specify each class the shares of which are to be without par value, and each class the shares of which are to have a par value and the par value of the shares of such class. The articles of incorporation must also set forth a statement of the designations and the powers, preferences and rights, and the qualifications, limitations or restrictions on each class of stock, and an express grant of such authority as it may then be desired to grant to the board of directors to fix by resolution or resolutions any of the foregoing which are not fixed by the articles of incorporation.
- The name and mailing address of the incorporator or incorporators; and
- If the powers of the incorporator or incorporators are to terminate upon the filing of the articles of incorporation, the names and mailing addresses of the persons who are to serve as directors until the first annual meeting of the stockholders or until their successors are elected and qualify.

You must file the articles of incorporation with the secretary of state. As of January 2001, the filing fee was $75.00.

The existence of the corporation begins upon the filing of the articles of incorporation with the secretary of state. Upon creation, the corporation may have a meeting of its incorporators or initial board members to elect directors, officers, adopt bylaws (which may contain any provision consistent with law and the articles of incorporation), and carry on any other business of the corporation. This meeting may be held inside or outside of Kansas.

Minimum Number of Incorporators: Any individual or entity may incorporate or organize a corporation.

Management Requirements: Directors or original incorporators, depending upon the terms of the articles of incorporation, may approve bylaws for the corporation. There must be at least one director on the corporation's board of directors.

State Tax Classification: The State assesses a corporate franchise tax at the rate of $1.00 per $1,000 of the corporation's shareholders' equity, with a minimum tax of $20.00 and a maximum tax of $2,500. The State also assesses a corporate income tax of 4%, with a surtax of 3.35% imposed on taxable income in excess of $50,000, and sales and use taxes assessed at the rate of 4.9%.

Contact Information: Kansas Secretary of State
Corporations Division
120 SW 10th Ave., Room 100
Topeka, KS 66612-1240
Phone: (785) 296-4564
Facsimile: (785) 296-4570
http://www.kssos.org/corpwelc.html

Kentucky

State Corporation Statute: KRS §§ 271B.01.010 through 271B.18.070.

Formation: Before filing its articles of incorporation, a domestic for-profit corporation may reserve a name with the secretary of state's office. The articles of incorporation must include the following:

- The name of the corporation, which must contain the word "corporation," "incorporated," "company," or "limited," or the abbreviation "corp.," "inc.," "co.," or "ltd.," or words or abbreviations of like import in another language. The name shall not contain language stating or implying that the corporation is organized for a purpose other than that permitted by Kentucky law and its articles of incorporation. Except as provided below, a corporate name must be distinguishable upon the records of the Secretary of State from: (1) the corporate name of a corporation incorporated or authorized to transact business in Kentucky; (2) a reserved or registered corporate name; (3) the fictitious name adopted by a foreign corporation authorized to transact business in Kentucky because its real name is unavailable; (4) the corporate name of a not-for-profit corporation incorporated or authorized to transact business in Kentucky; and (5) a name filed with the secretary of state. A corporation may apply to the secretary of state for authorization to use a name that is not distinguishable upon his records from one or more of the names described above. The secretary of state shall authorize use of the name applied for if: (1) the other corporation consents to the use in writing and submits an undertaking in form satisfactory to the secretary of state to change its name to a name that is distinguishable upon the records of the secretary of state from the name of the applying corporation; or (2) the applicant delivers to the secretary of state a certified copy of the final judgment of a court of competent jurisdiction establishing the applicant's right to use the name applied for in Kentucky. A corporation may use the name (including the fictitious name) of another domestic or foreign corporation that is used in Kentucky if the other corporation is incorporated or authorized to transact business in Kentucky and the proposed user corporation: (1) has merged with the other corporation; (2) has been formed by reorganization of the other corporation; or (3) has acquired all or substantially all of the assets, including the corporate name, of the other corporation.

- The number of shares the corporation is authorized to issue;
- The street address of the corporation's initial registered office and the name of its initial registered agent at that office;
- The mailing address of the corporation's principal office; and
- The name and mailing address of each incorporator.

You must file the articles of incorporation, along with two additional copies, with the secretary of state. As of January 2001, the filing fee was $40.00. Simultaneous with the filing of the articles of incorporation, you must pay the corporate organizational tax.

The existence of the corporation begins upon the filing of the certificate of incorporation with the secretary of state. Upon creation, the corporation may have a meeting of its incorporators or initial board members to elect directors, officers, adopt bylaws (which may contain any provision consistent with law and the articles of incorporation), and carry on any other business of the corporation. This meeting may be held inside or outside of Kentucky.

Minimum Number of Incorporators: Any one individual or entity may incorporate or organize a corporation.

Management Requirements: Directors or original incorporators, depending upon the terms of the articles of incorporation, may approve bylaws for the corporation. There must be at least one director on the corporation's board of directors.

State Tax Classification: The State assesses a corporate franchise tax at the rate of $2.10 per $1,000 of total capital employed in the corporation in the State. Kentucky also assesses a variable rate corporate organizational tax, corporate income tax, and sales and use taxes at the rate of 6%.

Contact Information:	Kentucky Secretary of State
	700 Capital Avenue
	Suite 152, State Capitol
	Frankfort, KY 40601
	Phone: (502) 564-3490
	Facsimile: (502) 564-5687
	http://www.sos.state.ky.us/

Louisiana

State Corporation Statute: La. R.S. §§ 12.1 through 12.178.

Formation: Before filing its articles of incorporation, a domestic for-profit corporation may reserve a name with the secretary of state's office. The articles of incorporation must include the following:

• The name of the corporation, which must contain the word "corporation," "incorporated," or "limited," or the abbreviation of any of those words, or may contain instead the word "company" or the abbreviation "co." if the latter word or abbreviation is not immediately preceded by the word "and" or the symbol "&." No corporate name may contain the phrase "doing business as" or the abbreviation "d/b/a." The corporate name must not imply that the corporation is an administrative agency of any parish or of Louisiana or of the United States. Except as provided below, the corporate name must be distinguishable from any reserved name, the name of any other corporation, limited liability company, or trade name registered with the secretary of state. The applying corporation may use a name which is not distinguishable upon the records of the secretary of state from any of the names mentioned above if: (1) the other corporation is about to change its name, or to cease doing business, or is being liquidated, or, if a foreign corporation, is about to withdraw from doing business in Louisiana, and the written consent of the other corporation to the adoption of its name or a nondistinguishable name has been given and is filed with the articles of incorporation; (2) the other corporation has previously been authorized to do business in Louisiana for more than two years and has never actively engaged in business in Louisiana; (3) the other corporation has failed to pay the corporate franchise tax or taxes due by it to the state for the preceding five years; or (4) the other corporation, if a foreign corporation, is not authorized to do business in Louisiana and has not filed a Louisiana corporate franchise tax return for two consecutive years.

- In general terms, the purpose or purposes for which the corporation is to be formed, or that its purpose is to engage in any lawful activity for which corporations may be formed under law;
- The duration of the corporation, if other than perpetual;
- The aggregate number of shares which the corporation shall have the authority to issue;
- If the shares are to consist of one class only, the par value of each share or a statement that all of the shares are without par value;
- If the shares are to be divided into classes, the number of shares of each class; the par value of the shares of each class or a statement that such shares are without par value; the designation of each class and, insofar as fixed in the articles, each series of each preferred or special class; a statement of the preferences, limitations and relative rights of the shares of each class and the variations in relative rights and preferences as between series, insofar as the same are fixed in the articles; and a statement of any authority vested in the board of directors to amend the articles to fix the preferences, limitations and relative rights of the shares of any class, and to establish, and fix variations in relative rights as between any series of any preferred or special class;

- The full name and post office address of each incorporator; and
- The taxpayer identification number of the corporation.

You must file the articles of incorporation with the commercial division of the secretary of state. As of January 2001, the filing fee was $60.00, with additional charges of $10.00 for each requested certified copy of the certificate.

The existence of the corporation begins upon the filing of the articles of incorporation with the secretary of state. Upon creation, the corporation may have a meeting of its incorporators or initial board members to elect directors, officers, adopt bylaws (which may contain any provision consistent with law and the articles of incorporation), and carry on any other business of the corporation. This meeting may be held inside or outside of Louisiana.

Minimum Number of Incorporators: Any individual or entity may incorporate or organize a corporation.

Management Requirements: Directors or original incorporators, depending upon the terms of the articles of incorporation, may approve bylaws for the corporation. There must be at least one director on the corporation's board of directors.

State Tax Classification: The State charges $25.00 for corporate annual reports, assesses a corporate franchise tax at the rate of $3.00 per $1,000 of capital stock, surplus, undivided profits, and borrowed capital, and a variable rate corporate income tax. Louisiana also assesses sales and use taxes at the rate of 4%.

   Contact Information: Louisiana Secretary of State
Commercial Division
P. O. Box 94125
Baton Rouge, LA 70804
Phone: (225) 925-4704
E-mail: commercial@sec.state.la.us
http://www.sec.state.la.us/comm/
comm-index.htm

Maine

State Corporation Statute: Me. Code §§ 13A.101 through 13A.1406.

Formation: Before filing its articles of incorporation, a domestic for-profit corporation may reserve a name with the secretary of state's office.

The articles of incorporation must include the following:

- The name of the corporation, which must not contain any word or phrase which indicates or implies that it is organized for any purpose for which a corporation may not be organized under Maine law. The name may not be the same as, or deceptively similar to, the name of any domestic entity, any foreign entity authorized to transact business or to carry on activities in Maine, or a name the exclusive right to which is, at the time, reserved, or the name of an entity that has in effect a registration of its name, or the assumed name of a entity, unless: (1) the other entity executes and files with the secretary of state proof of a resolution of its board of directors, members or management, authorizing the use of a similar name by the corporation seeking to use the similar name; or (2) a foreign corporation seeking to file under a similar or identical name executes and files with the secretary of state proof of a resolution of its board of directors that it will not do business under that similar or identical name, but instead will do business under an assumed name. The name may not be the same as, or deceptively similar to, any registered mark, unless: (1) the owner or holder of the mark executes and files with the secretary of state proof of authorization of the use of a similar name by the corporation seeking to use the similar name; (2) a foreign corporation seeking to file under a similar or identical name executes and files with the secretary of state proof of a resolution of its board of directors that it will not do business under that similar or identical name, but instead will do business under an assumed name; or (3) the registered owner or holder of the mark is the same person or entity as the corporation seeking to use the same or similar name and files proof of ownership with the secretary of state.

- The municipality or other place in Maine where the corporation is located;

- The address of the initial registered office and the name of the initial clerk;

- Either: (1) the number of directors constituting the initial board of directors and, if they have been selected and the powers of the incorporator or incorporators are to terminate upon filing of the articles, the names and addresses of the persons who are to serve as directors until the first annual meeting of shareholders or until their successors be elected and qualify; or

(2) the following statement: "There shall be no director initially; the shares of the corporation will not be sold to more than 20 persons; the business of the corporation will be managed by the shareholders."

• The relevant information regarding the shares, including classes and series of shares, which the corporation shall be authorized to issue.

• If the shares of a corporation are to consist of one class only, the articles shall state: (1) the total number of such shares which the corporation shall have authority to issue; and (2) the par value of each of such shares or a statement that all of such shares are to be without par value.

• If the shares of a corporation are divided into two or more classes, the articles of incorporation: (1) shall designate each class of shares; (2) as to each class, shall specify the total number of such shares which the corporation shall have authority to issue, and the par value, if any, or a statement that the shares are to be without par value; and (3) shall specify the relative rights, preferences and limitations of the shares of each class.

• If shares of any preferred or special class are to be issued in series, the articles of incorporation shall state whether the shares have par value or are without par value; and shall either (1) designate each series within any class of shares, and specify the relative rights, preferences and limitations as among such series, to the extent that such is to be specified in the articles, or (2) set forth any authority of the board of directors to establish and designate series within any class of shares and determine the relative rights, preferences and limitations as among such series.

• In addition, by way of summary, the articles shall state (1) the aggregate par value of all shares having par value which the corporation shall have authority to issue, and (2) the total number of shares without par value which the corporation shall have authority to issue.

• The articles of incorporation shall be signed by each incorporator, with his name and residence address legibly printed or typed beneath or opposite his signature; if an incorporator is a corporation, the title of the person signing for it shall be stated, and the address of its principal place of business shall be stated.

You must file the articles of incorporation with the secretary of state. As of January 2001, the filing fee was $95.00, with an additional minimum charge for stock of $30.00.

The existence of the corporation begins upon the filing of the articles of incorporation with the secretary of state. Upon creation, the corporation may have a meeting of its incorporators or initial board members to elect directors, officers, adopt bylaws (which may contain any provision consistent with law and the articles of incorporation), and carry on any other business of the corporation. This meeting may be held inside or outside of Maine.

Minimum Number of Incorporators: Any individual or entity may incorporate or organize a corporation.

Management Requirements: Directors or original incorporators, depending upon the terms of the articles of incorporation, may approve bylaws for the corporation. Unless there are fewer than 20 shareholders of the corporation, there must be at least three directors on the corporation's board of directors.

State Tax Classification: The State charges $60.00 for the corporate annual report, assesses a variable rate corporate income tax, and assesses sales and use taxes at the rate of 5%.

Contact Information:	Maine Department of the Secretary of State
	Bureau of Corporations, Elections and
	Commissions
	101 State House Station
	Augusta, ME 04333-0101
	Reporting and Information Section: (207)
	287-4190
	Examining Section: (207) 287-4195
	Facsimile: (207) 287-5874
	http://www.state.me.us/sos/cec/corp/
	corp.htm

Maryland

State Corporation Statute: Md. Code §§ 2-101 through 2-612.

Formation: Before filing its articles of incorporation, a domestic for-profit corporation may reserve a name with the secretary of state's office. The articles of incorporation must include the following:

- The corporate name, which must contain the word "Corporation," "Incorporated," "Limited," "Inc.," "Corp.," or "Ltd." The name must be distinguishable from all other entities on record in Maryland. You may call (410) 767-1330 for a non-binding check for name availability. Acceptance of a name guarantees only that the corporation will have that name. It does not mean you cannot be sued for trade name or trade-mark infringement.

- The name and address of the individuals who are incorporating. The address should be one where mail can be received. It can be anywhere, even a foreign country.

- A statement certifying that the incorporator is 18 years old or older, and that the incorporator(s) are forming a corporation under the general laws of Maryland;

- The description of the business of the corporation.

- The address of the principal place of business. It must be a specific address in Maryland and must include street, city and zip code. It cannot be a post office box.

- The name and address of an agent designated to accept service of process if the corporation is summoned to court for any reason. The agent must be either an adult citizen of Maryland or another existing Maryland corporation. The address must include the street, city and zip code. The address must be in Maryland and cannot be a post office box. A corporation cannot act as its own resident agent. That person must also sign the articles of incorporation.

- The number of shares of stock the corporation will have the authority to issue as well as the par value of each share. If the aggregate par value (number of shares multiplied by the par value) exceeds $100,000, or if over 5,000 shares of stock without par value is used, the filing fee will increase beyond $40.00 minimum. If stock without par value is used, insert "$0" as the par value per share.

- The number of directors and the names of those adult individuals who will be directors. These individuals do not have to be residents of Maryland.

- The incorporators must sign the articles of incorporation.

You must file the articles of incorporation with the secretary of state. As of January 2001, the recording fee was $20.00, and the organization and capitalization fee was $20.00, provided that the corporation is authorized to issue no more than 100,000 shares. If the corporation is authorized to issue more than 100,000 shares, call (410) 767-1340 for the fee.

The existence of the corporation begins upon the filing of the certificate of incorporation with the secretary of state. Upon creation, the corporation may have a meeting of its incorporators or initial board members to elect directors, officers, adopt bylaws (which may contain any provision consistent with law and the articles of incorporation), and carry on any other business of the corporation. This meeting may be held inside or outside of Maryland.

Minimum Number of Incorporators: Any individual over the age of 18 may form a corporation.

Management Requirements: Directors or original incorporators, depending upon the terms of the articles of incorporation, may approve bylaws for the corporation. There must be at least three directors on the corporation's board of directors, unless there is no outstanding stock or fewer than three shareholders. In such event, the number of directors shall not be less than the number of shareholders, unless there are greater than three shareholders. The corporation must have a president, secretary and treasurer.

State Tax Classification: The State charges $100 for corporate annual reports, assesses a corporate income tax at 7%, and sales and use taxes at the rate of 5%.

Contact Information: Corporate Records
301 W. Preston Street
Room 801
Baltimore, Maryland 21201-2395
Phone: (410) 767-1340
Toll-free in Maryland: (888) 246-5941
http://www.dat.state.md.us/sdatweb/
charter.html

Massachusetts

State Corporation Statute: MGL §§ 156.1 through 156.55

Formation: Before filing its articles of organization, a domestic for-profit corporation may reserve a name with the secretary of the commonwealth's office. The articles of organization must include the following:

• The name of the corporation, which must also include some indication that the business is incorporated. The secretary of the commonwealth has determined that the words "corporation", "incorporated", "limited," or any abbreviation thereof are sufficient to indicate corporate status. Further, the corporations division will not allow the use of symbols as part of a corporate name. For example, one cannot use $ensible $ales as a corporate name. Such symbols may be protected by filing a trademark or servicemark. A corporation cannot assume the name or trade name of another corporation, firm, association or person carrying on business in Massachusetts at the present time or within three years prior thereto, or assume a name which is under reservation in Massachusetts, or assume a name so similar to any of the forgoing as to be likely to be mistaken for it, except with the written consent of said corporation, firm, association, or person. The standard of similarity is that which would mislead a person of average intelligence taking into account all of the facts and circumstances.

- The purposes for which the corporation is formed;
- The total number of shares and the par value, if any, of each class of stock which the corporation is authorized to issue;
- If more than one class of stock is authorized, a distinguishing designation for each class and prior to the issuance of any shares of a class if shares of any other class are outstanding a description of the preferences, voting powers, qualifications and special or relative rights or privileges of that class and of each other class of which shares are outstanding, and of each series then established within any class;
- A statement in which the incorporators, state their names and post office addresses, and in which they associate themselves with the intention of forming a corporation.

You must file the articles of organization with the secretary of the commonwealth. As of January 2001, the minimum filing fee was $200.00, with the fee determined by the total capital employed by the corporation. Such fee is assessed at the rate of 0.1% of capital stock (minimum par value of $1.00).

The existence of the corporation begins upon the filing of the articles of organization with the secretary of the commonwealth. Upon creation, the corporation may have a meeting of its incorporators or initial board members to elect directors, officers, adopt bylaws (which may contain any provision consistent with law and the articles of organization), and carry on any other business of the corporation. This meeting may be held inside or outside of Massachusetts.

Minimum Number of Incorporators: Any individual over the age of 18 or any entity may incorporate or organize a corporation.

Management Requirements: Directors or original incorporators, depending upon the terms of the articles of incorporation, may approve bylaws for the corporation. The number of directors shall be fixed or determined in the manner provided in the by-laws but shall not be less than three, except where there are less than three stockholders. If there are two stockholders, the number of directors shall not be less than two. If there is only one stockholder or prior to the issue of any stock, there need only be one director.

State Tax Classification: The State charges $85.00 for corporate annual reports, assesses a corporate excise tax at the rate of $2.60 per $1,000 of value of Massachusetts tangible property, plus 9.5% of corporate net income. The state assesses a corporate franchise tax, and also assesses sales and use taxes at the rate of 5%.

| ***Contact Information:*** | The Corporations Division of the Secretary of the Commonwealth's Office One Ashburton Place Boston, MA 02108-1512 Phone: (617) 727-9640 http://www.state.ma.us/sec/cor/coridx.htm |

Michigan

State Corporation Statute: MCL §§ 450.1101 through 450.2099

Formation: Before filing its certificate of incorporation, a domestic for-profit corporation may reserve a name with the department of commerce. The articles of incorporation must include the following:

- The name of the corporation, which must contain the word "corporation," "company," "incorporated," or "limited," or any of the following abbreviations, corp., co., inc., or ltd. The name shall not contain a word or phrase, or abbreviation or derivative of a word or phrase, which indicates or implies that the corporation is formed for a purpose other than the purposes permitted by its articles of incorporation. The name shall distinguish the corporate name upon the records of the department of commerce from all of the following: (1) the corporate name of any other domestic corporation or foreign corporation authorized to transact business in Michigan; (2) the corporate name of any corporation subject to the nonprofit corporation act, or any corporation authorized to conduct affairs in Michigan under that act; (3) a corporate name currently reserved, registered, or assumed; (4) the name of any domestic limited partnership or foreign limited partnership as filed or registered under the Michigan revised uniform limited partnership act, or any name currently reserved or assumed under that act; (5) the name of any domestic limited liability company or foreign limited liability company as filed or registered under the Michigan limited liability company act, or any name currently reserved or assumed under that act. The name of a corporation shall not contain a word or phrase, an abbreviation, or derivative of a word or phrase, the use of which is prohibited or restricted by any other statute of Michigan, unless in compliance with that restriction. Furthermore, unless the corporation is engaged in such businesses, the corporate name shall not imply that the corporation is a banking corporation, an insurance or surety company, or a trust company, and the corporation shall not use the word "bank," "industrial bank," "deposit," "surety," "security," "trust," or "trust company" in its corporate name, or use a combination of the letters or words with other letters or words in its corporate name to indicate or convey the idea of a bank or banking or industrial banking activity or security unless from the other words constituting the name, it is clear that the business conducted does not include the business of banking.

- The purposes for which the corporation is formed. It is a sufficient to state that the corporation may engage in any activity within the purposes for which corporations may be formed under the business corporation act. Any corporation which proposes to conduct educational purposes shall state the purposes and shall comply with all requirements of the Public Acts of 1931.

- The aggregate number of shares that the corporation has the authority to issue.

- If the shares are, or are to be, divided into classes, or into classes and series, the designation of each class and series, the number of shares in each class and series, and a statement of the relative rights, preferences and limitations of the shares of each class and series, to the extent that the designations, numbers, relative rights, preferences, and limitations have been determined.

- If any class of shares is to be divided into series, a statement of any authority vested in the board to divide the class of shares into series, and to determine or change for any series its designation, number of shares, relative rights, preferences and limitations.

- The street address, and the mailing address if different from the street address, of the corporation's initial registered office and the name of the corporation's initial resident agent at that address.
- The names and addresses of the incorporators.
- The duration of the corporation, if other than perpetual.

You must file the articles of incorporation with the department of commerce. As of January 2001, the filing fee was $50.00 for corporations with 60,000 shares or fewer, and an additional $30.00 for each additional 20,000 shares.

The existence of the corporation begins upon the filing of the certificate of incorporation with the department of commerce. Upon creation, the corporation may have a meeting of its incorporators or initial board members to elect directors, officers, adopt bylaws (which may contain any provision consistent with law and the articles of incorporation), and carry on any other business of the corporation. This meeting may be held inside or outside of Michigan.

Minimum Number of Incorporators: Any individual or entity may incorporate or organize a corporation.

Management Requirements: Directors or original incorporators, depending upon the terms of the articles of incorporation, may approve bylaws for the corporation. There must be at least one director on the corporation's board of directors. The officers of a corporation shall consist of a president, secretary, treasurer, and, if desired, a chairman of the board, one or more vice-presidents, and such other officers as may be prescribed by the bylaws or determined by the board of directors.

State Tax Classification: The State charges $15.00 for corporate annual reports, along with a privilege fee, assesses a business tax at the rate of 2%, and assesses sales and use taxes at the rate of 6%.

Contact Information:	Bureau of Commercial Services
	Corporation Division
	P.O. Box 30054
	Lansing, MI 48909
	Phone: (517) 241-6470
	Fax Filing Service: (517) 334-8048
	E-mail: bcsinfo@cis.state.mi.us
	http://www.cis.state.mi.us/corp/

Minnesota

State Corporation Statute: Minn. Statutes §§ 302A.001 through 302A.917.

Formation: Before filing its articles of incorporation, a domestic for-profit corporation may reserve a name with the secretary of state's office. The articles of incorporation must include the following:

- The name of the corporation, which must contain the word "corporation," "incorporated," or "limited," or shall contain an abbreviation of one or more of these words, or the word "company," or the abbreviation "co." if that word or abbreviation is not immediately preceded by the word "and" or the character "&." The name must be in the English language or in any other language expressed in English letters or characters, and it must not contain a word or phrase that indicates or implies that it is incorporated for a purpose other than a legal business purpose. Furthermore, the name must be distinguishable upon the records in the office of the secretary of state from the name of each entity authorized or registered to do business in Minnesota, whether profit or nonprofit, and each name the right to which is, at the time of incorporation, reserved, unless there is filed with the articles one of the following: (1) the written consent of the entity authorized or registered to do business in Minnesota or the holder of a reserved name or a name filed by or registered with the secretary of state having a name that is not distinguishable; (2) a certified copy of a final decree of a court in Minnesota establishing the prior right of the applicant to the use of the name in Minnesota; or (3) the applicant's affidavit that the entity with the name that is not distinguishable has been incorporated or on file in Minnesota for at least three years prior to the affidavit, if it is a domestic entity, or has been authorized or registered to do business in Minnesota for at least three years prior to the affidavit, if it is a foreign entity, or that the holder of a name filed or registered with the secretary of state, filed or registered that name at least three years prior to the affidavit; that the entity or holder has not during the three-year period before the affidavit filed any document with the secretary of state; that the applicant has mailed written notice to the entity or the holder of a name filed or registered with the secretary of state, by certified mail, return receipt requested, properly addressed to the registered office of the entity or in care of the agent of the entity, or the address of the holder of a name filed or registered with the secretary of state, shown in the records of the secretary of state, stating that the applicant intends to use a name that is not distinguishable and the notice has been returned to the applicant as undeliverable to the addressee entity, or holder of a name filed or registered with the secretary of state; that the applicant, after diligent inquiry, has been unable to find any telephone listing for the entity with the name that is not distinguishable in the county in which is located the registered office of the entity shown in the records of the secretary of state or has been unable to find any telephone listing for the holder of a name filed or registered with the secretary of state in the county in which is located the address of the holder shown in the records of the secretary of state; and that the applicant has no knowledge that the entity or holder of a name filed or registered with the secretary of state is currently engaged in business in Minnesota.

- The address of the registered office of the corporation and the name of its registered agent, if any, at that address;
- The aggregate number of shares that the corporation has authority to issue; and
- The name and address of each incorporator.

You must file the articles of incorporation with the secretary of state. As of January 2001, the filing fee was $135.00.

The existence of the corporation begins upon the filing of the articles of incorporation with the secretary of state. Upon creation, the corporation may have a meeting of its incorporators or initial board members to elect directors, officers, adopt bylaws (which may contain any provision consistent with law and the articles of incorporation), and carry on any other business of the corporation. This meeting may be held inside or outside of Minnesota.

Minimum Number of Incorporators: One or more natural persons of at least 18 years of age.

Management Requirements: Directors or original incorporators, depending upon the terms of the articles of incorporation, may approve bylaws for the corporation. There must be at least one director on the corporation's board of directors. A corporation must have one or more natural persons exercising the functions of the offices of chief executive officer and chief financial officer.

State Tax Classification: The State charges $20.00 for corporate annual reports, assesses a corporate income tax at the basic rate of 9.8%, with additional tax on property, payrolls, and sales and receipts and the type of corporation. The State also assesses sales and use taxes at the rate of 6.5%.

Contact Information: Business Services Director
Minnesota Secretary of State
180 State Office Building
100 Constitution Avenue
Saint Paul, MN 55155-1299
Phone: (651) 296-2803
Toll free Phone: 1-877-551-6SOS (6767)
Facsimile: (651) 215-0683
E-mail: business.services@state.mn.us
http://www.sos.state.mn.us/business/
index.html

Mississippi

State Corporation Statute: Miss. Code §§ 79-4-1.01 through 79-4-17.03.

Formation: Before filing its articles of incorporation, a domestic for-profit corporation may reserve a name with the secretary of state's office. The articles of incorporation must include the following:

• The name of the corporation, which must contain the word "corporation," "incorporated," "company," or "limited," or the abbreviation "corp.," "inc.," "co.," or "ltd.," or words or abbreviations of like import in another language. The name may not contain language stating or implying that the corporation is organized for a purpose other than that permitted by law and its articles of incorporation. Except as provided below, a corporate name must be distinguishable upon the records of the secretary of state from: (1) the corporate name of a corporation incorporated or authorized to transact business in Mississippi; (2) a reserved or registered corporate name; (3) the fictitious name adopted by a foreign corporation authorized to transact business in Mississippi because its real name is unavailable; and (4) the corporate name of a not-for-profit corporation incorporated or authorized to transact business in Mississippi. A corporation may apply to the secretary of state for authorization to use a name that is not distinguishable upon his records from one or more of the names described above. The secretary of state shall authorize use of the name applied for if: (1) the other corporation consents to the use in writing and submits an undertaking in form satisfactory to the secretary of state to change its name to a name that is distinguishable upon the records of the secretary of state from the name of the applying corporation; or (2) the applicant delivers to the secretary of state a certified copy of the final judgment of a court of competent jurisdiction establishing the applicant's right to use the name applied for in Mississippi. A corporation may use the name (including the fictitious name) of another domestic or foreign corporation that is used in Mississippi if the other corporation is incorporated or authorized to transact business in Mississippi and the proposed user corporation; (1) has merged with the other corporation; (2) has been formed by reorganization of the other corporation; or (3) has acquired all or substantially all of the assets, including the corporate name, of the other corporation.

- The number of shares the corporation is authorized to issue and the classes of shares and the number of shares of each class that the corporation is authorized to issue. If more than one class of shares is authorized, the articles of incorporation must prescribe a distinguishing designation for each class, and prior to the issuance of shares of a class the preferences, limitations and relative rights of that class must be described in the articles of incorporation. All shares of a class must have preferences, limitations and relative rights identical with those of other shares of the same class except to the extent otherwise permitted by law. The articles of incorporation must authorize one or more classes of shares that together have unlimited voting rights, and one or more classes of shares (which may be the same class or classes as those with voting rights) that together are entitled to receive the net assets of the corporation upon dissolution.

- The street address of the corporation's initial registered office and the name of its initial registered agent at that office; and

- The name and address of each incorporator.

You must file the articles of incorporation with the secretary of state. As of January 2001, the filing fee was $50.00.

The existence of the corporation begins upon the filing of the articles of incorporation with the secretary of state. Upon creation, the corporation may have a meeting of its incorporators or initial board members to elect directors, officers, adopt bylaws (which may contain any provision consistent with law and the articles of incorporation), and carry on any other business of the corporation. This meeting may be held inside or outside of Mississippi.

Minimum Number of Incorporators: Any individual or entity may incorporate or organize a corporation.

Management Requirements: Directors or original incorporators, depending upon the terms of the articles of incorporation, may approve bylaws for the corporation. There must be at least one director on the corporation's board of directors. Said director must be an individual.

State Tax Classification: The State charges $25.00 for annual corporate reports, assesses a corporate franchise tax at the rate of $2.50 per $1,000 or fraction thereof of the value of capital used, invested, or employed by the corporation, and assesses a variable rate corporate income tax. The State also assesses sales and use taxes at the rate of 7%.

> **Contact Information:**   Business Services Division
> Mississippi Secretary of State
> P.O. Box 136
> Jackson, MS 39205
> Phone: (601) 359-1633
> Toll free: (800) 256-3494
> Facsimile: (601) 359-1499
> www.sos.state.ms.us/busserv/corp/
> corporations.html

Missouri

State Corporation Statute: RSMo.§§ 351.010 through 351.935.

Formation: Before filing its articles of incorporation, a domestic for-profit corporation may reserve a name with the secretary of state's office. The articles of incorporation must include the following:

• The name of the corporation, which must contain the word "corporation," "company," "incorporated," or "limited," or shall end with an abbreviation of one of said words. The name may not contain any word or phrase which indicates or implies that it is any governmental agency or organized for any purpose other than a purpose for which corporations may be organized under this Missouri law. It must be distinguishable from the name of any domestic corporation existing under any law of Missouri or any foreign corporation authorized to transact business in Missouri, or any limited partnership or limited liability company existing or transacting business in Missouri, or a name the exclusive right to which is, at the time, reserved. If the name is the same, a word shall be added to make such name distinguishable from the name of such other corporation, limited liability company or limited partnership.

- The address, including street and number, if any, of its initial registered office in Missouri, and the name of its initial registered agent at such address;
- The aggregate number of shares which the corporation shall have the authority to issue, and the number of shares of each class, if any, that are to have a par value and the par value of each share of each such class, and the number of shares of each class, if any, that are to be without par value and also a statement of the preferences, qualifications, limitations, restrictions, and the special or relative rights including convertible rights, if any, in respect of the shares of each class;
- The extent, if any, to which the preemptive right of a shareholder to acquire additional shares is limited or denied;
- The name and place of residence of each incorporator;
- The number of years the corporation is to continue, which may be any number or perpetual;
- The purposes for which the corporation is formed;
- If the incorporators, the directors or the shareholders choose to do so, a provision eliminating or limiting the personal liability of a director to the corporation or its shareholders for monetary damages for breach of fiduciary duty as a director, provided that such provision shall not eliminate or limit the liability of a director (1) for any breach of the director's duty of loyalty to the corporation or its shareholders, (2) for acts or omissions not in subjective good faith or which involve intentional misconduct or a knowing violation of law, or (3) for any transaction from which the director derived an improper personal benefit. No such provision shall eliminate or limit the liability of a director for any act or omission occurring prior to the date when such provision becomes effective;
- Either (1) the number of directors to constitute the first board of di-

rectors and a statement to the effect that thereafter the number of directors shall be fixed by, or in the manner provided in, the bylaws of the corporation, and that any changes shall be reported to the secretary of state within thirty calendar days of such change, or (2) the number of directors to constitute the board of directors, except that the number of directors to constitute the board of directors must be stated in the articles of incorporation if the corporation is to have less than three directors.

• Any other provisions, not inconsistent with law, which the incorporators, the directors or the shareholders may choose to insert.

You must file one original and one copy of the articles of incorporation with the secretary of state. As of January 2001, the incorporation fee was based on the authorized shares of the corporation. A corporation with $30,000 or less in authorized was required to pay a $50.00 incorporation fee. For each additional $10,000 in authorized shares, a corporation was required to pay an additional $5.00 incorporation fee.

The existence of the corporation begins upon the filing of the articles of incorporation with the secretary of state. Upon creation, the corporation may have a meeting of its incorporators or initial board members to elect directors, officers, adopt bylaws (which may contain any provision consistent with law and the articles of incorporation), and carry on any other business of the corporation. This meeting may be held inside or outside of Missouri.

Minimum Number of Incorporators: Any natural person over the age of 18 may incorporate or organize a corporation.

Management Requirements: Directors or original incorporators, depending upon the terms of the articles of incorporation, may approve bylaws for the corporation. A corporation shall have three or more directors, except that a corporation may have one or two directors provided the number of directors to constitute the board of directors is stated in the articles of incorporation. Every corporation must have a president and a secretary, who shall be chosen by the directors.

State Tax Classification: The State charges an annual registration fee of $40.00, assesses a corporate franchise tax at the rate of .05% of the par value of outstanding shares and surplus in excess of $200,000 (par value set at $5.00 or greater). The State also assesses a corporate income tax at the rate of 6.25% and sales and use taxes at the rate of 4.225%.

Contact Information: Corporations Division
James C. Kirkpatrick State Information
  Center
P.O. Box 778
Jefferson City, Missouri 65102
Phone: (573) 751-4153
http://mosl.sos.state.mo.us/bus-ser/
  soscor.html

Montana

State Corporation Statute: MCA §§ 35-1-101 through 35-1-1312.

Formation: Before filing its articles of incorporation, a domestic for-profit corporation may reserve a name with the secretary of state's office. The articles of incorporation must include the following:

- The name of the corporation, which must contain the word "corporation," "incorporated," "company," or "limited"; the abbreviation "corp.," "inc.," "co.," or "ltd."; or words or abbreviations of similar meaning in another language. The name may not contain language that states or implies that the corporation is organized for a purpose or purposes other than those permitted by law and its articles of incorporation. Except as set forth below, a corporate name must be distinguishable in the records of the secretary of state from: (1) the corporate name of another corporation incorporated or authorized to transact business in Montana; (2) a reserved or registered corporate name; (3) the fictitious name adopted by a foreign corporation authorized to transact business in Montana because its real name is unavailable; (4) the corporate name of a not-for-profit corporation incorporated or authorized to transact business in Montana; (5) the corporate name of a domestic corporation that has dissolved, but only distinguishable for a period of 120 days after the effective date of its dissolution; and (6) any assumed business name, limited partnership name, limited liability company name, trademark, or service mark registered or reserved with the secretary of state. A corporation may apply to the secretary of state for authorization to use a name that is not distinguishable in the secretary of state's records from one or more of the names described in above. The secretary of state shall authorize use of the name applied for if: (1) the other corporation consents to the use in writing and submits an undertaking in a form satisfactory to the secretary of state to change its name to a name that is distinguishable in the records of the secretary of state from the name of the applying corporation; or (2) the applicant delivers to the secretary of state a certified copy of the final judgment of a court of competent jurisdiction establishing the applicant's right to use the name applied for in Montana. A corporation, limited liability company, or limited partnership may use the name, including the fictitious name, of another domestic or foreign corporation, limited liability company, or limited partnership that is used in Montana if the other corporation, limited liability company, or limited partnership is incorporated or authorized to transact business in Montana and the proposed user corporation, limited liability company, or limited partnership: (1) has merged with the other corporation, limited liability company, or limited partnership; (2) has been formed by reorganization of the other corporation, limited liability company, or limited partnership; (3) has acquired all or substantially all of the assets, including the corporate name, of the other corporation, limited liability company, or limited partnership; or (4) has obtained written permission from the other corporation, limited liability company, or limited partnership for use of the name and has filed a copy of the grant of permission with the secretary of state.

- The number of shares the corporation is authorized to issue;
- The street address of the corporation's initial registered office and, if different, the mailing address;
- The name of its initial registered agent at that office;
- The name and address of each incorporator.

You must file the one original and one copy of the articles of incorporation with the secretary of state. As of January 2001, corporations were charged a filing fee of $20.00 and a license fee at the time of incorporation. The license fee was assessed based on the authorized shares of the corporation's stock. For corporations with 1 to 50,000 shares, the fee was $50.00, for corporations with 50,001 to 100,000 shares, the fee was $100.00, for corporations with 100,001 to 250,000 shares, the fee was $250, for corporations with 250,001 to 500,000 shares, the fee was $400, for corporations with 500,001 to 1,000,000 shares, the fee was $600, and for corporations with over 1,000,000 shares, the fee was $1,000.

The existence of the corporation begins upon the filing of the articles of incorporation with the secretary of state. Upon creation, the corporation may have a meeting of its incorporators or initial board members to elect directors, officers, adopt bylaws (which may contain any provision consistent with law and the articles of incorporation), and carry on any other business of the corporation. This meeting may be held inside or outside of Montana.

Minimum Number of Incorporators: Any individual or entity may incorporate or organize a corporation.

Management Requirements: Directors or original incorporators, depending upon the terms of the articles of incorporation, may approve bylaws for the corporation. There must be at least one director on the corporation's board of directors. Such director must be an individual.

State Tax Classification: The State charges $10.00 for corporate annual reports, and a corporate income tax at 6.75% ("S" corporations exempt).

Contact Information: Business Services Bureau
Secretary of State
State Capitol, Room 260
P.O. Box 202801
Helena, Montana 59620-2801
Phone: (406) 444-3665
Facsimile: (406) 444-3976
http://state.mt.us/sos/index.htm

Nebraska

State Corporation Statute: Ne. Code §§ 21-2001 through 21-20,192.

Formation: Before filing its articles of incorporation, a domestic for-profit corporation may reserve a name with the secretary of state's office. The articles of incorporation must include the following:

- The name of the corporation, which must contain the word corporation, incorporated, company, or limited, or the abbreviation corp., inc., co., or ltd., or words or abbreviations of like import in another language, except that a corporation organized to conduct a banking business may use a name which includes the word bank without using any such words or abbreviations. The name may not contain language stating or implying that the corporation is organized for a purpose other than that permitted by law and its articles of incorporation. Except as provided below, a corporate name shall be distinguishable upon the records of the secretary of state from: (1) the corporate name of a corporation incorporated or authorized to transact business in Nebraska; (2) a reserved or registered corporate name; (3) the fictitious name adopted by a foreign corporation authorized to transact business in Nebraska because its real name is unavailable; (4) the corporate name of a not-for-profit corporation incorporated or authorized to transact business in Nebraska; and (5) a trade name registered in Nebraska. A corporation may apply to the secretary of state for authorization to use a name that is not distinguishable upon his or her records from one or more of the names described above. The secretary of state shall authorize use of the name applied for if: (1) the other corporation consents to the use in writing and submits an undertaking in a form satisfactory to the secretary of state to change its name to a name that is distinguishable upon the records of the secretary of state from the name of the applying corporation; or (2) the applicant delivers to the secretary of state a certified copy of the final judgment of a court of competent jurisdiction establishing the applicant's right to use the name applied for in Nebraska. A corporation may use the name, including the fictitious name, of another domestic or foreign corporation that is used in Nebraska if the other corporation is incorporated or authorized to transact business in Nebraska and the proposed user corporation has: (1) merged with the other corporation; (2) been formed by reorganization of the other corporation; or (3) acquired all or substantially all of the assets, including the corporate name, of the other corporation.

• The number of shares the corporation is authorized to issue and, if such shares are to consist of one class only, the par value of each of such shares or, if such shares are to be divided into classes, the number of shares of each class and a statement of the par value of the shares of each such class;

• The street address of the corporation's initial registered office and the name of its initial registered agent at that office;

• The name and street address of each incorporator; and

• Any provision limiting or eliminating the requirement to hold an annual meeting of the shareholders if the corporation is registered or intends to register as an investment company under the federal Investment Company Act of 1940. The provision shall not be effective if such corporation does not become or ceases to be so registered.

You must file the articles of incorporation with the secretary of state. As of January 2001, the filing fee was determined by the corporation's number of authorized shares. If the capital stock was $10,000 or less, the fee was $60.00. If the capital stock was more than $10,000 but did not exceed $25,000, the fee was $100.00. If the capital stock was more than $25,000 but did not exceed $50,000, the fee was $150. If the capital stock was more than $50,000 but did not exceed $75,000, the fee was $225. If the capital stock was more than $75,000 but did not exceed $100,000, the fee was $300. If the capital stock was more than $100,000, the fee was $300, plus $3 additional for each $1,000 in excess of $100,000. In addition to the foregoing, the Secretary of State charged $5.00 per page to file and record the articles of incorporation.

The existence of the corporation begins upon the filing of the articles of incorporation with the secretary of state. Upon creation, the corporation may have a meeting of its incorporators or initial board members to elect directors, officers, adopt bylaws (which may contain any provision consistent with law and the articles of incorporation), and carry on any other business of the corporation. This meeting may be held inside or outside of Nebraska.

Minimum Number of Incorporators: Any individual or entity may incorporate or organize a corporation.

Management Requirements: Directors or original incorporators, depending upon the terms of the articles of incorporation, may approve bylaws for the corporation. There must be at least one director on the corporation's board of directors. Such director must be an individual.

State Tax Classification: The State assesses a graduated corporate franchise tax, a graduated corporate income tax, and sales and use taxes at the rate of 5%.

Contact Information: Nebraska Secretary of State, Corporate
                          Division
                          State Capitol, Room 1301
                          Lincoln, Nebraska 68509
                          Phone: 402-471-4079
                          http://www.nol.org/business.html

Nevada

State Corporation Statute: NRS §§ 78.010 through 78.795.

Formation: Before filing its articles of incorporation, a domestic for-profit corporation may reserve a name with the secretary of state's office. The articles of incorporation must include the following:

- The name of the corporation. A name appearing to be that of a natural person and containing a given name or initials must not be used as a corporate name except with an additional word or words such as "Incorporated," "Limited," "Inc.," "Ltd.," "Company," "Co.," "Corporation," "Corp.," or other word which identifies it as not being a natural person. The name proposed for a corporation must be distinguishable on the records of the secretary of state from the names of all other artificial persons formed, organized, registered or qualified that are on file in the office of the secretary of state and all names that are reserved in the office of the secretary of state. If a proposed name is not so distinguishable, the secretary of state shall return the articles of incorporation containing the proposed name to the incorporator, unless the written, acknowledged consent of the holder of the name on file or reserved name to use the same name or the requested similar name accompanies the articles of incorporation. A proposed name is not distinguishable from a name on file or reserved name solely because one or the other contains distinctive lettering, a distinctive mark, a trade-mark or a trade name, or any combination of these. The name of a corporation whose charter has been revoked, which has merged and is not the surviving entity or whose existence has otherwise terminated is available for use by any other artificial person.

- The name of the person designated as the corporation's resident agent, the street address of the resident agent where process may be served upon the corporation, and the mailing address of the resident agent if different from the street address.

- The number of shares the corporation is authorized to issue and, if more than one class or series of stock is authorized, the classes, the series and the number of shares of each class or series which the corporation is authorized to issue, unless the articles authorize the board of directors to fix and determine in a resolution the classes, series and numbers of each class or series.

- The number, names and post office box or street addresses, either residence or business, of the first board of directors or trustees, together with any desired provisions relative to the right to change the number of directors.
- The name and post office box or street address, either residence or business of each of the incorporators executing the articles of incorporation.

You must file the articles of incorporation with the secretary of state. As of August 2001, the filing fee was based on the number and par value of the authorized shares of the corporation. The minimum valuation of the par value of a share for computation of filing fees was a no par value of $1.00 per share, although a minimum stated par value of $.001 per share may be used. If the amount represented by the total number of shares provided for in the articles or agreement was $75,000 or less, the filing fee was $175, if over $75,000 and not over $200,000, the filing fee was $225, if over $200,000 and not over $500,000, the filing fee was $325, if over $500,000 and not over $1,000,000, the filing fee was $425, if over $1,000,000, the filing fee was $425 for the first $1,000,000 and for each additional $500,000 or fraction thereof, the filing fee was an additional $225. The maximum fee for the articles of incorporation was $25,000.

The existence of the corporation begins upon the filing of the certificate of incorporation with the Secretary of State. Upon creation, the corporation may have a meeting of its incorporators or initial board members to elect directors, officers, adopt bylaws (which may contain any provision consistent with law and the articles of incorporation), and carry on any other business of the corporation. This meeting may be held inside or outside of Nevada.

Minimum Number of Incorporators: Any person may incorporate or organize a corporation.

Management Requirements: Directors or original incorporators, depending upon the terms of the articles of incorporation, may approve bylaws for the corporation. There must be at least one director on the corporation's board of directors. Such director must be a natural person of at least 18 years of age. Every corporation must have a president, a secretary and a treasurer.

State Tax Classification: The State charges $85.00 for corporate annual reports, a business privilege tax at $25.00 per employee, and sales and use taxes vary by county but are generally 7.5%.

Contact Information: Corporate Recordings/Corporate
                                  Information
                                  Secretary of State—Annex Office
                                  202 N. Carson Street
                                  Carson City, NV 89701-4271
                                  Phone: (775) 684-5708
                                  Facsimile: (775) 684-5725
                                  E-mail: sosmail@govmail.state.nv.us
                                  http://sos.state.nv.us/

New Hampshire

State Corporation Statute: RSA §§ 293-A:1.01 through 293-A:17.04.

Formation: Before filing its articles of incorporation, a domestic for-profit corporation may reserve a name with the secretary of state's office. The articles of incorporation must include the following:

• The name of the corporation, which must contain the word "corporation," "incorporated," or "limited," or the abbreviation "corp.," "inc.," or "ltd.," or words or abbreviations of like import in another language. The name may not contain language stating or implying that the corporation is organized for a purpose other than that permitted by RSA 293-A:3.01 and its articles of incorporation. Except as provided below, a corporate name shall not be the same as, or deceptively similar to: (1) the corporate name of a corporation incorporated or authorized to transact business in New Hampshire; (2) a reserved or registered name; (3) the fictitious name of another foreign corporation authorized to transact business in New Hampshire; (4) the corporate name of a not-for-profit corporation incorporated or authorized to transact business in New Hampshire; (5) the name of an agency or instrumentality of the United States or New Hampshire or a subdivision thereof; (6) the name of any recognized political party, unless written consent is obtained from the authorized representative of the respective political organization; (7) the name of a registered foreign partnership; and (8) the name of a New Hampshire investment trust. A corporation may apply to the secretary of state for authorization to use a name that is the same as, or deceptively similar to, one or more of the names described above. The secretary of state shall authorize the use of the name applied for if: (1) the holder or holders of the name as described above gives written consent to use the same or deceptively similar name; and if the name is the same, one or more words are added to the name to make the new name distinguishable from the other name; or (2) the corporation consents to the use in writing and submits an undertaking in form satisfactory to the secretary of state to change its name to a name that is not the same as, or deceptively similar to, the name of the applying corporation; or (3) the applicant delivers to the secretary of state a certified copy of the final judgment of a court of competent jurisdiction establishing the applicant's right to use the name applied for in New Hampshire. A corporation may use the name (including the fictitious name) of another domestic or foreign corporation that is used in New Hampshire if the other corporation is incorporated or authorized to transact business in New Hampshire and the proposed user corporation: (1) has merged with the other corporation; (2) has been formed by reorganization of the other corporation; or (3) has acquired all or substantially all of the assets, including the corporate name, of the other corporation.

- The number of shares the corporation is authorized to issue;
- The street address of the corporation's initial registered office and the name of its initial registered agent at that office;
- The name and address of each incorporator.

You must file the articles of incorporation with the secretary of state. As of January 2001, the filing fee was $35.00, with additional charge of $50.00 for an addendum to the articles of incorporation.

The existence of the corporation begins upon the filing of the articles of incorporation with the Secretary of State. Upon creation, the corporation may have a meeting of its incorporators or initial board members to elect directors, officers, adopt bylaws (which may contain any provision consistent with law and the articles of incorporation), and carry on any other business of the corporation. This meeting may be held inside or outside of New Hampshire.

Minimum Number of Incorporators: Any individual or entity may incorporate or organize a corporation.

Management Requirements: Directors or original incorporators, depending upon the terms of the articles of incorporation, may approve bylaws for the corporation. There must be at least one director on the corporation's board of directors.

State Tax Classification: The State charges $100.00 for corporate annual reports, assesses a business profits tax at the rate of 8%, and a business enterprise tax at the rate of 0.25%.

Contact Information: New Hampshire Secretary of State
Corporate Division
25 Capitol Street Floor 3
Concord, NH 03301-6312
Phone: (603) 271-3244
Corporation Information Phone:
        (603) 271-3246
http://webster.state.nh.us/sos/corporate/

New Jersey

State Corporation Statute: NJ Code §§ 14A:1-1 through 14A:17-3.

Formation: Before filing its certificate of incorporation, a domestic for-profit corporation may reserve a name with the secretary of state's office. The certificate of incorporation must include the following:

• The name of the corporation, which must not contain any word or phrase, or abbreviation or derivative thereof, which indicates or implies that it is organized for any purpose other than one or more of the purposes permitted by its certificate of incorporation. The name shall be such as to distinguish it upon the records in the office of the secretary of state from the names of other for profit and nonprofit domestic corporations and for profit and nonprofit foreign corporations qualified to do business in New Jersey and from the names of domestic limited partnerships and foreign limited partnerships and from names subject to a current name reservation or a current name registration, unless there is filed a certified copy of a final judgment of a court of competent jurisdiction establishing the prior right of the corporation to the use of such name in New Jersey. The name must not contain any word or phrase, or any abbreviation or derivative thereof, the use of which is prohibited or restricted by any statute of New Jersey, unless any such restrictions have been complied with. Furthermore, the name must contain the word "corporation," "company," "incorporated," or shall contain an abbreviation of one of those words, or shall include the abbreviation "Ltd." or shall contain words or abbreviations of like import in other languages, except that a foreign corporation which does not have those words or an abbreviation thereof in its name shall add at the end of its name one of those words or an abbreviation thereof for use in New Jersey.

- The purpose or purposes for which the corporation is organized. It shall be sufficient to state, alone or with specifically enumerated purposes, that the corporation may engage in any activity within the purposes for which corporations may be organized under this law, and all such activities shall by such statement be deemed within the purposes of the corporation, subject to express limitations, if any;
- The aggregate number of shares which the corporation shall have authority to issue;
- If the shares are, or are to be, divided into classes, or into classes and series, the designation of each class and series, the number of shares in each class and series, and a statement of the relative rights, preferences and limitations of the shares of each class and series, to the extent that such designations, numbers, relative rights, preferences and limitations have been determined;
- If the shares are, or are to be, divided into classes, or into classes and series, a statement of any authority vested in the board to divide the shares into classes or series or both, and to determine or change for any class or series its designation, number of shares, relative rights, preferences and limitations;
- Any provision not inconsistent with law which the incorporators elect to set forth for the management of the business and the conduct of the affairs of the corporation, or creating, defining, limiting or regulating the powers of the corporation, its directors and shareholders or any class of shareholders, including any provision which is required or permitted to be set forth in the bylaws;
- The address of the corporation's initial registered office, and the name of the corporation's initial registered agent at such address. The address of the registered office as shown on the certificate of incorporation shall be a complete address, including the number and street location of the registered office and, if applicable, the post office box number;
- The number of directors constituting the first board and the names and addresses of the persons who are to serve as such directors;
- The names and addresses of the incorporators;

- The duration of the corporation if other than perpetual; and
- If the certificate of incorporation is to be effective on a date subsequent to the date of filing, the effective date of the certificate.

You must file the certificate of incorporation with the secretary of state. As of January 2001, the filing fee was $100.00.

The existence of the corporation begins upon the filing of the certificate of incorporation with the secretary of state, or upon the date specified therein. Upon creation, the corporation may have a meeting of its incorporators or initial board members to elect directors, officers, adopt bylaws (which may contain any provision consistent with law and the articles of incorporation), and carry on any other business of the corporation. This meeting may be held inside or outside of New Jersey.

Minimum Number of Incorporators: Any individual of at least 18 years of age or any entity may incorporate or organize a corporation.

Management Requirements: Directors or original incorporators, depending upon the terms of the articles of incorporation, may approve bylaws for the corporation. There must be at least one director on the corporation's board of directors. The officers of a corporation shall consist of a president, a secretary, a treasurer, and, if desired, a chairman of the board, one or more vice presidents, and such other officers as may be prescribed by the by-laws.

State Tax Classification: The State charges $40.00 for corporate annual reports, assesses a variable rate corporate franchise tax, a corporate income tax at the rate of 7.25%, and sales and use taxes at the rate of 6%.

Contact Information: Division of Revenue
                                 P.O. Box 308
                                 Trenton, NJ 08625
                                 Phone: (609) 292-9292
                                 http://www.state.nj.us/treasury/
                                        revenue/dcr/dcrpg1.html

New Mexico

State Corporation Statute: NMSA §§ 53-11-1 through 53-18-12.

Formation: Before filing its articles of incorporation, a domestic for-profit corporation may reserve a name with the secretary of state's office. The articles of incorporation must include the following:

- The name of the corporation, which must contain the word "corporation," "company," "incorporated," or shall contain an abbreviation of one of those words, or shall include the abbreviation Ltd. or shall contain words or abbreviations of like import in other languages. The name must not contain any word or phrase, or abbreviation or derivative thereof, which indicates or implies that it is organized for any purpose other than one or more of the purposes permitted by law or its certificate of incorporation. The name shall be such as to distinguish it upon the records in the office of the secretary of state from the names of other for profit and nonprofit domestic corporations and for profit and nonprofit foreign corporations qualified to do business in New Mexico and from the names of domestic limited partnerships and foreign limited partnerships and from names subject to a current name reservation or a current name registration, unless there is filed a certified copy of a final judgment of a court of competent jurisdiction establishing the prior right of the corporation to the use of such name in New Mexico. The name must not contain any word or phrase, or any abbreviation or derivative thereof, the use of which is prohibited or restricted by any statute of New Mexico, unless any such restrictions have been complied with.
- The period of duration, if other than perpetual;
- The purpose or purposes for which the corporation is organized, which may include the transaction of any lawful business for which corporations may be incorporated under the Business Corporation Act;
- The aggregate number of shares which the corporation shall have authority to issue and, if the shares are to be divided into classes, the number of shares of each class;
- If the shares are to be divided into classes, the designation of each class;
- If the corporation is to issue the shares of any preferred or special class in series, then the designation of each series and a statement of the variations in the relative rights and preferences as between series insofar as they are to be fixed in the articles of incorporation, and a statement of any authority to be vested in the board of directors to establish series and fix and determine the variations in the relative rights and preferences as between series;
- Any provisions limiting or denying to shareholders the preemptive right to acquire unissued shares of securities convertible into such shares or carrying a right to subscribe to or acquire shares;

- The address of its initial registered office, and the name of its initial registered agent at the address;

- The number of directors constituting the initial board of directors and the names and addresses of the persons who are to serve as directors until the first annual meeting of shareholders or until their successors are elected and qualify; and

- The name and address of each incorporator.

You must file duplicate originals of the articles of incorporation with the secretary of state. As of January 2001, the filing fee was based on the authorized shares of the corporation. The fee was assessed at the rate of $1.00 for each 1,000 shares of the total amount of authorized shares, but in no case was the fee less than $100.00 or more than $1,000.00.

The existence of the corporation begins upon the filing of the articles of incorporation with the secretary of state. Upon creation, the corporation may have a meeting of its incorporators or initial board members to elect directors, officers, adopt bylaws (which may contain any provision consistent with law and the Articles of Incorporation), and carry on any other business of the corporation. This meeting may be held inside or outside of New Mexico.

Minimum Number of Incorporators: Any individual or entity may incorporate or organize a corporation.

Management Requirements: Directors or original incorporators, depending upon the terms of the articles of incorporation, may approve bylaws for the corporation. There must be at least one director on the corporation's board of directors.

State Tax Classification: The State charges $25.00 for corporate biennial reports, and a franchise tax of $50.00, and also assesses a variable rate corporate income tax.

Contact Information: State Corporation Commission
Corporation Department
P.O. Box 1269
Sante Fe, New Mexico 87504-1269
Phone: (505) 827-4511

New York

State Corporation Statute: NYSCL §§ 855.4.101 through 855.4.2001.

Formation: Before filing its certificate of incorporation, a domestic for-profit corporation may reserve a name with the department of state. The certificate of incorporation must include the following:

- The name of the corporation, which must contain the word "corporation," "incorporated," or "limited," or an abbreviation of one of such words; or, in the case of a foreign corporation, it shall, for use in this state, add at the end of its name one of such words or an abbreviation thereof. The name must be such as to distinguish it from the names of corporations of any type or kind, or a fictitious name of an authorized foreign corporation, as such names appear on the index of names of existing domestic and authorized foreign corporations of any type or kind, including fictitious names of authorized foreign in the department of state, division of corporations, or a name the right to which is reserved. The name may not contain any word or phrase, or any abbreviation or derivative thereof, the use of which is prohibited or restricted by any other statute of New York, unless in the latter case the restrictions have been complied with. The name may not contain any word or phrase, or any abbreviation or derivative thereof, in a context which indicates or implies that the corporation, if domestic, is formed or, if foreign, is authorized for any purpose or is possessed in this state of any power other than a purpose for which, or a power with which, the domestic corporation may be and is formed or the foreign corporation is authorized. Specifically, a corporate name may not contain any of the following phrases, or any abbreviation or derivative thereof: board of trade; state police; urban development; chamber of commerce; state trooper; urban relocation; community renewal; or tenant relocation. A corporate name may not contain any of the following words or any abbreviation or derivative thereof: acceptance; endowment; loan; annuity; fidelity; mortgage; assurance; finance; savings; bank; guaranty; surety; benefit; indemnity; title; bond; insurance; trust; casualty; investment; underwriter; doctor; or lawyer; unless written approval from the appropriate authorities or regulatory bodies is included in the certificate of incorporation. The name must not, unless the approval of the state board of standards and appeals is attached to the certificate of incorporation, or application for authority or amendment thereof, contain any of the following words or phrases, or any abbreviation or derivative thereof: union, labor, council, industrial organization, in a context which indicates or implies that the domestic corporation is formed or the foreign corporation authorized as an organization of working men or women or wage earners or for the performance, rendition or sale of services as labor or management consultant, adviser or specialist, or as negotiator or arbitrator in labor-management disputes. The name must not, unless the approval of the state department of social services is attached to the certificate of incorporation, or application for authority or amendment thereof, contain the word "blind" or "handicapped." Such approval may be granted by the state department of social services, if in its opinion the word "blind" or "handicapped" as used in the corporate name proposed will not tend to mislead or confuse the public into believing that the corporation is organized for charitable or non-profit purposes related to the blind or the handicapped. The name must not contain any words or phrases, or any abbreviation or derivation thereof in a context which will tend to mislead the public into believing that the corporation is an agency or instrumentality of the United States or the state of New York or a subdivision thereof or is a public corporation. The name must not contain any word or phrase, or any abbreviation or derivation thereof, which, separately, or in context, shall be indecent or obscene, or shall ridicule or degrade any person, group, belief, business or agency of government, or indicate or imply any unlawful activity. A corporate name must not, unless the approval of the attorney general is attached to the certificate of incorporation, or application for authority or amendment thereof, contain the word "exchange" or any abbreviation or derivative thereof. Such approval shall not be granted by the attorney general, if in his opinion the use of the word "exchange" in the proposed corporate name would falsely imply that the corporation conducts its business at a place where trade is carried on in securities or commodities by brokers, dealers, or merchants.

• The purpose or purposes for which it is formed, it being sufficient to state, either alone or with other purposes, that the purpose of the corporation is to engage in any lawful act or activity for which corporations may be organized under the laws of New York, provided that it also state that it is not formed to engage in any act or activity requiring the consent or approval of any state official, department, board, agency or other body without such consent or approval first being obtained. By such statement all lawful acts and activities will be within the purposes of the corporation, except for express limitations therein or in law, if any.

- The county within New York in which the office of the corporation is to be located;
- The aggregate number of shares which the corporation shall have the authority to issue; if such shares are to consist of one class only, the par value of the shares or a statement that the shares are without par value; or, if the shares are to be divided into classes, the number of shares of each class and the par value of the shares having par value and a statement as to which shares, if any, are without par value.
- If the shares are to be divided into classes, the designation of each class and a statement of the relative rights, preferences and limitations of the shares of each class.
- If the shares of any preferred class are to be issued in series, the designation of each series and a statement of the variations in the relative rights, preferences and limitations as between series insofar as the same are to be fixed in the certificate of incorporation, a statement of any authority to be vested in the board to establish and designate series and to fix the variations in the relative rights, preferences and limitations as between series and a statement of any limit on the authority of the board of directors to change the number of shares of any series of preferred shares;
- A designation of the secretary of state as agent of the corporation upon whom process against it may be served and the post office address within or without this state to which the secretary of state shall mail a copy of any process against it served upon him;
- If the corporation is to have a registered agent, his name and address within New York and a statement that the registered agent is to be the agent of the corporation upon whom process against it may be served; and
- The duration of the corporation, if other than perpetual.

You must file the certificate of incorporation with the department of state. As of January 2001, the filing fee was $125.00.

The existence of the corporation begins upon the filing of the certificate of incorporation with the department of state. Within 120 days of the organization of the corporation, affidavits must be filed with the department of state attesting to the fact that the corporation shall have published its certificate of incorporation, once per week for six successive weeks, in two newspapers of the county in which the office of the corporations is located, to be designated by the county clerk, one of which newspapers must be a newspaper published in the city or town in which the office is intended to be located, if there is a newspaper such city or town; or, if no newspaper is published there, in the newspaper nearest to such city or town. An affidavit of the printer or publisher of each of such newspapers is sufficient proof of such publication and must be filed with the department of state. Upon creation, the corporation may have a meeting of its incorporators or initial board members to elect directors, officers, adopt bylaws (which may contain any provision consistent with law and the certificate of incorporation), and carry on any other business of the corporation. This meeting may be held inside or outside of New York.

Minimum Number of Incorporators: Any individual of at least 18 years of age may incorporate or organize a corporation.

Management Requirements: Directors or original incorporators, depending upon the terms of the articles of incorporation, may approve bylaws for the corporation. There must be at least one director on the corporation's board of directors. The board may elect or appoint a president, one or more vice-presidents, a secretary and a treasurer, and such other officers as it may determine, or as may be provided in the bylaws.

State Tax Classification: The State assesses a variable rate corporate franchise tax. New York also assesses a stock transfer tax at the rate of 2½¢ per share on transfers other than by sale, and a variable stock transfer tax when shares are sold. The State also assesses sales and use taxes at the rate of 4%.

Contact Information: New York State Department of State
Division of Corporations, State Records,
and Uniform Commercial Code
41 State Street
Albany, NY 12231-0001
Phone: (518) 473-2492
Facsimile: (518) 474-1418
E-mail: corporations@dos.state.ny.us
http://www.dos.state.ny.us/corp/
corpwww.html

North Carolina

State Corporation Statute: N.C. Code §§ 55-1-101 through 55-17-05.

Formation: Before filing its articles of incorporation, a domestic for-profit corporation may reserve a name with the secretary of state's office. The articles of incorporation must contain the following:

- The name of the corporation, which must contain the word "corporation," "incorporated," "company," or "limited," or the abbreviation "corp.," "inc.," "co.," or "ltd." The name must not contain language stating or implying that the corporation is organized for a purpose other than that permitted by law and its articles of incorporation. Except as provided below, a corporate name must be distinguishable upon the records of the secretary of state from: (1) the corporate name of a corporation incorporated or authorized to transact business in North Carolina; (2) a reserved or registered corporate name; (3) the fictitious name adopted by a foreign corporation authorized to transact business in North Carolina because its real name is unavailable; (4) the corporate name of a nonprofit corporation incorporated or authorized to transact business in North Carolina; and (5) the name used, reserved, or registered by a limited liability company or by a limited partnership. A person may apply to the secretary of state for authorization to use a name that is not distinguishable upon his records from one or more of the names described above. The secretary of state shall authorize use of the name applied for if: (1) the other corporation consents to the use in writing and submits an undertaking in form satisfactory to the secretary of state to change its name to a name that is distinguishable upon the records of the secretary of state from the name of the applicant; or (2) the applicant delivers to the secretary of state a certified copy of the final judgment of a court of competent jurisdiction establishing the applicant's right to use the name applied for in North Carolina.
- The number of shares the corporation is authorized to issue;
- The classes of shares and the number of shares of each class that the corporation is authorized to issue. If more than one class of shares is authorized, the articles of incorporation must prescribe a distinguishing designation for each class, and, prior to the issuance of shares of a class, the preferences, limitations, and relative rights of that class must be described in the articles of incorporation. All shares of a class must have preferences, lim-

itations, and relative rights identical with those of other shares of the same class unless the articles of incorporation divide a class into series. If a class is divided into series, all the shares of any one series must have preferences, limitations, and relative rights identical with those of other shares of the same series.

• The articles of incorporation must authorize: (1) one or more classes of shares that together have unlimited voting rights, and (2) one or more classes of shares (which may be the same class or classes as those with voting rights) that together are entitled to receive the net assets of the corporation upon dissolution.

• The street address, and the mailing address if different from the street address, of the corporation's initial registered office, the county in which the initial registered office is located, and the name of the corporation's initial registered agent at that address; and

• The name and address of each incorporator.

You must file the original and one copy of the articles of incorporation with the secretary of state. As of January 2001, the filing fee was $125.00.

The existence of the corporation begins upon the filing of the articles of incorporation with the secretary of state. Upon creation, the corporation may have a meeting of its incorporators or initial board members to elect directors, officers, adopt bylaws (which may contain any provision consistent with law and the articles of incorporation), and carry on any other business of the corporation. This meeting may be held inside or outside of North Carolina.

Minimum Number of Incorporators: Any individual or entity may incorporate or organize a corporation.

Management Requirements: Directors or original incorporators, depending upon the terms of the articles of incorporation, may approve bylaws for the corporation. There must be at least one director on the corporation's board of directors.

State Tax Classification: The State assesses a corporate franchise tax at the rate of $1.50 per $1,000 of whichever yields the highest tax: (a) capital stock, surplus and undivided profits allocable to North Carolina; (b) investments in North Carolina tangible property; or (c) 55% of the appraised tangible personal property plus all intangible property in the State. North Carolina also assesses a corporate income tax at the rate of 6.9% and sales and use taxes at the rate of 4%.

Contact Information: Corporations Division
P.O. Box 29622
Raleigh, NC 27626-0622
Phone: (919) 807-2225
Facsimile: (919) 807-2039
http://www.secretary.state.nc.us/
corporations/

North Dakota

State Corporation Statute: Cent. Code §§ 10-19.1-01 through 10-19.1-1-131.

Formation: Before filing its articles of incorporation, a domestic for-profit corporation may reserve a name with the secretary of state's office. The articles of incorporation must include the following:

• The name of the corporation, which must contain the word "corporation," "incorporated," "company," or "limited," or the abbreviation "corp.," "inc.," "co.," or "ltd.," or words or abbreviations of like import in another language. The name may not contain language stating or implying that the corporation is organized for any unlawful purpose. Except as provided below, a corporate name must not be the same as, or deceptively similar to, the name of a domestic or foreign corporation, limited liability company, or limited partnership, whether profit or nonprofit, authorized to do business in North Dakota, or a name the right to which is, at the time of incorporation, reserved, or is a fictitious name registered with the office of the secretary of state, or is a trade name registered with the office of the secretary of state. The secretary of state may authorize a corporation to use a name that is not distinguishable on its records from one or more of the names described above. The secretary of state shall authorize use of the name applied for if: (1) the other corporation, holder of a reserved or registered name, limited partnership, limited liability partnership or limited liability company consents to the use in writing and submits an undertaking in a form satisfactory to the secretary of state to change its name to a name that is distinguishable upon the records of the secretary of state from the name of the applying corporation; or (2) the applicant delivers to the secretary of state a certified copy of the final judgment of a court in North Dakota establishing the applicant's right to use the name applied for in North Dakota.

- The address of the registered office of the corporation and the name of its registered agent at that address;
- The aggregate number of shares that a corporation has authorized to issue;
- The name and address of each incorporator; and
- The effective date of incorporation if a later date that than on which the certificate of incorporation is issued by the secretary of state.

You must file an original of the articles of incorporation with the secretary of state. As of January 2001, the filing fee was $30.00, with additional charges of $10.00 for the required written consent of the registered agent, and a minimum license fee of $50.00.

The existence of the corporation begins upon the issuance of the certificate of incorporation by the secretary of state. Upon creation, the corporation may have a meeting of its incorporators or initial board members to elect directors, officers, adopt bylaws (which may contain any provision consistent with law and the Articles of Incorporation), and carry on any other business of the corporation. This meeting may be held inside or outside of North Dakota.

Minimum Number of Incorporators: Any individual or entity may incorporate or organize a corporation.

Management Requirements: Directors or original incorporators, depending upon the terms of the articles of incorporation, may approve bylaws for the corporation. There must be at least one director on the corporation's board of directors. The corporation must have the officers of president, one or more vice presidents, secretary, and treasurer.

State Tax Classification: The State charges $25.00 for annual corporate reports, assesses a variable rate corporate income tax, and sales and use taxes at the rate of 5%.

Contact Information: Secretary of State
600 E. Boulevard Ave. Dept. 108
Bismarck, ND 58505-0500
Phone: (701) 328-4284
Toll Free: (800) 352-0867 ext. 8-4284
Facsimile: (701) 328-2992
Email: sosbir@state.nd.us

Ohio

State Corporation Statute: Oh. Revised Code §§ 1701.01 through 1701.99.

Formation: Before filing its articles of incorporation, a domestic for-profit corporation may reserve a name with the secretary of state's office. The articles of incorporation must include the following:

• The name of the corporation, which must end with or include the word or abbreviation "company," "co.," "corporation," "corp.," "incorporated," or "inc." The name must be distinguishable upon the records of the secretary of state from all of the following: (1) the name of any other corporation, whether nonprofit or for profit and whether that of a domestic or of a foreign corporation authorized to do business in Ohio; (2) the name of any limited liability company registered in the office of the secretary of state, whether domestic or foreign; (3) the name of any limited liability partnership registered in the office of the secretary of state, whether domestic or foreign; (4) the name of any limited partnership registered in the office of the secretary of state, whether domestic or foreign; (5) any trade name the exclusive right to which is at the time in question registered in the office of the secretary of state. The name must not contain any language that indicates or implies that the corporation is connected with a government agency of Ohio, another state, or the United States.

• The place in Ohio where the principal office of the corporation is to be located;

• The authorized number and the par value per share of shares with par value, and the authorized number of shares without par value, except that the articles of a banking, safe deposit, trust, or insurance corporation shall not authorize shares without par value;

• The express terms, if any, of the shares; and, if the shares are classified, the designation of each class, the authorized number and par value per share, if any, of the shares of each class, and the express terms of the shares of each class;

• If the corporation is to have an initial stated capital, the amount of that stated capital.

You must file the articles of incorporation with the secretary of state. As of January 2001, the filing fee was $85.00.

The existence of the corporation begins upon the filing of the certificate of incorporation with the secretary of state. Upon creation, the corporation may have a meeting of its incorporators or initial board members to elect directors, officers, adopt bylaws (which may contain any provision consistent with law and the articles of incorporation), and carry on any other business of the corporation. This meeting may be held inside or outside of Ohio.

Minimum Number of Incorporators: Any individual or entity may incorporate or organize a corporation.

Management Requirements: Directors or original incorporators, depending upon the terms of the articles of incorporation, may approve bylaws for the corporation. The number of directors shall be not less than three or, if not so fixed, shall be three. If all of the shares of a corporation are owned by one or two shareholders, the number of directors may be less than three, but not less than the number of shareholders. The officers of a corporation shall consist of a president, a secretary, a treasurer, and, if desired, a chairman of the board, one or more vice presidents, and such other officers and assistant officers as may be deemed necessary.

State Tax Classification: The State assesses a variable rate corporate franchise tax and sales and use taxes at the rate of 5%.

Contact Information: Ohio Secretary of State
                             Business Services Division
                             180 E. Broad St., 16th Floor
                             Columbus, Ohio 43215
                             Phone: (614) 466-3910
                             Toll Free: 1-877-SOS-FILE (1-877-767-3453)
                             Facsimile: (614) 466-3899
                             http://www.state.oh.us/sos/

Oklahoma

State Corporation Statute: Ok. Statutes §§ 18.1001 through 18.1144.

Formation: Before filing its certificate of incorporation, a domestic for-profit corporation may reserve a name with the secretary of state's office. The certificate of incorporation must include the following:

- The name of the corporation, which must contain the word "association," "company," "corporation," "club," "foundation," "fund," "incorporated," "institute," "society," "union," "syndicate," or "limited," or the abbreviation "corp.," "inc.," "co.," or "ltd.," or words or abbreviations of like import in another language; provided that such abbreviations are written in Roman characters or letter. A corporate name must be distinguishable upon the records of the secretary of state from (1) names of other corporations organized under the laws of Oklahoma then existing or which existed at any time during the preceding three years; (2) names of foreign corporations registered in accordance with the laws of Oklahoma then existing or which existed at any time during the preceding three years; (3) names of then existing limited partnerships whether organized pursuant to the laws of Oklahoma or registered as foreign limited partnerships in Oklahoma: (4) trade names or fictitious names filed with the secretary of state; (5) corporate, limited liability company or limited partnership names registered with the secretary of state; or (6) names of then existing limited liability companies, whether organized pursuant to the laws of Oklahoma or registered as foreign limited liability companies in Oklahoma.

- The address, including the street, number, city and county, of the corporation's registered office in Oklahoma, and the name of the corporation's registered agent at such address;
- The nature of the business or purposes to be conducted or promoted. It shall be sufficient to state, either alone or with other business purposes, that the purpose of the corporation is to engage in any lawful act or activity for which corporations may be organized under the general corporation law of Oklahoma, and by such statement, all lawful acts and activities shall be within the purposes of the corporation, except for express limitations, if any.
- If the corporation is to be authorized to issue only one class of stock, the total number of shares of stock which the corporation shall have authority to issue and the par value of each of such shares, or a statement that all such shares are to be without par value. If the corporation is to be authorized to issue more than one class of stock, the certificate of incorporation must set forth the total number of shares of all classes of stock which the corporation shall have authority to issue and the number of shares of each class, and shall specify each class the shares of which are to have par value and the par value of shares of each such class.
- The name and mailing address of the incorporator or incorporators; and

- If the powers of the incorporator or incorporators are to terminate upon the filing of the certificate of incorporation, the names and mailing addresses of the persons who are to serve as directors until the first annual meeting of shareholders or until their successors are elected and qualify.

You must file the certificate of incorporation with the secretary of state. As of January 2001, the filing fee was based upon the authorized capital stock of the corporation. The filing fees were assessed at the rate of 0.1% of the authorized capital stock for such corporation; provided that the minimum fee for any such service was $50.00.

The existence of the corporation begins upon the filing of the certificate of incorporation with the Secretary of State. Upon creation, the corporation may have a meeting of its incorporators or initial board members to elect directors, officers, adopt bylaws (which may contain any provision consistent with law and the Articles of Incorporation), and carry on any other business of the corporation. This meeting may be held inside or outside of Oklahoma.

Minimum Number of Incorporators: Any individual or entity may incorporate or organize a corporation.

Management Requirements: Directors or original incorporators, depending upon the terms of the articles of incorporation, may approve bylaws for the corporation The stock, property and affairs, of such corporation shall be managed by the board of directors, which shall consist of 5 members, all of whom must be stockholders, and who shall be elected at the annual meeting of the stockholders. At the first meeting of the stockholders, there shall be elected 5 directors, one of whom shall serve one year, two of whom shall serve two years, and the remaining two of whom shall serve three years.

State Tax Classification: The State assesses a corporate franchise tax at the rate of $1.25 per $1,000 or fraction thereof used, invested or employed in Oklahoma. Oklahoma also assesses a corporate income tax at the rate of 6% and sales and use taxes at the rate of 4.5%.

Contact Information: Business Records Department
2300 N. Lincoln Blvd., Room 101
Oklahoma City, OK 73105-4897
Phone: (900) 555-2424 (A flat fee of $5.00)
Facsimile: (405) 521-3771
http://www.sos.state.ok.us/

Oregon

State Corporation Statute: ORS §§ 60.001 through 60.992.

Formation: Before filing its articles of incorporation, a domestic for-profit corporation may reserve a name with the secretary of state's office. The articles of incorporation must include the following:

- The name of the corporation, which must contain one or more of the words "corporation," "incorporated," "company," or "limited," or an abbreviation of one or more of those words. A corporate name must not contain the word "cooperative." The name must be written in the alphabet used to write the English language and may include Arabic and Roman numerals and incidental punctuation. Except as provided below, it must be distinguishable upon the records of the secretary of state from any other corporate name, professional corporate name, nonprofit corporate name, cooperative name, limited partnership name, business trust name, reserved name, registered corporate name or assumed business name of active record with the secretary of state. The corporate name need not satisfy the requirement mentioned above if the applicant delivers to the secretary of state a certified copy of a final judgment of a court of competent jurisdiction that finds that the applicant has a prior or concurrent right to use the corporate name in Oregon. Corporations are not prohibited from transacting business under an assumed business name.
- The number of shares the corporation is authorized to issue;
- The address, including street and number, and mailing address, if different, of the corporation's initial registered office and the name of its initial registered agent at that office;
- The name and address of each incorporator; and
- A mailing address to which notices may be mailed until an address has been designated by the corporation in its annual report.

You must file the articles of incorporation with the secretary of state. As of January 2001, the filing fee was $50.00.

The existence of the corporation begins upon the filing of the articles of incorporation with the secretary of state. Upon creation, the corporation may have a meeting of its incorporators or initial board members to elect directors, officers, adopt bylaws (which may contain any provision consistent with law and the articles of incorporation), and carry on any other business of the corporation. This meeting may be held inside or outside of Oregon.

Minimum Number of Incorporators: Any individual of at least 18 years of age or any entity may incorporate or organize a corporation.

Management Requirements: Directors or original incorporators, depending upon the terms of the articles of incorporation, may approve bylaws for the corporation. There must be at least one director on the corporation's board of directors. Such director must be an individual of at least 18 years of age. The corporation must have both a president and secretary as officers.

State Tax Classification: The State charges $30 for corporate annual reports, assesses a corporate excise tax at the rate of 6.6%, and a corporate income tax at the rate of 6.6%.

Contact Information: Janet Sullivan, Director
Corporations Division
Public Service Building
255 Capitol St. NE, Suite 151
Salem, OR 97310-1327
Phone: (503) 986-2200
E-mail: business-info.sos.bic@state.or.us
http://www.sos.state.or.us/corporation/
bic/bic.htm

Pennsylvania

State Corporation Statute: Penn. Consol. Statutes §§ 15.1101 through 15.1997.

Formation: Before filing its articles of incorporation, a domestic for-profit corporation may reserve a name with the department of state. The articles of incorporation must include the following:

• The name of the corporation, which must contain one of the following corporate designators: Corporation, Corp., Company, Co., Incorporated, Inc., Limited, Ltd., Association, Fund, Syndicate, or other such words or abbreviations of like import in languages other than English. The words "Company" or "Co." may be immediately preceded by "and" or "&" whether or not they are immediately followed by one of the words "Incorporated," "Inc.," "Limited," or "Ltd." For example, John Doe & Co. The corporate name shall be distinguishable upon the records of the department from: (1) the name of any other domestic corporation for profit or not-for-profit which is either in existence or for which articles of incorporation have been filed but have not yet become effective, or of any foreign corporation for profit or not-for-profit which is either authorized to do business in Pennsylvania or for which an application for a certificate of authority has been filed but has not yet become effective, or the name of any registered association. A name the exclusive right to which is at the time reserved by any other person whatsoever in the manner provided by statute.

- The address, including street and number, if any, of its initial registered office in Pennsylvania;
- A statement that the corporation is incorporated under the provisions of the Business Corporation Law of 1988.
- A statement that the corporation is to be organized upon a nonstock basis, or if it is to be organized on a stock basis: (1) the aggregate number of shares that the corporation shall have authority to issue (it shall not be necessary to set forth in the articles the designations of the classes of shares of the corporation, or the maximum number of shares of each class that may be issued); (2) a statement of the voting rights, designations, preferences, limitations and special rights in respect of the shares of any class or any series of any class, to the extent that they have been determined; (3) a statement of any authority vested in the board of directors to divide the authorized and unissued shares into classes or series, or both, and to determine for any such class or series its voting rights, designations, preferences, limitations and special rights.
- The name and address, including street and number, if any, of each of the incorporators.
- The term for which the corporation is to exist, if not perpetual.
- If the articles are to be effective on a specified date, the hour, if any, and the month, day and year of the effective date.
- Any other provisions that the incorporators may choose to insert.

You must file the articles of incorporation with the department of state. As of January 2001, the filing fee was $100.00.

The existence of the corporation begins upon the filing of the articles of incorporation with the department of state. Upon creation, the corporation may have a meeting of its incorporators or initial board members to elect directors, officers, adopt bylaws (which may contain any provision consistent with law and the articles of incorporation), and carry on any other business of the corporation. This meeting may be held inside or outside of Pennsylvania.

Minimum Number of Incorporators: Any individual of at least 18 years of age or any entity may incorporate or organize a corporation.

Management Requirements: Directors or original incorporators, depending upon the terms of the articles of incorporation, may approve bylaws for the corporation. There must be at least one director on the corporation's board of directors. Such director must be at least 18 years of age. Every business corporation shall have a president, a secretary and a treasurer, or persons who shall act as such, regardless of the name or title by which they may be designated, elected or appointed.

State Tax Classification: The State assesses a corporate income tax at the rate of 9.99%, a capital stock tax at the rate of 7.49 mills per dollar of capital stock value, and sales and use taxes at the rate of 6%.

Contact Information:	Department of State
	Corporation Bureau
	P.O. Box 8722
	Harrisburg, PA 17105-8722
	Phone: (717) 787-1057
	http://www.dos.state.pa.us/corp/index.htm

Rhode Island

State Corporation Statute: R.I. Code §§ 7-1.1-1 through 7-1.1-141.

Formation: Before filing its articles of incorporation, a domestic for-profit corporation may reserve a name with the secretary of state's office. The articles of incorporation must include the following:

• The name of the corporation, which must contain the word "corporation," "company," "incorporated," or "limited," or shall contain an abbreviation of one of the words. The name must not contain any word or phrase which indicates or implies that it is organized for any purpose other than one or more of the purposes contained in its articles of incorporation. Except as provided below, the name must not be the same as, or deceptively similar to, the name of any domestic corporation, whether for profit or not for profit, or limited partnership existing under the laws of Rhode Island or any foreign corporation, whether for profit or not for profit, or limited partnership authorized to transact business in Rhode Island, or domestic or foreign limited liability company or a name the exclusive right to which is, at the time filed, reserved or registered, or the name of a corporation or a limited partnership which has in effect a registration of its corporate or limited partnership. The foregoing does not apply if the applicant files with the secretary of state either of the following: (1) the written consent of the other corporation, limited partnership, limited liability company or holder of a filed, reserved or registered name to use that name or deceptively similar name, and one or more words are added to make the name distinguishable from the other name; or (2) a certified copy of a final decree of a court of competent jurisdiction establishing the prior right of the applicant to the use of the name in Rhode Island. Furthermore, the name may be the same as, or deceptively similar to, the name of a corporation or other association the certificate of incorporation or organization of which has been revoked by the secretary of state as permitted by law and the revocation has not been withdrawn within one year from the date of the revocation. A corporation with which another corporation, domestic or foreign, is merged, or which is formed by the reorganization or consolidation of one or more domestic or foreign corporations or upon a sale, lease, or other disposition to, or exchange with, a domestic corporation of all or substantially all the assets of another corporation, domestic or foreign, including its name, may have the same name as that used in Rhode Island by any of the corporations if at the time the other corporation was organized under the laws of, or is authorized to transact business in, Rhode Island.

- The period of duration, which may be perpetual.
- The specific purpose or purposes for which the corporation is organized and which may include the transaction of any or all lawful business for which corporations may be incorporated.
- If the corporation is to be authorized to issue only one class of stock, the total number of shares of stock which the corporation has authority to issue; and: (1) the par value of each of the shares; or (2) a statement that all the shares are to be without par value;
- If the corporation is to be authorized to issue more than one class of stock, the total number of shares of all classes of stock which the corpora-

tion has authority to issue and: (1) the number of the shares of each class of stock that are to have a par value and the par value of each share of each class; and/or (2) the number of the shares that are to be without par value; and (3) a statement of all or any of the designations and the powers, preferences, and rights, including voting rights, and the qualifications, limitations, or restrictions of them, which are permitted by Rhode Island law in respect of any class or classes of stock of the corporation and the fixing of which by the articles of association is desired, and an express grant of the authority as it may then be desired to grant to the board of directors to fix by vote or votes any of them that may be desired but which is not fixed by the articles.

- Any provisions dealing with the preemptive right of shareholders.
- Any provision, not inconsistent with law, which the incorporators elect to set forth in the articles of incorporation for the regulation of the internal affairs of the corporation, including, but not limited to, a provision eliminating or limiting the personal liability of a director to the corporation or to its stockholders for monetary damages for breach of the director's duty as a director; provided that the provision does not eliminate or limit the liability of a director for: (1) any breach of the director's duty of loyalty to the corporation or its stockholders; (2) acts or omissions not in good faith or which involve intentional misconduct or a knowing violation of law; (3) liability imposed pursuant to the provisions of § 7-1.1-43 of the Rhode Island Code; or (4) any transaction from which the director derived an improper personal benefit; and also including; (5) any provision which is required or permitted to be set forth in the bylaws. No provision eliminating or limiting the personal liability of a director will be effective with respect to causes of action arising prior to the inclusion of the provision in the articles of incorporation of the corporation.
- The address of its initial registered office, and the name of its initial registered agent at the address.
- The number of directors, if any, constituting the initial board of directors, or, if none, the titles of the initial officers of the corporation and the names and addresses of the persons who are to serve as directors or officers until the first annual meeting of shareholders or until their successors are elected and qualify.
- The name and address of each incorporator.
- If the corporate existence is to begin at a time subsequent to the is-

suance of the certificate of incorporation by the secretary of state, the date when corporate existence begins.

You must file two notarized original copies of the articles of incorporation with the secretary of state. As of January 2001, the filing fee was $70.00.

The existence of the corporation begins upon the filing of the certificate of incorporation with the secretary of state, or upon a later date specified therein. Upon creation, the corporation may have a meeting of its incorporators or initial board members to elect directors, officers, adopt bylaws (which may contain any provision consistent with law and the articles of incorporation), and carry on any other business of the corporation. This meeting may be held inside or outside of Rhode Island.

Minimum Number of Incorporators: Any individual or entity may incorporate or organize a corporation.

Management Requirements: Directors or original incorporators, depending upon the terms of the articles of incorporation, may approve bylaws for the corporation. There must be at least one director on the corporation's board of directors. The officers of a corporation consist of a chairperson of the board of directors, if prescribed by the bylaws, a president, one or more vice presidents, if prescribed by the bylaws, a secretary, and a treasurer.

State Tax Classification: The State charges $50.00 for corporate annual reports, assesses a variable rate corporate franchise tax, and assesses sales and use taxes at the rate of 7%.

Contact Information: First Stop Business Center
100 North Main Street, 2nd Floor
Providence, RI 02903-1335
Phone: (401) 222-2185
Facsimile: (401) 222-3890
E-mail: firststop@sec.state.ri.us
http://www.sec.state.ri.us/bus/frststp.htm

South Carolina

State Corporation Statute: S.C. Code §§ 33-1-101 through 33-19-630.

Formation: Before filing its articles of incorporation, a domestic for-profit corporation may reserve a name with the secretary of state's office. The articles of incorporation must include the following:

- The name of the corporation, which must contain the word "corporation," "incorporated," "company," or "limited," the abbreviation "corp.," "inc.," "co.," or "ltd.," or words or abbreviations of like import in another language. The name may not contain language stating or implying that the corporation is organized for a purpose other than that permitted by law and its articles of incorporation. Except as provided below, a corporate name must be distinguishable upon the records of the secretary of state from: (1) the corporate name of a corporation incorporated or authorized to transact business in South Carolina; (2) a reserved or registered corporate name; (3) the fictitious name adopted by a foreign corporation authorized to transact business in South Carolina because its real name is unavailable; (4) the corporate name of a not-for-profit corporation incorporated or authorized to transact business in South Carolina; (5) the name of a limited partnership authorized to transact business in South Carolina. A corporation may apply to the secretary of state for authorization to use a name that is not distinguishable upon his records from one or more of the names described above. The secretary of state shall authorize use of the name applied for if: (1) the other corporation consents to the use in writing and submits an undertaking in form satisfactory to the secretary of state to change its name to a name that is distinguishable upon the records of the secretary of state from the name of the applying corporation; or (2) the applicant delivers to the secretary of state a certified copy of the final judgment of a court of competent jurisdiction establishing the applicant's right to use the name applied for in South Carolina. A corporation may use the name (including the fictitious name) of another domestic or foreign corporation that is used in South Carolina if the other corporation is incorporated or authorized to transact business in South Carolina and the proposed user corporation: (1) has merged with the other corporation; (2) has been formed by reorganization of the other corporation; or (3) has acquired all or substantially all of the assets, including the corporate name, of the other corporation.
- The number of shares the corporation is authorized to issue, itemized by classes;
- The street address of the corporation's initial registered office and the name of its initial registered agent at that office;
- The name and address of each incorporator;
- The signature of each incorporator; and

- A certificate, signed by an attorney licensed to practice in South Carolina, that all of the requirements of South Carolina law governing corporate formation have been complied with.

You must file the original signed copy, and one additional copy of the articles of incorporation with the secretary of state. As of January 2001, the filing fee was $135.00, with an additional charge of $2.00 for the certificate of incorporation. The articles of incorporation must be accompanied by the corporation's initial annual report.

The existence of the corporation begins upon the filing of the articles of incorporation with the secretary of state. Upon creation, the corporation may have a meeting of its incorporators or initial board members to elect directors, officers, adopt bylaws (which may contain any provision consistent with law and the articles of incorporation), and carry on any other business of the corporation. This meeting may be held inside or outside of South Carolina.

Minimum Number of Incorporators: Any individual or entity may incorporate or organize a corporation.

Management Requirements: Directors or original incorporators, depending upon the terms of the articles of incorporation, may approve bylaws for the corporation. There must be at least one director on the corporation's board of directors.

State Tax Classification: The State assesses a corporate franchise tax at the rate of $15.00 plus 1 mill per $1.00 paid to capital stock and surplus, a corporate income tax at the rate of 5%, and sales and use taxes at the rate of 4%.

Contact Information: South Carolina Secretary of State
Business Filings
P.O. Box 11350
Columbia, SC 29211
Customer Services: (803) 734-2158
http://www.scsos.com/

South Dakota

State Corporation Statute: S.D. Code §§ 47-2 through 47-9.

Formation: Before filing its articles of incorporation, a domestic for-profit corporation may reserve a name with the secretary of state's office. The articles of incorporation must include the following:

- The name of the corporation, which must contain the word "corporation," "company," "incorporated," or "limited," or shall contain an abbreviation of one of such words. The name must not contain any word or phrase which indicates or implies that it is organized for any purpose other than one or more of the purposes stated in its articles of incorporation. The name must be distinguishable upon the records of the secretary of state from the name of any other corporation, whether for profit or not for profit, organized under the laws of South Dakota; the name of any foreign corporation, whether for profit or not for profit, authorized to engage in any business in South Dakota; or any corporate name reserved or registered as permitted by the laws of South Dakota; or the name of any limited partnership certified or registered in South Dakota; or the name of any limited liability company. Corporate names or limited partnership names already in use, with generic, proper, geographical or descriptive terms which have acquired a secondary meaning shall be protected. The foregoing does not apply if the applicant files with the secretary of state either: (1) the written consent signed by the president or a vice president and by the secretary or an assistant secretary of the other corporation; by a holder of a reserved or registered name; or by a general partner of a limited partnership to use the same or a distinguishable name; (2) a certified copy of a final decree of a court of competent jurisdiction establishing the prior right of the applicant to the use of such name in South Dakota; or (3) in the case of a foreign corporation, if the corporate name is not available for use, a resolution of its board of directors adopting an assumed name for use in transacting business in South Dakota, which assumed name is not distinguishable from the name of any domestic corporation, any foreign corporation authorized to engage in any business in South Dakota, or any corporate name reserved or registered as permitted by the laws of South Dakota, or the name of any limited partnership certified or registered in South Dakota or any other assumed name filed with the secretary of state by a foreign corporation authorized to transact business in South Dakota. The name must be transliterated into letters of the English alphabet, if it is not in English. A corporation with which another corporation, domestic or foreign, is merged, or which is formed by the reorganization or consolidation of one or more domestic or foreign corporations or upon a sale, lease or other disposition to or exchange with, a domestic corporation of all or substantially all the assets of another corporation, domestic or foreign, including its name, may have the same name as that used in South Dakota by any of such corporations if the other corporation was organized under the laws of, or is authorized to transact business in South Dakota.

- The period of duration, which may be perpetual;
- The purpose or purposes for which the corporation is organized;
- The aggregate number of shares which the corporation shall have authority to issue; if such shares are to consist of one class only, the par value of each of such shares, or a statement that all of such shares are without par value; or, if such shares are to be divided into classes, the number of shares of each class, and a statement of the par value of the shares of each such class, or that such shares are to be without par value;
- If the shares are to be divided into classes, the designation of each class and a statement of the preferences, limitations and relative rights in respect of the shares of each class;
- If the corporation is to issue the shares of any preferred or special class in series, then the designation of each series and a statement of the variations in the relative rights and preferences as between series insofar as the same are to be fixed in the articles of incorporation, and a statement of any authority to be vested in the board of directors to establish series and fix and determine the variations in the relative rights and preferences as between series;
- A statement that the corporation will not commence business until consideration of the value of at least one thousand dollars has been received for the issuance of shares;
- Any provision limiting or denying to shareholders the preemptive right to acquire additional or treasury shares of the corporation;
- Any provision, not inconsistent with law, which the incorporators elect to set forth in the articles of incorporation for the regulation of the internal affairs of the corporation, including any provision restricting the transfer of shares and any provision which is required or permitted to be set forth in the bylaws;
- The street address, or a statement that there is no street address, of the registered office, the name of its registered agent at such address and his written consent to the appointment;
- The number of directors constituting the initial board of directors and the names and addresses of the persons who are to serve as directors until

the first annual meeting of shareholders or until their successors be elected and qualify;

- The name and address of each incorporator.

You must file the articles of incorporation with the secretary of state. As of January 2001, the filing fee was based on the par value of the authorized stock of the corporation. The minimum par value was $100 per share, the minimum filing fee was $90.00, and the maximum filing fee assessed was $16,000.

The existence of the corporation begins upon the issuance of the certificate of existence by the secretary of state. Upon creation, the corporation may have a meeting of its incorporators or initial board members to elect directors, officers, adopt bylaws (which may contain any provision consistent with law and the articles of incorporation), and carry on any other business of the corporation. This meeting may be held inside or outside of South Dakota.

Minimum Number of Incorporators: Any natural person of at least 18 years of age may incorporate or organize a corporation.

Management Requirements: Directors or original incorporators, depending upon the terms of the articles of incorporation, may approve bylaws for the corporation. There must be at least one director on the corporation's board of directors.

State Tax Classification: The State charges $90.00 for the original corporate report, $50.00 for annual corporate reports, and assesses sales and use taxes at the rate of 4%.

     Contact Information: Secretary of State
                                         Capitol Building
                                         500 East Capitol Avenue Ste 204
                                         Pierre, SD 57501-5070
                                         Phone: (605) 773-4845
                                         Facsimile: (605) 773-4550
                                         E-mail: mary.heidelberger@state.sd.us
                                         http://www.state.sd.us/sos/sos.htm

Tennessee

State Corporation Statute: TN Statutes §§ 48-11-101 through 48-27-103.

Formation: Before filing its corporate charter, a domestic for-profit corporation may reserve a name with the secretary of state's office. The corporate charter must include the following:

- The name of the corporation, which must contain the word "corporation," "incorporated," "company," or the abbreviation "corp.," "inc.," "co.," or words or abbreviations of like import in another language (provided they are written in roman characters or letters); provided, that if such corporation is formed for the purpose of an insurance or banking business, the name of such corporation need not contain any of the aforementioned words or abbreviations. The name may not contain language stating or implying that the corporation: (1) transacts or has power to transact any business for which authorization in whatever form and however denominated is required under the laws of Tennessee, unless the appropriate commission or officer has granted such authorization and certifies that fact in writing; (2) is organized as, affiliated with, or sponsored by, any fraternal, veterans', service, religious, charitable, or professional organization, unless that fact is certified in writing by the organization with which affiliation or sponsorship is claimed; (3) is an agency or instrumentality of, affiliated with or sponsored by the United States or the state of Tennessee or a subdivision or agency thereof, unless such fact is certified in writing by the appropriate official of the United States or the state of Tennessee or subdivision or agency thereof; or (4) is organized for a purpose other than that permitted by law and its charter. Except as provided below, a corporate name must be distinguishable upon the records of the secretary of state from: (1) the corporate name or assumed corporate name of a corporation incorporated or authorized to transact business in Tennessee; (2) an assumed, reserved or registered corporate name; (3) the corporate name of a not-for-profit corporation incorporated or authorized to transact business in Tennessee; (4) a limited partnership name reserved or organized under the laws of Tennessee or registered as a foreign limited partnership in Tennessee; and (5) the name of a limited liability company authorized to do business as a foreign limited liability company in Tennessee. A corporation may apply to the secretary of state for authorization to use a name that is not distinguishable upon the secretary of state's records from one or more of the names described above. The secretary of state shall authorize use of the name applied for if: (1) the other corporation, limited partnership or foreign limited liability company consents to the use in writing and submits an undertaking in form satisfactory to the secretary of state to change its name to a name that is distinguishable upon the records of the secretary of state from the name of the applying corporation; or (2) the applicant delivers to the secretary of state a certified copy of the final judgment of a court of competent jurisdiction establishing the applicant's right to use the name applied for in Tennessee. A domestic corporation or a foreign corporation authorized to transact business or applying for a certificate of authority to transact business may elect to adopt an assumed corporate name.

- The number of shares the corporation is authorized to issue;
- The street address and zip code of the corporation's initial registered office, the county in which the office is located, and the name of its initial registered agent at that office;
- The name and address and zip code of each incorporator;
- The street address and zip code of the initial principal office of the corporation;
- The number of shares of each class that the corporation is authorized to issue. If more than one class of shares is authorized, the charter must prescribe a distinguishing designation for each class, and prior to the issuance of shares of a class, the preferences, limitations, and relative rights of that class must be described in the charter. All shares of a class must have preferences, limitations, and relative rights identical with those of other shares of the same class, except to the extent that the board of directors may be authorized in the charter to determine such rights; and
- A statement that the corporation is for profit.

You must file the corporate charter with the secretary of state. As of January 2001, the filing fee was $100.00.

The existence of the corporation begins upon the filing of the corporate charter with the secretary of state. Upon creation, the corporation may have a meeting of its incorporators or initial board members to elect directors, officers, adopt bylaws (which may contain any provision consistent with law and the corporate charter), and carry on any other business of the corporation. This meeting may be held inside or outside of Tennessee.

Minimum Number of Incorporators: Any individual of at least 18 years of age may incorporate or organize a corporation.

Management Requirements: Directors or original incorporators, depending upon the terms of the articles of incorporation, may approve bylaws for the corporation. There must be at least one director on the corporation's board of directors. Such director must be an individual. There must be a president and secretary of the corporation.

State Tax Classification: The State charges $20.00 for annual corporate reports, assesses annual franchise taxes at the rate of $.25 per $100.00 of net worth, assesses an excise tax at the rate of 6%, and sales and use taxes at the rate of 6%.

Contact Information:	Division of Business Services
	312 Eighth Avenue North
	6th Floor, William R. Snodgrass Tower
	Nashville, TN 37243
	Corporate Certification Phone:
	(615) 741-6488
	Corporate Information Phone:
	(615) 741-2286
	E-mail: services@mail.state.tn.us
	http://www.state.tn.us/sos/service.htm

Texas

State Corporation Statute: Business Corporation Act §§ 1.01 through 13.08.

Formation: Before filing its articles of incorporation, a domestic for-profit corporation may reserve a name with the secretary of state's office. The articles of incorporation must include the following:

• The name of the corporation, which must contain the word "corporation," "company," or "incorporated," or shall contain an abbreviation of one of such words, and shall contain such additional words as may be required by law. It must not contain any word or phrase which indicates or implies that it is organized for any purpose other than one or more of the purposes contained in its articles of incorporation. A corporate name may not contain the word "lottery." It may not be the same as, or deceptively similar to, the name of any domestic corporation, limited partnership, or limited liability company existing under the laws of Texas, or the name of any foreign corporation, non-profit corporation, limited partnership, or limited liability company authorized to transact business in Texas, or a name the exclusive right to which is, at the time, reserved or registered. A name may be similar if written consent is obtained from the existing corporation, limited partnership, or limited liability company having the name deemed to be similar or the person for whom the name deemed to be similar is reserved in the office of the secretary of state. Any domestic or foreign corporation having authority to transact business in Texas may do so under an assumed name by filing an assumed name certificate.

- The period of duration, which may be perpetual;
- The purpose or purposes for which the corporation is organized which may be stated to be, or to include, the transaction of any or all lawful business for which corporations may be incorporated;
- The aggregate number of shares which the corporation shall have authority to issue; if such shares are to consist of one class only, the par value of each of such shares, or a statement that all of such shares are without par value; or, if such shares are to be divided into classes, the number of shares of each class, and a statement of the par value of the shares of each class or that such shares are to be without par value;
- If the shares are to be divided into classes, the designation of each class and statement of the preferences, limitations, and relative rights in respect of the shares of each class;
- If the corporation is to issue the shares of any class in series, then the designation of each series and a statement of the variations in the preferences, limitations and relative rights as between series insofar as the same are to be fixed in the articles of incorporation, and a statement of any authority to be vested in the board of directors to establish series and fix and determine the preferences, limitations and relative rights of each series;
- A statement that the corporation will not commence business until it has received for the issuance of shares consideration of the value of a stated sum which shall be at least $1,000;
- Any provision limiting or denying to shareholders the preemptive right to acquire additional or treasury shares of the corporation;
- If a corporation elects to become a close corporation, any provision (1) required or permitted to be stated in the articles of incorporation of a close corporation, but not in the articles of incorporation of an ordinary corporation, (2) contained or permitted to be contained in a shareholders' agreement which the incorporators elect to set forth in articles of incorporation, or (3) that makes a shareholders' agreement part of the articles of incorporation of a close corporation, but any such provision shall be preceded by a statement that the provision shall be subject to the corporation remaining a close corporation;

- Any provision, not inconsistent with law providing for the regulation of the internal affairs of the corporation;
- The street address of its initial registered office and the name of its initial registered agent at such address;
- The number of directors constituting the initial board of directors and the names and addresses of the person or persons who are to serve as directors until the first annual meeting of shareholders or until their successors be elected and qualify, or, in the case of a close corporation that, is to be managed in some other manner pursuant to a shareholders' agreement by the shareholders or by the persons empowered by the agreement to manage its business and affairs, the names and addresses of the person or persons who, pursuant to the shareholders' agreement, will perform the functions of the initial board of directors;
- The name and address of each incorporator, unless the corporation is being incorporated pursuant to a plan of conversion or a plan of merger, in which case the articles need not include such information; and
- If the corporation is being incorporated pursuant to a plan of conversion or a plan of merger, a statement to that effect, and in the case of a plan of conversion, the name, address, date of formation, and prior form of organization and jurisdiction of incorporation or organization of the converting entity.

You must file an original and a copy of the articles of incorporation with the secretary of state. As of January 2001, the filing fee was $300.00.

The existence of the corporation begins upon the filing of the articles of incorporation with the secretary of state. Upon creation, and subsequent to its receipt of at least $1,000 as consideration for shares of stock, the corporation may have a meeting of its incorporators or initial board members to elect directors, officers, adopt bylaws (which may contain any provision consistent with law and the articles of incorporation), and carry on any other business of the corporation. This meeting may be held inside or outside of Texas.

Minimum Number of Incorporators: Any individual of at least 18 years of age may incorporate or organize a corporation.

Management Requirements: Directors or original incorporators, depending upon the terms of the articles of incorporation, may approve bylaws for the corporation. There must be at least one director on the corporation's board of directors. There also must be a president and secretary of the corporation.

State Tax Classification: The State assesses a corporate franchise tax at the rate of .25% per year of net taxable capital and 4.5% of net taxable earned surplus, and sales and use taxes at the rate of 6.25%.

Contact Information: Corporations Section
Secretary of State
P.O. Box 13697
Austin, Texas 78711
Phone: (512) 463-5583
E-mail: corphelp@sos.state.tx.us
http://www.sos.state.tx.us/corp/index.shtml

Utah

State Corporation Statute: Utah Code §§ 16-10a-102 through 16-10a-1705.

Formation: Before filing its articles of incorporation, a domestic for-profit corporation may reserve a name with the department of commerce. The articles of incorporation must include the following:

• The name of the corporation, which must contain the word "corporation," "incorporated," or "company," the abbreviation "corp.," "inc.," or "co.," or words or abbreviations of like import to the words or abbreviations listed above in another language. The name may not contain language stating or implying that the corporation is organized for a purpose other than that permitted by law and the corporation's articles of incorporation. Without the written consent of the United States Olympic Committee, the name may not contain the words "Olympic," "Olympiad," or "Citius Altius Fortius." Without the written consent of the State Board of Regents, may not contain the words "university," "college," or "institute." Except as provided below, the name of a corporation must be distinguishable upon the records of the corporations division from the following: (1) the name of any domestic corporation incorporated in or foreign corporation authorized to transact business in Utah; (2) the name of any domestic or foreign non-profit corporation incorporated or authorized to transact business in Utah; (3) the name of any domestic or foreign limited liability company formed or authorized to transact business in Utah; (4) the name of any limited partnership formed or authorized to transact business in Utah; (5) any name reserved or registered with the corporations division for a corporation, limited liability company, or general or limited partnership, under the laws of Utah; and (6) any business name, fictitious name, assumed name, trademark, or service mark registered by the division. A corporation may apply to the division for authorization to file its articles of incorporation under, or to register or reserve, a name that is not distinguishable upon its records from one or more of the names described above. The division shall approve the application if: (1) the other person whose name is not distinguishable from the name under which the applicant desires to file, or which the applicant desires to register or reserve: (A) consents to the filing, registration, or reservation in writing; and (B) submits an undertaking in a form satisfactory to the division to change its name to a name that is distinguishable from the name of the applicant; or (2) the applicant delivers to the division a certified copy of the final judgment of a court of competent jurisdiction establishing the applicant's right to make the requested filing in Utah under the name applied for. A corporation may make a filing under the name, including the fictitious name, of another domestic or foreign corporation that is used or registered in Utah if: (1) the other corporation is incorporated or authorized to transact business in this state; and (2) the filing corporation: (a) has merged with the other corporation; or (b) has been formed by reorganization of the other corporation.

- The purpose or purposes for which the corporation is organized;
- The number of shares the corporation is authorized to issue;
- With respect to each class of shares the corporation is authorized to issue, the classes of shares and the number of shares of each class that the corporation is authorized to issue. If more than one class of shares is authorized, the articles of incorporation must prescribe a distinguishing designation for each class, and prior to the issuance of shares of a class the preferences, limitations, and relative rights of that class must be described in the articles of incorporation. All shares of a class must have preferences, limitations, and relative rights identical with those of other shares of the same class except to the extent otherwise permitted by Sections 16-10a-601 and 602 of the Utah Code.
- The street address of the corporation's initial registered office and the name and signature of its initial registered agent at that office; and
- The name and address of each incorporator.

You must file the articles of incorporation with the department of commerce. As of January 2001, the filing fee was $50.00.

The existence of the corporation begins upon the filing of the articles of incorporation with the department of commerce. Upon creation, the corporation may have a meeting of its incorporators or initial board members to elect directors, officers, adopt bylaws (which may contain any provision consistent with law and the articles of incorporation), and carry on any other business of the corporation. This meeting may be held inside or outside of Utah.

Minimum Number of Incorporators: Any individual or entity may incorporate or organize a corporation.

Management Requirements: Directors or original incorporators, depending upon the terms of the articles of incorporation, may approve bylaws for the corporation. Prior to the issuance of shares of stock, there must be at least one director on the corporation's board of directors. Once the corporation has issued shares of stock, there must be two directors if there are two shareholders, or at least three directors if there are at least three shareholders. Directors must be natural persons.

State Tax Classification: The State charges $10.00 for corporate annual reports, assesses a corporate franchise tax at the rate of 5% of Utah taxable income, a corporate income tax of 5%, and sales and use taxes at the rate of 4.75%.

Contact Information:	Utah Department of Commerce
	Division of Corporations and
	Commercial Code
	160 E. 300th Street
	Salt Lake City, UT 84111
	Phone: (801) 530-4849
	http://www.commerce.state.ut.us/
	corporat/corpcoc.htm

Vermont

State Corporation Statute: Vt. Statutes §§ 11A-1.01 through 11A-20.16.

Formation: Before filing its certificate of incorporation, a domestic for-profit corporation may reserve a name with the secretary of state's office. The certificate of incorporation must include the following:

- The name of the corporation, which must contain the word "corporation," "incorporated," "company," or "limited," or the abbreviation "corp.," "inc.," "co.," or "ltd.," or words or abbreviations of like import in another language. The name may not contain language stating or implying that the corporation is organized for a purpose other than that permitted by law and its articles of incorporation. A corporate name must not have the word "cooperative" or any abbreviation thereof as part of its name unless the corporation is a worker cooperative corporation or the articles of incorporation contain all of the provisions required of a corporation organized as a cooperative association. The name must not include any word not otherwise authorized by law. Except as provided below, a corporate name, based upon the records of the secretary of state, must be distinguishable from, and not the same as, deceptively similar to, or likely to be confused with or mistaken for any name granted, registered, or reserved under this chapter, or the name of any other entity, whether domestic or foreign, that is reserved, registered, or granted by or with the secretary of state. A corporation may apply to the secretary of state for authorization to use a name that is not distinguishable from, or is the same as, deceptively similar to, or likely to be confused with or mistaken for one or more of the names described above, as determined from review of the records of the secretary of state. The secretary of state shall authorize use of the name applied for if: (1) the other corporation or business consents to the use in writing and submits an undertaking in form satisfactory to the secretary of state to change its name to a name that is distinguishable from, and not the same as, deceptively similar to, or likely to be confused with or mistaken for the name of the applying corporation; or (2) the applicant delivers to the secretary of state a certified copy of the final judgment of a court of competent jurisdiction establishing the applicant's right to use the name applied for in Vermont. A corporation may use the name (including the fictitious name) of another domestic or foreign corporation that is used in Vermont if the other corporation is incorporated or authorized to transact business in Vermont and the proposed user corporation: (1) has merged with the other corporation; (2) has been formed by reorganization of the other corporation; or (3) has acquired all or substantially all of the assets, including the corporate name, of the other corporation.

- The classes of shares, if any, and the number of shares in each class that the corporation is authorized to issue;
- The number of shares the corporation is authorized to issue;
- The street address of the corporation's initial registered office and the name of its initial registered agent at that office;

- The name and address of each incorporator;
- One or more classes of shares must have unlimited voting rights; and
- One or more classes of shares (which may be the same class or classes as those with voting rights) must be entitled to receive the net assets of the corporation upon dissolution.

You must file the articles of incorporation with the secretary of state. As of January 2001, the filing fee was $75.00, with an additional charge of $5.00 for the certificate of incorporation.

The existence of the corporation begins upon the filing of the articles of incorporation with the secretary of state. Upon creation, the corporation may have a meeting of its incorporators or initial board members to elect directors, officers, adopt bylaws (which may contain any provision consistent with law and the articles of incorporation), and carry on any other business of the corporation. This meeting may be held inside or outside of Vermont.

Minimum Number of Incorporators: Any individual of at least 18 years of age may incorporate or organize a corporation.

Management Requirements: Directors or original incorporators, depending upon the terms of the articles of incorporation, may approve bylaws for the corporation. A board of directors of a corporation, which is not a close corporation, must consist of three or more individuals, with the number specified in or fixed in accordance with the articles of incorporation or bylaws. If the number of shareholders in any corporation is less than three, the number of directors may be as few as the number of shareholders. A corporation must have a president and a secretary.

State Tax Classification: The State charges $15.00 for annual corporation reports, assesses a variable rate corporate income tax, and assesses sales and use taxes at the rate of 5%.

Contact Information: Vermont Secretary of State
Corporations Division
81 River Street, Drawer 09
Montpelier, Vt 05609-1104
Phone: (802) 828-2386
Facsimile: (802) 828-2853
http://www.sec.state.vt.us/corps/
corpindex.htm

Virginia

State Corporation Statute: Va. Code §§ 13.1-601 through 13.1-781.

Formation: Before filing its certificate of incorporation, a domestic for-profit corporation may reserve a name with the state corporation commission. The certificate of incorporation must include the following:

- The name of the corporation, which must contain the word "corporation," "incorporated," "company," or "limited," or the abbreviation "corp.," "inc.," "co.," or "ltd." Such words and their corresponding abbreviations may be used interchangeably for all purposes. A corporate name shall not contain: (1) any language stating or implying that it will transact one of the special kinds of businesses listed in Section 13.1-620 of the Virginia Code, unless it proposes in fact to engage in such special kind of business; or (2) any word or phrase that is prohibited by law for such corporation. Except as provided below, a corporate name shall be distinguishable upon the records of the commission from: (1) the corporate name of a domestic corporation or a foreign corporation authorized to transact business in Virginia; (2) a reserved or registered corporate name; (3) the designated name adopted by a foreign corporation, whether issuing or not issuing shares, because its real name is unavailable; and (4) the corporate name of a nonstock corporation incorporated or authorized to transact business in Virginia. A domestic corporation may apply to the commission for authorization to use a name that is not distinguishable upon its records from one or more of the names described above. The commission shall authorize use of the name applied for if: (1) the other entity consents to the use in writing and submits an undertaking in form satisfactory to the commission to change its name to a name that is distinguishable upon the records of the commission from the name of the applying corporation.
- The number of shares the corporation is authorized to issue;
- If more than one class of shares is authorized, the number of authorized shares of each class and a distinguishing designation for each class;
- The address of the corporation's initial registered office (including both (1) the post-office address with street and number, if any and (2) the name of the city or county in which it is located), and the name of its initial registered agent at that office;

• A statement which declares that the agent is either (1) a resident of Virginia and either a director of the corporation or a member of the Virginia State Bar or (2) a professional corporation, professional limited liability company, or registered limited liability partnership registered with the Virginia State Bar.

You must file the articles of incorporation with the state corporation commission. As of January 2001, the filing fee was $25.00. In addition, domestic and foreign corporations must pay a charter fee, assessed at the rate of $50 for each 25,000 shares or fraction thereof. For any domestic or foreign corporation whose number of authorized shares is more than 1,000,000 shares, the fee was $2,500.

The existence of the corporation begins upon the issuance of a certificate of incorporation by the state corporation commission. Upon creation, the corporation may have a meeting of its incorporators or initial board members to elect directors, officers, adopt bylaws (which may contain any provision consistent with law and the articles of incorporation), and carry on any other business of the corporation. This meeting may be held inside or outside of Virginia.

Minimum Number of Incorporators: Any individual or entity may incorporate or organize a corporation.

Management Requirements: Directors or original incorporators, depending upon the terms of the articles of incorporation, may approve bylaws for the corporation. There must be at least one director on the corporation's board of directors.

State Tax Classification: The State charges $50.00 on the first 5,000 authorized share, and $15.00 for each additional 5,000 shares, as an annual registration fee. Virginia also assesses a corporate income tax at the rate of 6% and sales and use taxes at the rate of 3.5%.

Contact Information: Office of the Clerk
Virginia State Corporation Division
P. O. Box 1197
Richmond, Virginia 23218
Phone: (804) 371-9733
http://www.state.va.us/scc/division/clk/
index.htm

Washington

State Corporation Statute: RCW §§ 23B.01 through 23B.900.

Formation: Before filing its certificate of incorporation, a domestic for-profit corporation may reserve a name with the secretary of state's office. The certificate of incorporation must include the following:

- The name of the corporation, which must contain the word "corporation," "incorporated," "company," or "limited," or the abbreviation "corp.," "inc.," "co.," or "ltd." The name must not contain language stating or implying that the corporation is organized for a purpose other than those permitted by law and its articles of incorporation. It must not contain any of the following words or phrases: "Bank," "banking," "banker," "trust," "cooperative," or any combination of the words "industrial" and "loan," or any combination of any two or more of the words "building," "savings," "loan," "home," "association," and "society," or any other words or phrases prohibited by any statute of Washington. Except provided below, the name must be distinguishable upon the records of the secretary of state from: (1) the corporate name of a corporation incorporated or authorized to transact business in Washington; (2) a reserved or registered corporate name; (3) the fictitious name adopted by a foreign corporation authorized to transact business in Washington because its real name is unavailable; (4) the corporate name or reserved name of a not-for-profit corporation incorporated or authorized to conduct affairs in Washington; (5) the name or reserved name of a mutual corporation or miscellaneous corporation incorporated or authorized to do business in Washington; (6) the name or reserved name of a foreign or domestic limited partnership formed or registered under the laws of Washington; (7) the name or reserved name of a limited liability company organized or registered under the laws of Washington; and (8) the name or reserved name of a limited liability partnership registered under Washington law. A corporation may apply to the secretary of state for authorization to use a name that is not distinguishable upon the records from one or more of the names described above. The secretary of state shall authorize use of the name applied for if: (1) the other corporation, company, holder, limited liability partnership, or limited partnership consents to the use in writing and files with the secretary of state documents necessary to change its name or the name reserved or registered to a name that is distinguishable upon the records of the secretary of state from the name of the applying corporation; or (2) the applicant delivers to the secretary of state a certified copy of the final judgment of a court of competent jurisdiction establishing the applicant's right to use the name applied for in Washington. A corporation may use the name, including the fictitious name, of another domestic or foreign corporation, limited liability company, limited partnership, or limited liability partnership, that is used in Washington if the other entity is formed or authorized to transact business in Washington, and the proposed user corporation: (1) has merged with the other corporation, limited liability company, or limited partnership; or (2) has been formed by reorganization of the other corporation.

- The number of shares the corporation is authorized to issue;
- The street address of the corporation's initial registered office and the name of its initial registered agent at that office;
- The name and address of each incorporator; and
- The articles of incorporation or bylaws must either specify the number of directors or specify the process by which the number of directors will be fixed, unless the articles of incorporation dispense with a board of directors.

You must file the articles of incorporation with the secretary of state. As of January 2001, the filing fee was $175.00, with an additional charge of $175.00 for the corporation's initial report. Within 120 days of the formation of the corporation, you must file the corporation's initial report.

The existence of the corporation begins upon the filing of the articles of incorporation with the secretary of state. Upon creation, the corporation may have a meeting of its incorporators or initial board members to elect directors, officers, adopt bylaws (which may contain any provision consistent with law and the articles of incorporation), and carry on any other business of the corporation. This meeting may be held inside or outside of Washington.

Minimum Number of Incorporators: Any individual or entity may incorporate or organize a corporation.

Management Requirements: Directors or original incorporators, depending upon the terms of the articles of incorporation, may approve bylaws for the corporation. Unless the board is disposed of in the articles of incorporation pursuant to Washington law, there must be at least one director on the corporation's board of directors.

State Tax Classification: The State charges $50.00 as an annual license fee, and assesses a retail sales tax at the rate of 6.5%.

Contact Information: Corporations Division
801 Capitol Way S.
P.O. Box 40234
Olympia, WA 98504-0234
Phone: (360) 753-7115
E-mail: corps@secstate.wa.gov
http://www.secstate.wa.gov/corps/
default.htm

West Virginia

State Corporation Statute: WV Code §§ 31-1-1 through 31-1-160.

Formation: Before filing its certificate of incorporation, a domestic for-profit corporation may reserve a name with the secretary of state's office. The articles of incorporation must include the following:

• The name of the corporation, which must contain the word "corporation," "company," "incorporated," or "limited," or shall contain an abbreviation of one of such words. The name must not contain any word or phrase which indicates or implies that it is organized for any purpose other than one or more of the purposes contained in its articles of incorporation. The name must be transliterated into letters of the English alphabet, if it is not in English. No corporation may be chartered in West Virginia under any name which includes the word "engineer," "engineers," "engineering" or any combination of the same unless the purpose of the corporation is to practice professional engineering, and one or more of the incorporators is a registered professional engineer. The name must not be the same as, and shall be distinguishable from: (1) the name of any domestic corporation, domestic limited partnership, domestic limited liability partnership, or domestic limited liability company existing under the laws of West Virginia; (2) the name of any foreign corporation, foreign limited partnership, foreign limited liability partnership, foreign limited liability company, or any other foreign business entity authorized to conduct affairs or transact business in West Virginia; (3) a name the exclusive right to which is, at the time, reserved in the manner provided by law; or (4) the name of a corporation, limited partnership, limited liability partnership, or limited liability company which has in effect a registration of its business name as provided by law. The foregoing requirements do not apply if the applicant files with the secretary of state either: (1) a written consent to the use and a written undertaking by the present user, registrant or owner of a reserved name submitted in a form satisfactory to the secretary of state to change the name to a name that is distinguishable from the name applied for; or (2) a certified copy of a final order of a court of competent jurisdiction establishing the prior right of the applicant to the use of such name in West Virginia. Any terms or abbreviations required to be included in the business name to identify the type of business entity shall not alone be sufficient to make one name distinguishable from another. A corporation with which another corporation, domestic or foreign, is merged, or which is formed by the reorganization or consolidation of one or more domestic or foreign corporations or upon a sale, lease or other disposition to or exchange with, a domestic corporation of all or substantially all the assets of another corporation, domestic or foreign, including its name, may have the same name as that used in West Virginia by any of such corporations if such other corporation was organized under the laws of, or is authorized to conduct affairs or do or transact business in West Virginia.

- The period of duration, which may be perpetual;
- The purpose or purposes for which the corporation is organized, which may be stated to be, or to include, the transaction of any or all lawful business for which corporations may be incorporated under law;
- The address of its principal office, and the name and address of the person to whom shall be sent notice or process served upon, or service of which is accepted by, the secretary of state, if such person has been appointed by the corporation;
- The number of directors constituting the initial board of directors and the names and addresses of the persons who are to serve as such directors;
- The name and address of each incorporator;
- The aggregate number of shares which the corporation shall have authority to issue; if such shares are to consist of one class only, the par value of each of such shares, or a statement that all of such shares are without par value; or, if such shares are to be divided into classes, the number of shares

of each class, and a statement of the par value of the shares of each such class or that such shares are to be without par value.

• If the shares are to be divided into classes, the designation of each class and a statement of the preferences, limitations and relative rights in respect of the shares of each class.

• If the corporation is to issue the shares of any preferred or special class in series, the designation of each series and a statement of the variations in the relative rights and preferences as between series insofar as the same are to be fixed in the articles of incorporation, and a statement of any authority to be vested in the board of directors to establish series and fix and determine the variations in the relative rights and preferences as between series;

• Any provision limiting or denying to shareholders the preemptive right to acquire additional unissued or treasury shares of the corporation;

• Any provision, not inconsistent with law, which the incorporators elect to set forth in the articles of incorporation for the regulation of the internal affairs of the corporation, including any provision restricting the transfer of shares and any provision which under this article is required or permitted to be set forth in the bylaws.

You must file the articles of incorporation with the secretary of state. As of January 2001, the registration fee was $50.00. In addition, domestic for-profit corporations were charged an attorney of fact fee and a license tax fee, which were determined by the value of the authorized capital stock of the corporation.

The existence of the corporation begins upon the issuance of a certificate of incorporation by the secretary of state. Upon creation, the corporation may have a meeting of its incorporators or initial board members to elect directors, officers, adopt bylaws (which may contain any provision consistent with law and the articles of incorporation), and carry on any other business of the corporation. This meeting may be held inside or outside of West Virginia.

Minimum Number of Incorporators: Any individual or entity may incorporate or organize a corporation.

Management Requirements: Directors or original incorporators, depending upon the terms of the articles of incorporation, may approve bylaws for the corporation. There must be at least one director on the corporation's board of directors, and the corporation must have a president, secretary, and treasurer.

State Tax Classification: The State charges a graduated corporate license tax, a business franchise tax, a corporate net income tax at the rate of 9%, and sales and use taxes at the rate of 6%.

Contact Information:

Corporations Division
Secretary of State
Bldg. 1, Suite 157-K
1900 Kanawha Blvd. East
Charleston, WV 25305-0770
Phone: (304) 558-8000
Facsimile: (304) 558-0900
E-mail: wvsos@secretary.state.wv.us
(include the division name in the subject line)
http://www.state.wv.us/sos/corp/default.htm

Wisconsin

State Corporation Statute: Wi. Statutes §§ 180.0101 through 180.1008.

Formation: Before filing its articles of corporation, a domestic for-profit corporation may reserve a name with the secretary of state's office. The articles of incorporation must include the following:

• The name of the corporation, which must contain the word "corporation," "incorporated," "company," or "limited," or the abbreviation "corp.," "inc.," "co.," or "ltd.," or words or abbreviations of like import in another language. The name may not contain language stating or implying that the corporation is organized for a purpose other than that permitted by law and its articles of incorporation. Except as provided below, the corporate name of a domestic corporation must be distinguishable upon the records of the department from all of the following names: (1) the corporate name of a domestic corporation or a foreign corporation authorized to transact business in Wisconsin; (2) a reserved or registered corporate name; (3) the corporate name of a dissolved corporation or a dissolved nonstock corporation that has retained the exclusive use of its name; (4) the fictitious name adopted by a foreign corporation or a foreign nonstock corporation authorized to transact business in Wisconsin; (5) the corporate name of a nonstock corporation incorporated in Wisconsin; (6) the name of a limited partnership formed under the laws of, or registered in, Wisconsin; (7) the name of a cooperative association incorporated or authorized to transact business in Wisconsin; and (8) the name of a limited liability company organized under the laws of, or registered in, Wisconsin; the name of a limited liability partnership formed under the laws of, or registered in, Wisconsin. The corporate name of a corporation is not distinguishable from a name referred to above if the only difference between it and the other name is the inclusion or absence of the words "limited partnership," "limited liability partnership," "cooperative," or "limited liability company," or an abbreviation of these words. A corporation may apply to the department for authorization to use a name that is not distinguishable upon the records of the department from one or more of the names described above. The department shall authorize use of the name applied for if any of the following occurs: (1) the other corporation or the foreign corporation, limited liability company, nonstock corporation, limited partnership, limited liability partnership or cooperative association consents to the use in writing and submits an undertaking in a form satisfactory to the department to change its name to a name that is distinguishable upon the records of the department from the name of the applicant; or (2) the applicant delivers to the department a certified copy of a final judgment of a court of competent jurisdiction establishing the applicant's right to use the name applied for in Wisconsin. A corporation may use the name, including the fictitious name, that is used in Wisconsin by another domestic corporation or a foreign corporation authorized to transact business in Wisconsin if the corporation proposing to use the name has done any of the following: (1) merged with the other domestic corporation or foreign corporation; (2) been formed by reorganization of the other domestic corporation or foreign corporation; (3) acquired all or substantially all of the assets, including the corporate name, of the other domestic corporation or foreign corporation.

• The number of authorized shares, except that an investment company may declare an indefinite number of authorized shares.

• If more than one class of shares is authorized, all of the following: (1) the distinguishing designation of each class; (2) the number of shares of each class that the corporation is authorized to issue, except that an investment company may declare that each class has an indefinite number of authorized shares.

Before the issuance of shares of a class, a description of the preferences, limitations and relative rights of that class;

- If one or more series of shares are created within a class of shares, all of the following before the issuance of shares of a series: (1) the distinguishing designation of each series within a class; (2) the number of shares of each series that the corporation is authorized to issue, except that an investment company may declare that each series has an indefinite number of authorized shares; (3) the preferences, limitations and relative rights of that series.
- Any provision authorizing the board of directors to act;
- Any provision granting or limiting preemptive rights.
- The street address of the corporation's initial registered office and the name of its initial registered agent at that office.
- The name and address of each incorporator.

You must file the articles of incorporation with the secretary of state. As of January 2001, the filing fee was based on the number of authorized shares. The fee was $.01 for each authorized share, except the minimum fee was $90 and the maximum fee was $10,000.

The existence of the corporation begins upon the filing of the articles of incorporation with the secretary of state. Upon creation, the corporation may have a meeting of its incorporators or initial board members to elect directors, officers, adopt bylaws (which may contain any provision consistent with law and the articles of incorporation), and carry on any other business of the corporation. This meeting may be held inside or outside of Wisconsin.

Minimum Number of Incorporators: Any individual or entity may incorporate or organize a corporation.

Management Requirements: Directors or original incorporators, depending upon the terms of the articles of incorporation, may approve bylaws for the corporation. There must be at least one director on the corporation's board of directors.

State Tax Classification: The State charges $25.00 for annual corporate reports, assesses a corporate franchise and income tax at the rate of 7.9%, and sales and use taxes at the rate of 5%.

Contact Information: Corporations Section, 3rd Floor
P.O. Box 7846
Madison, WI 53707-7846
Phone: (608) 261-7577
Facsimile: (608) 267-6813
E-mail: info@dfi.state.wi.us
www.wdfi.org/corporations/

Wyoming

State Corporation Statute: Wy. Statutes §§ 17-16-101 through 17-16-1803.

Formation: Before filing its articles of incorporation, a domestic for-profit corporation may reserve a name with the secretary of state's office. The articles of incorporation must include the following:

- The name of the corporation. A corporate name may not contain language stating or implying that the corporation is organized for a purpose other than that permitted by law and its articles of incorporation. Except as provided below, a corporate name may not be the same as, or deceptively similar to any trademark or service mark registered in Wyoming and shall be distinguishable upon the records of the secretary of state from the name of any profit or nonprofit corporation, trade name, limited liability company, statutory trust company, limited partnership or other business entity organized, continued or domesticated under the laws of Wyoming or licensed or registered as a foreign profit or nonprofit corporation, foreign limited partnership, foreign joint stock company, foreign statutory trust company, foreign limited liability company or other foreign business entity in Wyoming or any fictitious or reserved name. A corporation may apply to the secretary of state for authorization to use a name that is not distinguishable from one or more of the names described above. The secretary of state shall authorize use of the name applied for if: (1) the other person whose name is not distinguishable from the name which the applicant desires to register or reserve, irrevocably consents to the use in writing and submits an undertaking in a form satisfactory to the secretary of state to change its name to a name that is distinguishable from the name of the applicant; or (2) the applicant delivers to the secretary of state a certified copy of the final judgment of a court of competent jurisdiction establishing the applicant's right to use the name applied for in Wyoming. A corporation may use the name, including the fictitious name, of another domestic or foreign corporation that is used in Wyoming if the other corporation is incorporated or authorized to transact business in Wyoming and the proposed user corporation: (1) has merged with the other corporation; or (2) has been formed by reorganization of the other corporation; or (3) has acquired all or substantially all of the assets, including the corporate name, of the other corporation.

- The number of shares the corporation is authorized to issue, which may be unlimited if so stated;
- The street address of the corporation's initial registered office and the name of its initial registered agent at that office; and
- The name and address of each incorporator.

You must file the articles of incorporation with the secretary of state. As of January 2001, the filing fee was $100.00.

The existence of the corporation begins upon the filing of the articles of incorporation with the secretary of state. Upon creation, the corporation may have a meeting of its incorporators or initial board members to elect directors, officers, adopt bylaws (which may contain any provision consistent with law and the articles of incorporation), and carry on any other business of the corporation. This meeting may be held inside or outside of Wyoming.

Minimum Number of Incorporators: Any individual or entity may incorporate or organize a corporation.

Management Requirements: Directors or original incorporators, depending upon the terms of the articles of incorporation, may approve bylaws for the corporation. There must be at least one director on the corporation's board of directors.

State Tax Classification: The State assesses a corporate franchise tax at the rate of $50.00 or 2/10 of one mill on the dollar, whichever is greater, based upon the sum of the corporation's capital, property, and assets reported. Wyoming also assesses sales and use taxes at the rate of 4%.

Contact Information: Secretary of State
Corporations Division
200 West 24th Street
The Capitol Building
Cheyenne 82002-0020

Phone: (307) 777-7311
Facsimile: (307) 777-5339
E-mail: corporations@state.wy.us
http://soswy.state.wy.us/corporat/
corporat.htm

About the Author

 **Garrett Sutton, Esq.**, author of *Own Your Own Corporation* in the Rich Dad's Advisor series, is an attorney with over twenty years of experience in assisting individuals and businesses to determine their appropriate corporate structure, limit their liability, protect their assets, and advance their financial and personal goals.

Garrett and his law firm represent hundreds of corporations, limited liability companies, limited partnerships, and individuals in their business-related law matters, including incorporation, contracts, mergers and acquisitions, private and public company securities offerings, and ongoing business-related legal advice.

Garrett attended Colorado College and the University of California at Berkeley, where he received a B.S. in business administration in 1975. He graduated with a J.D. in 1978 from Hastings College of the Law, the University of California's law school in San Francisco. While at Hastings, he served as an editor of *Comm/Ent, the Journal of Communications and Entertainment Law*, and co-authored an article on the taxation of professional sports franchises.

Garrett is a member of the State Bar of Nevada, the State Bar of California, and the American Bar Association. He has written numerous professional articles and serves on the Publication Committee of the State Bar of Nevada.

Garrett enjoys speaking with entrepreneurs on the advantages of forming business entities. He is a frequent lecturer for the Nevada Microenterprise Institute and the Small Business Administration.

Garrett serves on the boards of the American Baseball Foundation, located in Birmingham, Alabama, and the Reno, Nevada–based Tech Alliance.

For more information on Garrett Sutton and his firm, please visit his website at www.sutlaw.com.

HOW CAN I INCORPORATE?

For additional information about incorporating your company in all 50 states, suggestions concerning other types of entities, and helpful tips and entrepreneur resources regarding related fields of business law, visit www.successdna.com.

SAVINGS OFFER FOR YOU

If you ask us to help you incorporate,
mention this book and receive a 5% discount
on the basic incorporation fee.

I NEED MORE INFORMATION– WHERE CAN I GO?

For further information about the author and his law firm, visit www.sutlaw.com, where you can review biographical notes, explanations of the various practice areas and services offered by the firm, and how to contact the firm for information about initial consultation arrangements and engagement of the firm for an array of legal services.

CASHFLOW® TECHNOLOGIES, INC.

CASHFLOW® Technologies, Inc., and richdad.com, the collaborative efforts of Robert and Kim Kiyosaki and Sharon Lechter, produce innovative financial education products.

The Company's mission Statement is:
 "To elevate the financial well-being of humanity."

CASHFLOW® Technologies, Inc., presents Robert's teaching through books: *Rich Dad Poor Dad™, Rich Dad's CASHFLOW® Quadrant™, Rich Dad's Guide to Investing™,* and *Rich Kid Smart Kid™*; board games *CASHFLOW® 101, CASHFLOW® 202,* and *CASHFLOW for Kids®*; and tape sets. Additional products are available and under development for people searching for financial education to guide them on their path to financial freedom. For updated information see <u>richdad.com</u> or contact <u>info@richdad.com</u>.

Rich Dad's
ADVISORS™

Rich Dad's Advisors is a collection of books and educational products, reflecting the expertise of the professional advisors that *CASHFLOW®* Technologies, Inc., and its principals, Robert and Kim Kiyosaki and Sharon Lechter, use to build their financial freedom. Each advisor is a specialist in their respective areas of the B-I Triangle, the business foundation taught by *CASHFLOW®* Technologies, Inc.

Robert Kiyosaki's Edumercial
An Educational Commercial

The Three Incomes

In the world of accounting, there are three different types of income: earned, passive, and portfolio. When my real dad said to me, "Go to school, get good grades and find a safe secure job," he was recommending I work for earned income. When my rich dad said, "The rich don't work for money, they have their money work for them," he was talking about passive income and portfolio income. Passive income, in most cases, is derived from real estate investments. Portfolio income is income derived from paper assets, such as stocks, bonds, and mutual funds.

Rich dad used to say, "The key to becoming wealthy is the ability to convert earned income into passive income and/or portfolio income as quickly as possible." He would say, "The taxes are highest on earned income. The least taxed income is passive income. That is another reason why you want your money working hard for you. The government taxes the income you work hard for more than the income your money works hard for."

The Key to Financial Freedom

The key to financial freedom and great wealth is a person's ability or skill to convert earned income into passive income and/or portfolio income. That is the skill that my rich dad spent a lot of time teaching Mike and me. Having that skill is the reason my wife, Kim, and I are financially free, never needing to work again. We continue to work because we choose to. Today we own a real estate investment company for passive income and participate in private placements and initial public offerings of stock for portfolio income.

Investing to become rich requires a different set of personal skills, skills essential for financial success as well as low-risk and high-investment returns. In other words, the knowledge to create assets that buy other assets. The problem is that gaining the basic education and experience required is often time consuming, frightening, and expensive, especially when you make mistakes with your own money. That is why I created my patented education board games trademarked as CASHFLOW.

Three Different Games

CASHFLOW, Investing 101®:

CASHFLOW® *101* teaches you the basics of fundamental investing, but it also does much more. *CASHFLOW*® *101* teaches you how to take control of your personal finances, build a business through proper cash flow management, and learn how to invest with greater confidence in real estate and other businesses.

This educational product is for you if you want to improve your business and investing skills by learning how to take your ideas and turn them into assets such as your own business. Many small businesses fail because the owner lacks capital, real-life experience, and basic accounting skills. Many investors think investing is risky simply because they cannot read financial statements. *CASHFLOW*® *101* teaches the fundamental skills of financial literacy and investing. This educational product includes the board game, a video, and audiotapes. It takes approximately two complete times playing the game to understand it. Then we recommend that you play the game at least six times to begin to master the fundamentals of cash flow management and investing. **Price $195 U.S.**

CASHFLOW, Investing 202®:

CASHFLOW® *202* teaches you the advanced skills of technical investing. After you are comfortable with the fundamentals of *CASHFLOW*® *101*, the next educational challenge is learning how to manage the ups and downs of the markets, often called volatility. *CASHFLOW*® *202* uses the same board game as *101*, but it comes with a completely different set of cards and score sheets and more advanced audiotapes. *CASHFLOW*® *202* teaches you to use the investment techniques of qualified investors—techniques such as short selling, call options, put options, and straddles—techniques that can be very expensive to learn in the real market. Most investors are afraid of a market crash. A qualified investor uses the tools taught in *CASHFLOW*® *202* to make money when the markets go up and when the markets come down.

After you have mastered *101*, *CASHFLOW*® *202* becomes very exciting because you learn to react to the highs and lows of the markets, and you make a lot of paper money. Again, it is a lot less expensive to learn these advanced trading techniques on a board game using paper money than trading in the market with real money. While these games cannot guarantee your investment success, they will improve your financial vocabulary and knowledge of these advanced investing techniques.
Price $95 U.S.

CASHFLOW, Investing for Kids®:

Could your child be the next Bill Gates, Anita Roddick of the Body Shop, Warren Buffett, or Donald Trump? If so, then *CASHFLOW for Kids*® could be the family's educational and fun game that gives your child the same educational head start my rich dad gave me. Few people know that Warren Buffett's father was a stockbroker and Donald Trump's father was a real estate developer. A parent's influence at an early age can have long-term financial results. *CASHFLOW for Kids*® includes the board game, book, and audiotape.

Price $59.95 U.S.

Please visit our Web site,
www.richdad.com
to review:

- Additional Information About Our Financial Education Products
- Frequently Asked Questions (FAQs) About Our Products
- Seminars, Events, and Appearances with Robert Kiyosaki

Thank You